IoT and Big Data Analytics

(Volume 4)

Industry 4.0 Convergence with AI, IoT, Big Data and Cloud Computing: Fundamentals, Challenges and Applications

Edited by

Parikshit N. Mahalle
Vishwakarma Institute of Information Technology
Pune, Maharashtra, India

Gitanjali R. Shinde
Vishwakarma Institute of Information Technology
Pune, Maharashtra, India

&

Prachi M. Joshi
DES Pune University
Pune, Maharashtra, India

IoT and Big Data Analytics

(Volume 4)

Industry 4.0 Convergence with AI, IoT, Big Data and Cloud Computing:

Fundamentals, Challenges and Applications

Editors: Parikshit N. Mahalle, Gitanjali R. Shinde and Prachi M. Joshi

ISSN (Online): 2972-4155

ISSN (Print): 2972-4147

ISBN (Online): 978-981-5179-18-7

ISBN (Print): 978-981-5179-19-4

ISBN (Paperback): 978-981-5179-20-0

First published in 2023.

need for a court order if at any point you breach any terms of this License Agreement. In no event will any delay or failure by Bentham Science Publishers in enforcing your compliance with this License Agreement constitute a waiver of any of its rights.

3. You acknowledge that you have read this License Agreement, and agree to be bound by its terms and conditions. To the extent that any other terms and conditions presented on any website of Bentham Science Publishers conflict with, or are inconsistent with, the terms and conditions set out in this License Agreement, you acknowledge that the terms and conditions set out in this License Agreement shall prevail.

Bentham Science Publishers Pte. Ltd.
80 Robinson Road #02-00
Singapore 068898
Singapore
Email: subscriptions@benthamscience.net

BENTHAM SCIENCE

CONTENTS

FOREWORD

The boundaries between the physical and virtual worlds are becoming progressively blurred in what are known as cyber-physical production systems as a result of information and communications technology (ICT) being widely used by the manufacturing industry and traditional production operations (CPPSs). Intelligent machines are constantly exchanging data regarding current stock levels, issues, and modifications in orders or demand levels. In order to increase productivity and optimise throughput times, capacity utilisation, and quality in development, production, marketing, and purchasing, processes and deadlines are coordinated. Robotics, drones, nanotechnology, 3D printing, and artificial intelligence are just a few examples of the exponentially developing technologies that are accelerating and reshaping industrial processes.

The book outline and contents show that the major topic of the book is the brief introduction to the domain, research challenges, literature reviews and state-of-the-art, different algorithms/techniques/deployment methods. The book is divided into three sections that include challenges, convergence with AI and IoT Applications and Industry 4.0.

It starts with a comprehensive study of AI, IoT, Cloud Computing, and Blockchain Technologies. The Internet of Things (IoT), blockchain technology, and Artificial Intelligence (AI) are now acknowledged as advancements with the potential to change entire industries and enhance existing business processes. Blockchain, for instance, offers a shared and decentralized distributed ledger that can improve corporate operations' trust, transparency, security, and privacy. Similar to a register, a distributed ledger or blockchain can be used to hold any type of asset. For the German and European industries, automation of industries and user-friendliness of business processes are crucial. Finally, AI enhances business processes by identifying trends and maximizing their results. AI is structured based on a human mindset and an approach that is human-centered.

These key enablers for Industry 4.0 focusing on IoT, AI and Blockchain Technologies will help readers to empower their research and learning in these areas. Buyers, who belong to the category of researchers, will be benefited from the state-of-art and future research directions provided in the book. Practicing engineers will be benefited from the knowledge of the current challenges in technology, deployment methods and solutions. Postgraduate students will be introduced to new AI domains, and their related recent advancements. They will also be made aware of the rapid growth in the technology.

Pathan Mohd. Shafi
Department of Computer Science and Engineering
MIT ADT University, Loni Kalbhor
Pune, Maharashtra, India

PREFACE

Artificial Intelligence (AI), the branch that has now captured the entire world with its power in dealing, predicting, and estimating with large amounts of data is on a roll. The need to apply intelligence, augment knowledge and enhance communication has made the AI domain more prevalent in emerging technologies. Moreover, the wide availability of varied types of media has made it desired to deliver and provide a robust communicating platform. The existence of potential approaches and techniques to deal with them has opened new avenues for researchers to combine AI methodologies to utilize the media and produce efficient outcomes in the process.

Further, the transformation and automation of traditional practices in industries – manufacturing and production have geared up in Industry 4.0. Integrating IoT, communication media and this digital transformation has become valuable as it has revolutionized the technology. The potential to transform with increasing demand to deliver smart solutions is opening broad perspectives for researchers and thus demanding more attention.

Working towards these new dimensions of AI - to deliver, communicate and process is gaining momentum. New solutions are being looked at to accommodate and improve the business domain. Detecting trends with analytics, interpreting the communicating data, and capturing futuristic estimates are the key factors required in today's networking world. In recent years, researchers are gaining interest in this domain for various ubiquitous applications. To develop and deliver robust next-generation solutions with the applicability of Machine Learning, Deep learning and Data Sciences are used to overcome the challenges possessed by traditional approaches. This ranges from robotics to healthcare, and agriculture to sustainability.

This book focuses on the recent research that introduces new methods and techniques of AI for communicating media along with Industry 4.0.

Parikshit N. Mahalle
Vishwakarma Institute of Information Technology
Pune, Maharashtra, India

Gitanjali R. Shinde
Vishwakarma Institute of Information Technology
Pune, Maharashtra, India

&

Prachi M. Joshi
DES Pune University
Pune, Maharashtra, India

List of Contributors

Avinash Patil	Maharashtra Institute of Technology World Peace University, Pune, India Human Inspired AI Research Pvt. Ltd - HumInspAIRe, Pune, Maharashtra, India
Eudes Smith M. Linheiro	Department of Computer Engineering, Vishwakarma Institute of Information Technology, Pune, Maharashtra, India
Gitanjali R. Shinde	Vishwakarma Institute of Information Technology, Pune, Maharashtra, India
Hriday Pandurang Khandagale	Department of Technology, Shivaji University, Vidyanagar, Kolhapur, India
Jayashri Bagade	Department of Information Technology, Bansilal Ramnath Agarwal Charitable Trust's, Vishwakarma Institute of Information Technology, Pune, India
Milind Pande	Maharashtra Institute of Technology World Peace University, Pune, India Human Inspired AI Research Pvt. Ltd - HumInspAIRe, Pune, Maharashtra, India
Mangesh Bedekar	Maharashtra Institute of Technology World Peace University, Pune, India Human Inspired AI Research Pvt. Ltd. - HumInspAIRe, Pune, Maharashtra, India
Neha Mandora	Human Inspired AI Research Pvt. Ltd. - HumInspAIRe, Pune, Maharashtra, India
Nilesh P. Sable	Department of Information Technology, Bansilal Ramnath Agarwal Charitable Trust's, Vishwakarma Institute of Information Technology, Pune, India
Priyanka Kuklani	Human Inspired AI Research Pvt. Ltd. - HumInspAIRe, Pune, Maharashtra, India Northeastern University, Boston, Massachusetts, United States
Priya Shelke	Department of Information Technology, Vishwakarma Institute of Information Technology, Pune, Maharashtra, India
Pratap Pandurang Halkarnikar	Dr. D.Y. Patil Institute of Engineering, Management and Research, Nigdi Pradhikaran, Akurdi, Pune, India
Prasad Raghunath Mutkule	Vishwakarma Institute of Information Technology, Pune, Maharashtra, India
Prachi M. Joshi	DES Pune University, Pune, Maharashtra, India
Pawan S. Wawage	Vishwakarma University, Pune, Maharashtra, India
Pranali Chavhan	Department of Computer Engineering, Vishwakarma Institute of Information Technology, Pune, Maharashtra, India
Priyanka More	Department of Computer Engineering, Vishwakarma Institute of Information Technology, Pune, Maharashtra, India
Parikshit N. Mahalle	Vishwakarma Institute of Information Technology, Pune, Maharashtra, India
Prashant C. Dhas	Vishwakarma Institute of Information Technology, Pune, Maharashtra, India

Riddhi Mirajkar	Department of Information Technology, Vishwakarma Institute of Information Technology, Pune, Maharashtra, India
Ravesa Akhter	National Institute of Technology Srinagar, Srinagar, Jammu and Kashmir, India
Rajesh Phursule	Department of Information Technology, Pimpri Chinchwad College of Engineering, Pune, India
Snehal Rathi	Department of Computer Engineering, Vishwakarma Institute of Information Technology, Pune, Maharashtra, India
Saniya Zahoor	National Institute of Technology Srinagar, Srinagar, Jammu and Kashmir, India
Vijay U. Rathod	Department of Artificial Intelligence and Data Science, G H Raisoni College of Engineering and Management, Wagholi, Pune, India
Varad Vishwarupe	Amazon Research and Development Centre, Bangalore, Karnataka, India Human Inspired AI Research Pvt. Ltd. - HumInspAIRe, Pune, Maharashtra, India
Vijay P. Bhatkar	Maharashtra Institute of Technology World Peace University, Pune, India
Vishal Pawar	Maharashtra Institute of Technology World Peace University, Pune, India Human Inspired AI Research Pvt. Ltd. - HumInspAIRe, Pune, Maharashtra, India
Yogesh D. Deshpande	Vishwakarma Institute of Information Technology, Pune, Maharashtra, India Vishwakarma University, Pune, Maharashtra, India
Yuvraj V. Parkale	Department of Electronics and Telecommunication Engineering, SVPM's College of Engineering, Malegaon (BK), Baramati, Maharashtra, India

CHAPTER 1

A Comprehensive Study of State-of-the-Art Applications and Challenges in IoT, and Blockchain Technologies for Industry 4.0

Saniya Zahoor[2,*], **Ravesa Akhter**[2], **Varad Vishwarupe**[1,4], **Mangesh Bedekar**[3,4], **Milind Pande**[3,4], **Vijay P. Bhatkar**[3], **Prachi M. Joshi**[5], **Vishal Pawar**[3,4], **Neha Mandora**[4] and **Priyanka Kuklani**[4,6]

[1] *Amazon Research and Development Centre, Bangalore, Karnataka, India*

[2] *National Institute of Technology Srinagar, Srinagar, Jammu and Kashmir, India*

[3] *Maharashtra Institute of Technology World Peace University, Pune, India*

[4] *Human Inspired AI Research Pvt. Ltd. - HumInspAIRe, Pune, Maharashtra, India*

[5] *DES Pune University, Pune, Maharashtra, India*

[6] *Northeastern University, Boston, Massachusetts, United States*

Abstract: The Internet of Things (IoT) is a network of smart and self-configuring devices that exchange data by interacting with the environment to make decisions without human intervention. Endowed to sense surrounding events, these physical objects generate large amounts of real-time data that need an acceptable architecture with better security to process and convert it into meaningful information. Implementation of blockchain in IoT offers a secure, transparent and efficient mechanism to store and manage data generated by connected IoT devices. Even though the integration of blockchain with IoT is pretty recent, there are at present a huge number of applications that include smart healthcare, smart homes, e-government, automotive industry, smart education, precision agriculture *etc*. However, there are several challenges encountered in Blockchain-IoT integration which include anonymity, standardization, interoperability, heterogeneity, data privacy, smart contracts, legal issues, transparency, storage capacity and scalability, security, *etc*. This chapter presents the current state-of-the-art Blockchain-IoT integration in order to examine how blockchain could possibly improve the IoT ecosystem catered towards Industry 4.0. This chapter investigates the various application domains of Blockchain-IoT integration. It also discusses the main challenges faced in the adoption of blockchain in IoT environments for I4.0.

Keywords: Blockchain technology, Internet of things, Industry 4.0, Smart home, Smart education.

* **Corresponding author Saniya Zahoor:** National Institute of Technology Srinagar, Srinagar, Jammu and Kashmir, India; E-mail: saniyazahoor@yahoo.com

Parikshit N. Mahalle, Gitanjali R. Shinde and Prachi M. Joshi (Eds.)

1. INTRODUCTION

The rapid advancement of Internet of Things (IoT) technology has led to the increased use of a number of devices in a wide range of applications contributing to an extraordinary improvement in our day-to-day lives. IoT has led to an abrupt shift toward the digital world and has changed an ordinary world into a smart world. It has been estimated that there will be 20 to 50 billion IoT devices connected over the Internet by 2025. Therefore, the aim of IoT is to connect the entire world where objects sense the data about the surroundings and interact with each other making a digital representation of the real world. In an IoT system, a number of IoT devices, equipped with sensors and actuators, monitor surroundings and take necessary actions *via* intensive sensing and data aggregation over a network. The collected data from the IoT devices are transferred to fog or cloud *via* gateways (or edge) that perform pre-processing of data before transmitting over the network. IoT devices take the necessary action by executing commands using their actuators. The cloud gateway facilitates secure data transmission between the edge gateway and cloud servers. Cloud servers perform data processing such as data cleaning and structuring to store the required data in a particular context. Various data analytics techniques are used to find the insight into the data such as correlations and pattern findings, outlier detections, *etc*. Various machine learning models are used to create precise models for IoT control applications that send automatic alerts to actuators. The concept of blockchain came into existence in recent times because of its decentralized and peer-to-peer architecture. Blockchain finds its applicability in many fields such as healthcare, industry, supply chain management, *etc*. In most of these applications, there is a tremendous problem of trust due to a lack of the verification mechanism for sensitive information. Blockchain provides a mechanism where transactions are verified by a group of unreliable actors *via* a secure, distributed, transparent and audible ledger. Blockchain provides open and full access to all transactions occurred to date at any time. There are a number of protocols in blockchain for organizing the information in the form of blocks with each block storing the set of transactions performed at a given time. These blocks are linked together by a reference to the previous block, forming a chain of blocks. In blockchain systems, there are various services that should be provided by network peers to operate in the blockchain environment. The services include routing, storage, wallet, and mining. Fig. (**1**) shows the architecture for blockchain. Blockchain is considered an application software that is installed on several computers (nodes) in a network for registrations and transactions. In blockchain systems, a new block of information for each new register is created to the system. This new block is combined with the previous block of information using complex mathematical algorithms. The node which first calculates the new block transfers it to the other node on the network for approval. If approval comes, it is added as a new block in the blockchain system and accordingly updated on all nodes. Therefore, this creates a chain of blocks and is hence referred to as the blockchain.

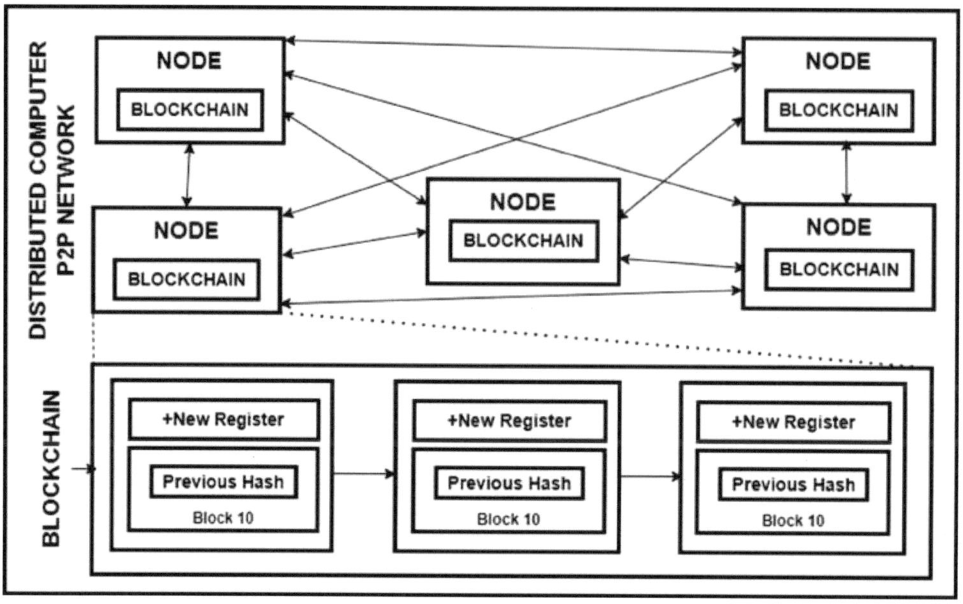

Fig. (1). Blockchain architecture.

Mining, storage, routing and wallet services should be provided by network peers to operate with the blockchain [4]. Different types of nodes can be part of the network as per the functions they provide. Table **1** summarizes some of the common node types in the Bitcoin network. Depending upon the level of security required and budget and nature of problem, we can have different types of nodes in a Bitcoin network based on the following characteristics.

Table 1. Common node types in bitcoin network.

Characteristics	Open	Secluded	Hybrid
Consensus Mechanism	Pricey Proof of work (Pow) required	Light Pow	Light Pow
Identity Secrecy	Malicious	Trusted	Trusted
Ownership and Supervision	Public	Centralised	Semi-centralised
Time taken for Transaction	Minutes	Microseconds	Microseconds

In IoT environments, devices sense and produce a large amount of data which are transmitted over the Internet to other devices. Therefore, it requires the involvement of many participant devices for data sensing, transmission, aggregation, storage, processing, *etc.* Any data breach in these chains of participants can lead to fraud leading to huge economic losses to companies. Better control for secure data sharing between participants in these applications is required. The integration of blockchain with Internet of Things is a revolutionary step where information is shared between the participants in a secure manner. There has been recent research in the integration of blockchain with the Internet of Things and allied fields such as Wireless Sensor Networks (WSNs), cloud computing and fog computing. Blockchain provides a trusted information sharing service to the IoT environment, thereby enhancing the security of such systems. The other challenges addressed by integrated Blockchain-IoT environments include central point of failure, fault tolerance, scalability, authentication and authorization of IoT devices, reliability, *etc.*

A lot of work has been done in the field of Blockchain-IoT. In section 1.2 we have discussed the Blockchain IoT applications currently present in the literature and summarised the literature survey in Table **2**.

Table 2. Blockchain based security solution for few applications of IoT.

S. No.	Applications	Issues Encountered	Solution using Blockchain	Remarks
1.	Smart IoT-Healthcare	Malicious attacks [1], Resource constrained [2, 3], Incorrect prescription and wrong treatment [6], Information leakage [7], cyber accidents [8].	Privacy preserving, data encryption, ethereum based smart contracts,	Confidentiality, privacy, reduced single point failure, integrity, identity management, tamper resistance, immutability, QoS, Secure data sharing.
2.	Smart Home	Robbing, fire, carelessness towards elderly people.	Home security controls, home monitoring, smart contract, Smart meter, CCTV.	Security, privacy, homecare, automatic utility payment.
3.	Smart education	Quality of service issues (QoS) issues, Privacy leakage, Data integrity and repudiation issues.	IoT-BC framework was implemented to communicate securely.	Privacy, availability, integrity, confidentiality.
4.	Drug traceability	QoS(Quality of service) issues, counterfeiting of drugs	Drug ledger, Hyper ledger have been implemented for supply using blockchain to prevent forging,	Supply chain management, enhance security, discernibility, traceability.

(Table 2) cont.....

S. No.	Applications	Issues Encountered	Solution using Blockchain	Remarks
5.	Power grid	Unreliability, energy wastage, unavailability of services.	Extended Petra builds ledgers using blockchain to provide secrecy for communiqué, request and trading [25, 26].	Smart metring, microgrid energy, energy trading.
6.	Smart transportation system	Inconvenience faced in terms of traffic jam issues, parking issues.	Smart devices, Collaborative info collecting by public blockchain [31].	Enhances device security and privacy.
7.	Commercial world	QoS (Quality of service) issues.	Smart agreement policy [32, 33], Media's digital rights management system [34].	Effective management of construction industries, user's behaviour.
8.	Supply chain	Forging of items, mutability, lack of integrity.	RFID tags have been used in blockchain for agri-food supply management.	Supply chain management throughout the process.
9.	Automotive Industry	Forging of products like spare parts, lack of satisfaction and trust on brands.	Supply chain management in whole automotive system.	Supply chain management, reduced automotive system overheads.
10.	e-government	Information leakage, Cross-site scripting(XSS), structured query language (SQL) injection, Denial of service attacks (DoS), malware targeting [46].	Secure information exchange technology for security.	Confidentiality, integrity and availability.

2. INTEGRATED BLOCKCHAIN-IOT APPLICATIONS

The integration of blockchain with the Internet of Things has paved the way to a multitude of applications in many sectors as discussed below.

2.1. Smart IoT-Healthcare

IoT in healthcare aids in real-time fitness monitoring and data access to bring about for patients' well-being, enhanced healthcare procedures. In the medical field, the realm of IoT comprises justification, spontaneous info compilation, and perception. Since smart healthcare (IoT-enabled) systems deal typically with patients' personal data and results, this data is tremendously under the influence of malicious attacks if not protected with innovative and formidable security methods [1]. Most of the smart healthcare devices like sensors, and actuators are resource-constrained. As a result, auxiliary security protocols cannot be incorporated in them [2, 3]. In addition, such devices are moveable and may need public network connections, such as in clinics, hospitals, cafeteria, homes, workplaces, *etc*., which further enhance to their exposure. Due to the exponential rise in connected IoT devices, designing vigorous and firm security mechanisms is a difficult task [4, 5]. For instance, the record of patients' health condition is personal, and it necessities a security technique to prevent the information dispersion to an unofficial group. By working in this way, no one can perceive and influence the facts or get access to a patient's health record. Besides this, it also averts a doctor from mistreatment of the patients. If no security practice is implemented, the physicians may give incorrect prescriptions or endow the wrong treatment to their patients [6]. For example, alterations to a blood investigation report might overstate a patient's condition for transfusing mismatched blood in the course of the blood transfusion procedure. Severe cyber-attack alerts have happened in healthcare services in the past few years. In the year 2019, a high number of cases have been reported where HIPAA (Health Insurance Portability and Accountability Act) offense touched 418, and an about 34.9 million US nations had their protected health information (PHI) conceded in that year [7]. The prevailing infrastructure is not proficient to provide security contrary to such data breaches, which can eventually question the confidentiality and privacy of patients' health information. The existing techniques in smart healthcare record another gap towards a challenging scenario, *i.e*., the presence of patients' data in the guardianship of health administrations, leaving patients' information at risk, and generating futile data distribution towards patients' healthcare. For instance, just because the info of a patient's well-being is not referred from one service provider to the other on time, the patient's cure might get delayed. *Electronic Health Record* (HER) has such limits practically, which can be overwhelmed by using the blockchain technology. In recent times, it has been adopted by numerous government, private, and hybrid (both public and private) partnered projects [8]. In the field of healthcare, the benefits of blockchain technology were perceived when IBM Watson Health and the US Food and Drug Administration (FDA) dedicated a blockchain framework to guard data allied to oncology [9]. Blockchain obtains data from several sources and save it in the transaction audit log, which eventually aids in keeping track of the transparency and liability of data at the time of data interchange. It is supposed by the FDA (U.S. Food and Drug Administration) and IBM that blockchain has the ability to support data sharing collected from various sources with the consensus of patients and the terms equally agreed on [27]. Present working models are dependent on passwords, which may contain secret data (sensitive information) that have to be shared and are usually kept on untrustworthy and less protected clouds [4]. This resulted in several renowned cyber accidents. In the year 2014, the most well-known of which was the one, when hackers intruded into US Health insurer

Anthem's servers and the delicate info of about 80 million people (patients and employees) got stolen [8]. It is also of high significance that the healthcare data access must be handled with high precautions. Likewise, standardized checking is inevitable for ensuring data integrity. Blockchain decreases the threats of such calamitous breaches and ensures data privacy, integrity and robust storage. Moreover, single-point-of-failure is also lessened as this model stores data in a distributive computing way.

2.2. Smart Home

Smart homes using IoT lead to home automation. It is the mechanism that enables to control home appliances by electronically using internetworking systems. It includes setting up intricate heating, and lighting systems in advance, setting alarms, locking and unlocking the rooms, home security controls (watching homes), *etc.* all linked by a central system /hub and remote-controlled by end users.

Smart home info can easily be determined using blockchain technology as it is very easy to incorporate with heterogeneous IoT devices used in smart homes. Fig. (**2**) shows the blockchain-based ecosystem smart home using IoT. It is a conceptual framework of four layers consisting of the IoT layer, blockchain platform layer, application layer, and access layer [10].

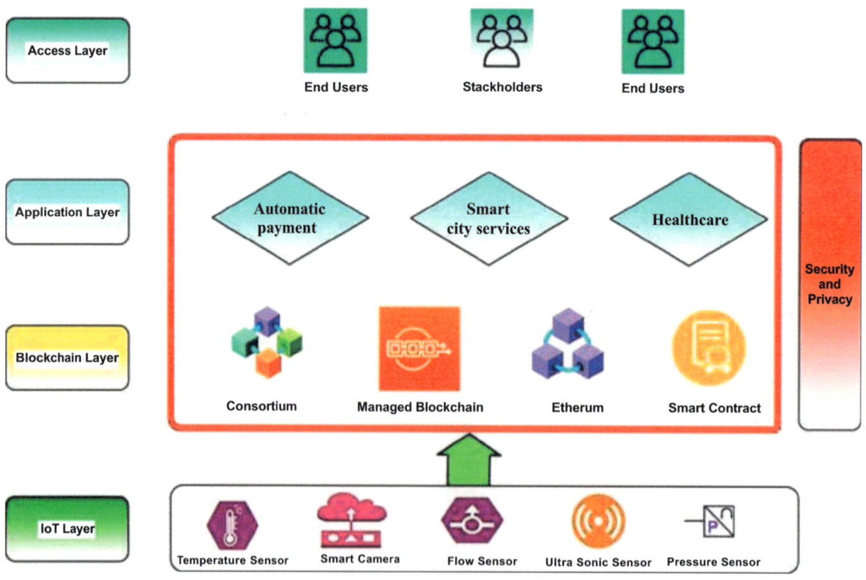

Fig. (2). Framework for blockchain based smart home ecosystem.

The IoT layer collects data from devices that are significant for measuring the state, environment, and inhabitants of smart homes. The requirements of IoT devices for smart homes are roughly characterized into three foremost categories; sensors, healthcare and multimedia. Environmental factors are measured using sensors. For instance, the thermostat sensor measures and regulates the temperature of a room. A closed-circuit television (CCTV), *etc*. is called a blockchain node. Facts from these nodes are merged and stored either in a centralized server or in a decentralized fashion like blockchain which makes the basic layer of the stack.

On top of the IoT ecosystem resides a blockchain technology. It comprises two main components: data structure, and a smart contract. Hash values are used to cryptographically link blocks. As a miner for authenticating and adding new relations to new blocks, a home server computer can be used. Smart contracts follow the rules which are predefined, and assist the decentralized relations. There are numerous ways to implement blockchain; private, public and hybrid, but generally in a smart home network, a private blockchain is preferred to reduce the overhead cost.

Application layer eases to use diverse smart home applications and their incorporation with prevailing blockchain platforms. It comprises smart home applications for instance homecare, data souk, management in accessing services, healthcare, automatic payment and smart city services. Most of these growing applications are adopting blockchain platform. Some are still under research.

Finally, at the topmost of the stack comes the Access layer. It allows stakeholders to value from smart home applications based on blockchain such as; microgrid, service providers, caregivers, retail shop, *etc*.

2.3. Smart Education

Education using the information and communication system (ICT) is known as the e-education system. Today's whole education system is dependent on internet and its technologies. Mostly in the pandemic era of Covid-19, every task related to academics is performed using ICT. One of the prevalent accomplishments [11] was to build a framework for the education system to interconnect by means of blockchain and IoT technology on the Internet. This framework was mainly appropriate for the end users wherever the info is frequently taken to the linked devices on the internet. Besides that they have used a re-transmission policy, variable packet-length, to increase the system performance. Hence the implementation of IOT-BC dual framework is proposed [12]. The entire system has been realized as a three-tier architecture, fog, blockchain (BC), and Internet of

Things (IoT). A token or symbol given by the accepted blockchain repository to the IoT device has the authority to link the model, get a notification key from the workstation, and gather info from the fog [13]. The IoT device can be a student, an employee or a tutor. IoT portable device determines the smart contacts from within the acceptable blockchain depository [14]. A primary server verifies the token or symbol from such an accepted blockchain repository or produces a key for each smart device as well as a reaction down to a device [15].

2.4. Drug Traceability

In medicine supply chain management blockchain plays a very important role in traceability and monitoring medicinal products while transportation. A lot of work has been done in this research area by incorporating IoT in blockchain. Huang Y *et al.* [17] used Drug ledger that has been designed to maintain the workflow of drug supply chain including packing, unpacking and repacking using blockchain technology. In [18, 19] blockchain technology has been used to track the counterfeiting of drugs by using encrypted QR for authentic manufacturers and Hyperledger using permissioned blockchain respectively. In a study [20], authors have clarified how to use Blockchain to enhance security, discernibility and traceability to the medicine supply chain. They were able to track the drugs from the producer to the end user.

2.5. Power Grid

Currently, everything is directly or indirectly dependent on the power grid. Maintenance of it is very tough. But using blockchain technology with IoT makes it very easy. Energy trading [21, 22], smart metering [23], and microgrid energy [24] are the power grid areas in which blockchain technology aids to offer a quick facility to consumers. A study [25, 26] clarified a strategy of blockchain-based transactive microgrid that can deliver transactional reliability through distributed computing nodes. The extension of PETra (builds on dispersed ledgers, such as Blockchains, and provides secrecy for communiqué, request, and trading) trading workflow have be used by them. In a study [27], a hybrid blockchain system has been used by combining public and private blockchain systems. It offers novel services to the power grid system.

2.6. Smart Transportation System

Transportation is the physical way by which one can connect to the rest of the world. Using Smart Transportation, it can be made more convenient and safe.

Smart Transportation system comprises seven [28] layers. Each layer consists of either some hardware devices or application oriented services that help in providing smart service. Once incorporating with blockchain technology, it improves the device security and privacy in both devices and data [29]. Secure key management is one of the vital concerns in the heterogeneous system of networks [30]. In a study [31], authors have suggested a model for collaborative info collecting by public blockchain.

2.7. Commercial World

Commerce is the backbone of economy for every nation. In order to boost it to the advanced stage, we should incorporate novel technologies like blockchain, IoT, *etc*.

In another study [32, 33], authors suggested innovative architecture for commercial world using Blockchain with a mention of some special strategies for smart agreements policy. Some [34] authors have proposed Media's Digital rights management system using blockchain for effective management of each commercial area like, user's behaviour in media, construction industries [35]. Authors [36, 37] revealed that it is promising to employ M2M electricity market in the commercial world successfully using blockchain.

2.8. Supply Chain

Supply chain management involves the whole process from the beginning of the production of goods till their consumption. In order to keep the proper track of each step in this process, one may need to introduce novel techniques and technologies to enhance its reliability, security, and transparency. For authentication, blockchain as a service has been used by the Chinese Government for the supply chain. In a study [38], authors used RFID tags and blockchain for agri-food supply chain management. To trace this process through its lifecycle, one can get awareness of a true producer. Some [39] authors have proposed blockchain solution to the problems of supply chain such as Double Demotion and Info Disproportionateness. In a study [40], authors built a food supply chain tracing system for agri-food using HACCP (Hazard Analysis and Critical Control Points), blockchain and IoT that can enhance its reliability, security, and transparency.

2.9. Automotive Industry

Currently, the automotive industry looks for more personalized, on-demand and integrated services including interconnected, shared and autonomous environment for instance e-healthcare, smart parking system, *etc*. It is closely linked to novel technologies. In fact, in the automotive industry, autonomous cars are the most outstanding revolution. Autonomous Industry will make the automobile in 2050 self-driving. As in a recent study that predicts that about 250 million connected cars- each will be made of hundreds of sensors for information gathering. The growth in implementation of autonomous cars in the automotive industry seems to interfere with government protocols, insurance, industrial manufacturing, maintenance services, *etc*.

The automotive system of the supply chain industry has grown into a complex and extensive ecosystem, which is considered one of the utmost innovative sectors with contributors ranging from government supervisory parties, industrialists, dealers, and sellers to spare parts suppliers. Conversely, one of the prevalent concerns in the automotive supply chain industry is forging products, which is presently expected at plentiful billion dollars' worth of spare parts. Forged spare parts usually have low quality, because they move in the supply chain directly or through online sources. This led to an influence on the original accoutrements manufacturer and spare part providers. This results in a lack of satisfaction in customers and affects badly the trust on the brand. Effective development of manufacturing capacity, tracking and locating of specific parts through the supply chain, and precise and on-time info become vital in building the automotive industry in the smart city.

Blockchain technology has made a revolution and fascinates many stakeholders who ascertain the benefits of this technology, affecting the financial industry along with other sectors. The combination of the automotive industry with blockchain technology results in smart solutions to certain automotive problems, specifically those associated with the interconnected automotive industry. The influence of this technology can lead to innovation and solutions across the whole automotive ecosystem.

2.10. E-government

E-government or electronic government basically refers to the "utilization of information technology, information and communication technologies, other web-based technologies to advance and/or increase the competence and success of service delivery in the public sector domain". The extensive availability of the internet has inspired diverse countries across the globe to utilize technologies as; a means of communication and service sharing in tween inhabitants and other associates. E-government users use online services while sitting in their comfortable homes, evading time-consuming queues in public organizations, without using any transportation costs, *etc*. in the most efficient way. Mostly speaking, government networks can connect to each other much better than commercial networks, since most of them are connected for transmitting info to the public without any sort of competition. It has been predicted that the number of devices using e-government services will increase exponentially because of the fast advancement of smart homes, smart healthcare, smart grid smart cities, and other interconnected services [41, 42]. In the year 2014, the United Nation e-government survey said that around the world almost every government is providing its inhabitants and other shareholders e-services through websites and mobile applications [43].

E-government systems gather, save and process an essential amount of trustworthy info about inhabitants, employees, workers, customers, goods, researches, financial status, using computers. The compromise of such info ordinarily leads to the harm of users' expectation and trust, opportunities, and financial rewards, *etc.* [44]. It has been found that above 80% of e-government web sites around the world were exposed to cross-site scripting (XSS) and structured query (SQL) injection because of the dearth of appropriate authentication mechanism [45]. In recent times, many countries across the globe have experienced a great danger from various online attacks like denial of service attacks (DoS) and malware targeting their systems [46].

In the year 2015 and 2016, Unites States government and Tanzania government were attacked while using e-government services and around 4 million government staff's personal info was leaked and about 85 million US dollars were lost respectively [47, 48].

It is hence of important to make sure that the CIA(Confidentiality, integrity, and availability) triangle is being followed. The current e-government systems [49, 50, 56, 59 - 62], are centralized where it is probable to suffer from a single point of failure and have become a target to cyber-attacks. It implies that an e-government system will face these issues in the future if not secured. Blockchain is one of the best solutions for a secure info exchange technology in such systems [51, 52, 67 - 70, 72 - 75]. Blockchain has been found in other systems as well like education [55], healthcare [56], smart cities [41], IoT [53], and smart homes [54]. The blockchain technology is in the early stage of e-government system [57, 71] and not following any common framework to implement it [64 - 66]. Authors have summarised security solutions for IoT-based applications using blockchain technology as shown in Table **2**.

3. CHALLENGES IN THE ADOPTION OF BLOCKCHAIN IN IOT ENVIRONMENTS FOR INDUSTRY 4.0.

This section focuses on the challenges faced while integrating blockchain technology in the IoT environments. Some of the major challenges are discussed.

3.1. Consensus

There has been recent research in leveraging the distributed nature and global potential of Internet of Things to adapt the consensus in the IoT. But in many IoT applications, there are resource constraints in devices which impose a lot of challenges in taking part in consensus mechanism. The resource requirements vary from one consensus protocol to the other in the blockchain networks. Few solutions include inclusion of few resourceful devices capable of addressing this issue, an off-chain solution to reduce the high latency in blockchain, consensus protocol called Proof of Understanding (PoU) for IoT applications having energy constraint, *etc*. These consensus protocols focus on tacking key issues of resource overhead in IoT systems.

3.2. Storage Capacity and Scalability

In many IoT applications, there are resource constraints in devices such as limited energy, limited storage, limited processing and limited communication capabilities which make the integration of blockchain with IoT more challenging. Most of the current blockchain implementations are capable of processing few transactions per second, therefore imposing challenge for the integration of data intensive IoT with blockchain. Further, blockchain is not meant to store large amounts of data which is opposite to the case of data intensive IoT applications demanding high storage. A lot of IoT data are stored but not all the data are relevant for extracting knowledge in a particular context. Different compression techniques to filter out the useful data have been employed. These techniques reduce the load on storage, processing and communication in IoT systems generating data in huge quantity.

3.3. Security

Internet of Things face security issues at different levels viz. node and network level. There are many reasons for security issues in IoT and these include mobility, heterogeneity, wireless communication, resource constraints, *etc*. There are many threats such as denial of service, eavesdropping, *etc* that can affect the IoT. Further, there are cases when data from IoT devices has a chance to get corrupt because of failure of any sensor or damage of the device as a whole. Blockchain has emerged as a key technology to provide security in IoT but there are many other challenges faced in integration of blockchain with IoT. IoT communication issue is one of the challenges faced in integrated Blockchain-IoT. Many IoT protocols such as MQTT integrate security protocols such as TLS to provide security during communication among IoT devices.

3.4. Smart Contracts

Smart contract refers to a computer based transaction protocol that provides a way to auto-execute contractual clauses. Blockchain is considered an ideal solution to support smart contracts and this integration has led to the emergence of blockchain 2.0. This automatic contract execution in a trusted manner is much required in IoT environments. Smart contract is stored on the blockchain and each is identified by a unique address and whenever a transaction is done, it is send to this unique code. The benefits of using smart contracts in IoT systems include reduced cost overhead, efficiency, transparency, precision, *etc*.

3.5. Legal Issues

The emergence of blockchain has raised a controversy in one of its application viz bitcoin. The bitcoin users are accused of fraud and illegal conduct while using the network. Many countries have restricted the use of bitcoin by developing rules and regulations that govern the use of virtual currencies. This situation creates a lot of legal issues and can be considered as the reason behind its recent failure. There has been recent research in secure blockchain applications where permissions such as write are granted to a predefined peer devices or set of peer devices. This resolves many issues such as authorization and authentication mechanisms leading to less chance of frauds in bitcoin systems. Other IoT applications include information distributed among different sectors such as government, companies, universities, *etc*. Hence, a proper solution is required to ensure legal issues do not arise in such environments and there occurs a seamless integration between population, companies, government and universities.

Note, however, that there are still various research directions to take to address issues and challenges in the future.

3.6. Co-integration with IoT Platform

Co-integration of the automotive industry with the smart home, transportation, healthcare, *etc*. is required to create a single sign-on platform for making life easy, efficient, and smarter in the future.

3.7. Virtual Ecosystem

A virtual ecosystem for the individual user is needed to customize the services and balance power between users, automotive manufacturers, and tech industries.

3.8. Structurally Adaptable

The structural design of smart contracts directly affects the adaptability of the entire framework as an attribute of quality needed by many industries.

3.9. Dynamic Expandability

To maintain the performance and efficiency of the framework, the framework should expand dynamically alongside the increased size of distributed ledgers or organizations.

3.10. Standardization

Currently, due to the lack of common standards, different organizations are developing their own blockchain and standards. In the public domain, blockchain-based applications are supposed to work within the regulatory framework.

CONCLUSION

In this paper, we have initially highlighted the importance of IoT in most of the application scenarios pertaining to Industry 4.0. Blockchain technology is considered to be amongst such emerging platform in industry 4.0 which can provide such services on integrating with IoT technology because of its distributed and transparent nature. Since in Industry 4.0 we are facing the tremendous issues but the most concerned is the security. We carried out an extensive survey on the efforts made to integrate blockchain technology with the existing IoT networks. This chapter presents the current state of art of Blockchain-IoT integration in order to examine how blockchain could possibly improve the IoT ecosystem catered towards Industry 4.0. This chapter investigates the various application domains of Blockchain-IoT integration. It also discusses the main challenges faced in the adoption of blockchain in IoT environments for Industry 4.0. To conclude, we aimed to highlight the main challenges and best techniques and protocols in blockchain based IoT ecosystems which will efficiently impact the global economy.

REFERENCES

[1] Z. Maamar, E. Kajan, M. Asim, and T. Baker Shamsa, "Open challenges invetting the internet of things", *Internet Technol. Lett.,* vol. 2, no. 5, 2019.

[2] N. Tariq, M. Asim, Z. Maamar, M.Z. Farooqi, N. Faci, and T. Baker, "A Mobile Code-driven Trust Mechanism for detecting internal attacks in sensor node-powered IoT", *J. Parallel Distrib. Comput.,* vol. 134, pp. 198-206, 2019. [http://dx.doi.org/10.1016/j.jpdc.2019.08.013]

[3] N. Abbas, M. Asim, N. Tariq, T. Baker, and S. Abbas, "A Mechanism for Securing IoT-enabled Applications at the Fog Layer", *Journal of Sensor and Actuator Networks,* vol. 8, no. 1, p. 16, 2019. [http://dx.doi.org/10.3390/jsan8010016]

[4] N. Tariq, M. Asim, F. Al-Obeidat, M. Zubair Farooqi, T. Baker, M. Hammoudeh, and I. Ghafir, "The Security of Big Data in Fog-Enabled IoT Applications Including Blockchain: A Survey", *Sensors (Basel),* vol. 19, no. 8, p. 1788, 2019. [http://dx.doi.org/10.3390/s19081788] [PMID: 31013993]

[5] N. Tariq, M. Asim, and F.A. Khan, "Securing scada-based critical infrastructures: Challenges and open issues", *Procedia Comput. Sci.,* vol. 155, pp. 612-617, 2019. [http://dx.doi.org/10.1016/j.procs.2019.08.086]

[6] F.A. Khan, N.A.H. Haldar, A. Ali, M. Iftikhar, T.A. Zia, and A.Y. Zomaya, "A continuous change detection mechanism to identify anomalies in ecg signals for wban-based healthcare environments", *IEEE Access,* vol. 5, pp. 13531-13544, 2017. [http://dx.doi.org/10.1109/ACCESS.2017.2714258]

[7] Available from: https://www.physicianspractice.com/hipaa/hipaa-breaches-2019-year-review.

[8] N. Kshetri, "Blockchain and electronic healthcare records", *Computer,* vol. 51, no. 12, pp. 59-63, 2018. [http://dx.doi.org/10.1109/MC.2018.2880021]

[9] Available from: https://www.computerworld.com/article/3156504/ibm-watson-fda-to-explore-blockchain-for-secure-patient-data-exchange.html

[10] M. Moniruzzaman, S. Khezr, A. Yassine, and R. Benlamri, "Blockchain for smart homes: Review of current trends and research challenges", *Comput. Electr. Eng.,* vol. 83, 2020. [http://dx.doi.org/10.1016/j.compeleceng.2020.106585]

[11] F.T de O. Sergio, da Silva Junior Joao F, and MR de Alencar Fernanda, "The Blockchain-based Internet of Things Development: Initiatives and Challenges", *ICSEA,* vol. 39, 2017.

[12] A. Dorri, S.S. Kanhere, and R Jurdak, "Blockchain in internet of things: challenges and solutions", *Cryptography and Security,* 2016. [http://dx.doi.org/10.48550/arXiv.1608.05187]

[13] M. Samaniego, and R. Deters, "Blockchain as a Service for IoTIoT" In Internet of Things (iThings) and IEEE Green Computing and Communications (GreenCom) and IEEE Cyber, Physical and Social Computing (CPSCom) and IEEE Smart Data (SmartData), 2016 IEEE International Conference on, 433-436, IEEE, 2016.

[14] A. Kuzmin, "Blockchain-based structures for a secure and operate IoT,", In: *Internet of Things Business Models, Users, and Networks.* IEEE, 2017.

[15] R. Han, V. Gramoli, and X. Xu, "Evaluating Blockchains for IoT", New Technologies, Mobility and Security (NTMS), 9th IFIP International Conference on, IEEE. 2018. [http://dx.doi.org/10.1109/NTMS.2018.8328736]

[16] T. Bocek, B.B. Rodrigues, T. Strasser, and B. Stiller, "Blockchains everywhere -a use-case of blockchains in the pharma supply-chain", In: *2017 IFIP/IEEE symposium on integrated network and service management (IM),*. Lisbon, Portugal, pp.772-777, 2017. http: //ieeexplore. ieee. org/ document

/7987376 /
[http://dx.doi.org/10.23919/INM.2017.7987376]

[17] Y. Huang, "WuJ, Long C. Drugledger: a practical blockchain system for drug traceability and regulation. In: 2018 IEEE international conference on Internet of things (iThings) and IEEE green computing and communications (GreenCom) and IEEE cyber, physical and social computing (CPSCom) and IEEE smart data (SmartData)", Halifax, NS, Canada, pp.1137-1144, 2018. https://ieeexplore.ieee.org/document /8726740/

[18] R. Kumar, and R. Tripathi, "Traceability of counterfeit medicine supply chain through Blockchain", *2019 11th international conference on communication sys-tems & networks (COMSNETS),* https://ieeexplore .ieee .org /document /8711418/ Bengaluru, India, pp.568-570, 2019. [http://dx.doi.org/10.1109/COMSNETS.2019.8711418]

[19] R. Raj, N. Rai, and S. Agarwal, "Anticounterfeiting in pharmaceutical supply chain by establishing proof of ownership", In: *TENCON 2019 -2019 IEEE region 10 con-ference (TENCON).* IEEE: Kochi, India, 2019, pp. 1572-1577.
[http://dx.doi.org/10.1109/TENCON.2019.8929271]

[20] M. Sahoo, S.S. Singhar, B. Nayak, and B.K. Mohanta, "A Blockchain Based Framework Secured by ECDSA to Curb Drug Counterfeiting,", In: *2019 10th International Conference on Computing, Communication and Networking Technologies (ICCCNT).* Kanpur, India, pp. 1-6, 2019.
[http://dx.doi.org/10.1109/ICCCNT45670.2019.8944772]

[21] A. Nordrum, "Govern by blockchain dubai wants one platform to rule them all, while Illinois will try anything", *IEEE Spectr.,* vol. 54, no. 10, pp. 54-55, 2017.
[http://dx.doi.org/10.1109/MSPEC.2017.8048841]

[22] M.E. Peck, and D. Wagman, "Energy trading for fun and profit buy your neighbor's rooftop solar power or sell your own-it'll all be on a blockchain", *IEEE Spectr.,* vol. 54, no. 10, pp. 56-61, 2017.
[http://dx.doi.org/10.1109/MSPEC.2017.8048842]

[23] C. Rottondi, and G. Verticale, "A privacy-friendly gaming framework in smart electricity and water grids", *IEEE Access,* vol. 5, pp. 14221-14233, 2017.
[http://dx.doi.org/10.1109/ACCESS.2017.2727552]

[24] E. Mengelkamp, J. Gärttner, K. Rock, S. Kessler, L. Orsini, and C. Weinhardt, "Designing microgrid energy markets", *Appl. Energy,* vol. 210, pp. 870-880, 2018.
[http://dx.doi.org/10.1016/j.apenergy.2017.06.054]

[25] J. Bergquist, A. Laszka, M. Sturm, and A. Dubey, "On the design of communication and transaction anonymity in blockchain-based transactive microgrids", *Proceedings of the 1st Workshop on Scalable and Resilient Infrastructures for Distributed Ledgers ACM.* Las Vegas Nevada, December 11 - 15, pp.3, 2017.
[http://dx.doi.org/10.1145/3152824.3152827]

[26] A. Laszka, A. Dubey, M. Walker, and D. Schmidt, "Providing privacy, safety, and security in IoT-based transactive energy systems using distributed ledgers", In: *Proceedings of the Seventh International Conference on the Internet of Things* ACM, 2017, p. 13.
[http://dx.doi.org/10.1145/3131542.3131562]

[27] L. Wu, K. Meng, S. Xu, S. Li, M. Ding, and Y. Suo, "Democratic centralism: a hybrid blockchain architecture and its applications in energy internet", In: *Proceedings of the IEEE International Conference on Energy Internet (ICEI)* IEEE, 2017, pp. 176-181.
[http://dx.doi.org/10.1109/ICEI.2017.38]

[28] Y. Yuan, and F-Y. Wang, "Towards blockchain-based intelligent transportation systems", *Proceedings of the 2016 IEEE 19th International Conference on Intelligent Transportation Systems (ITSC),.* pp.2663-2668, 2016.

[29] J. Kang, R. Yu, X. Huang, S. Maharjan, Y. Zhang, and E. Hossain, "Enabling localized peer-to-peer electricity trading among plug-in hybrid electric vehicles using consortium blockchains", *IEEE Trans.*

Industr. Inform., vol. 13, no. 6, pp. 3154-3164, 2017. [http://dx.doi.org/10.1109/TII.2017.2709784]

[30] A. Lei, H. Cruickshank, Y. Cao, P. Asuquo, C.P.A. Ogah, and Z. Sun, "Blockchain-based dynamic key management for heterogeneous intelligent transportation systems", *IEEE Internet Things J.*, vol. 4, no. 6, pp. 1832-1843, 2017. [http://dx.doi.org/10.1109/JIOT.2017.2740569]

[31] A. Fujihara, "PoWaP: proof of work at proximity for a crowdsensing system for collaborative traffic information gathering", Internet Things, vol. 10, 2019.

[32] S. Mansfield-Devine, "Beyond Bitcoin: using blockchain technology to provide assurance in the commercial world", *Comput. Fraud Secur.*, vol. 2017, no. 5, 2017. 14–18. [http://dx.doi.org/10.1016/S1361-3723(17)30042-8]

[33] W. Li, A. Sforzin, S. Fedorov, and G.O. Karame, "Towards scalable and private industrial blockchains", In: *Proceedings of the ACM Workshop on Blockchain, Cryptocurrencies and Contracts* ACM, 2017, pp. 9-14. [http://dx.doi.org/10.1145/3055518.3055531]

[34] R. Xu, L. Zhang, H. Zhao, and Y. Peng, "Design of network medias digital rights management scheme based on blockchain technology", *Proceedings of the 2017 IEEE 13th International Symposium on Autonomous Decentralized System (ISADS),* IEEE, pp. 128-133, 2017. [http://dx.doi.org/10.1109/ISADS.2017.21]

[35] Ž. Turk, R. Klinc, , and , "Potentials of blockchain technology for construction management", *Procedia Engineering.,* vol. 196, pp. 638-645, 2017.

[36] S. Delgado-Segura, C. Pérez-Solà, G. Navarro-Arribas, and J. Herrera-Joancomartí, "A fair protocol for data trading based on Bitcoin transactions", *Fut. Gen. Comput. Syst.,* 2017. [http://dx.doi.org/10.1016/j.future.2017.08.021]

[37] J.J. Sikorski, J. Haughton, and M. Kraft, "Blockchain technology in the chemical industry: Machine-to-machine electricity market", *Appl. Energy,* vol. 195, pp. 234-246, 2017. [http://dx.doi.org/10.1016/j.apenergy.2017.03.039]

[38] F. Tian, "An agri-food supply chain traceability system for China based on RFID & blockchain technology", In: *Proceedings of the 2016 13th International Conference on Service Systems and Service Management (ICSSSM)* IEEE, 2016, pp. 1-6.

[39] M. Nakasumi, "Information sharing for supply chain management based on block chain technology", In: *Proceedings of the 2017 IEEE 19th Conference on Business Informatics (CBI)* vol. volume 1. IEEE, 2017, pp. 140-149. [http://dx.doi.org/10.1109/CBI.2017.56]

[40] F. Tian, "A supply chain traceability system for food safety based on HACCP, blockchain & internet of things", In: *Proceedings of the 2017 International Conference on Service Systems and Service Management (ICSSSM)* IEEE, 2017, pp. 1-6.

[41] K. Biswas, and V. Muthukkumarasamy, Securing smart cities using blockchain technology. In 2016 IEEE 18th international conference on high performance computing and communications; IEEE 14th international conference on smart city; IEEE 2nd international conference on data science and systems (HPCC/SmartCity/DSS) (pp. 1392–1393). IEEE. [http://dx.doi.org/10.1109/HPCC-SmartCity-DSS.2016.0198]

[42] L. Yang, N. Elisa, and N. Eliot, *Privacy and security aspects of E-government in smart cities.* Elsevier Press: New York, 2018.

[43] E-Government survey 2014. E-Government in support of sustainable development/UN Department of Economic and Social Affairs.,

[44] C. Lambrinoudakis, S. Gritzalis, F. Dridi, and G. Pernul, "Security requirements for e-government services: a methodological approach for developing a common PKI-based security policy", *Comput.*

Commun., vol. 26, no. 16, pp. 1873-1883, 2003. [http://dx.doi.org/10.1016/S0140-3664(03)00082-3]

[45] V. Moen, A.N. Klingsheim, K.I.F. Simonsen, and K.J. Hole, "Vulnerabilities in e-governments", *International Journal of Electronic Security and Digital Forensics,* vol. 1, no. 1, pp. 89-100, 2007. [http://dx.doi.org/10.1504/IJESDF.2007.013595]

[46] L-F. Pau, *Business and social evaluation of denial of service attacks of communications networks in view of scaling economic counter-measures. In 2010 IEEE/IFIP network operations and management symposium workshops (NOMS Wksps).* IEEE, 2010, pp. 126-133.

[47] Available from: https://www.cryptomathic.com/news-events/blog/keyfor-egovernment-secur-ty-central-signing-authentication/

[48] Available from: https://www.ippmedia. com/en/business/how-tanzania-lost-187bn-cyber-crim-nals-2016/

[49] P. Seltsikas, and R.M. O'Keefe, "Expectations and outcomes in electronic identity management: the role of trust and public value", *Eur. J. Inf. Syst.,* vol. 19, no. 1, pp. 93-103, 2010. [http://dx.doi.org/10.1057/ejis.2009.51]

[50] O. Ali, J. Soar, and J. Yong, Impact of cloud computing technology on e-government. In International conference on information and software technologies pp. 272–290. [http://dx.doi.org/10.1007/978-3-319-11958-8_22]

[51] Available from: https://www.bitcoin.org/bitcoin.pdf

[52] U. Mukhopadhyay, A. Skjellum, O. Hambolu, J. Oakley, L. Yu, and R. Brooks, A brief survey of cryptocurrency systems. In 2016 14th annual conference on privacy, security and trust (PST) pp. 745–752. [http://dx.doi.org/10.1109/PST.2016.7906988]

[53] S. Huh, S. Cho, and S. Kim, Managing iot devices using blockchain platform. In 2017 19th international conference on advanced communication technology (ICACT) pp. 464–467. [http://dx.doi.org/10.23919/ICACT.2017.7890132]

[54] A. Dorri, S.S. Kanhere, R. Jurdak, and P. Gauravaram, "Blockchain for iot security and privacy: The case study of a smart home", In: *2017 IEEE international conference on pervasive computing and communications workshops (PerCom workshops).* IEEE, 2017, pp. 618-623.

[55] M. Turkanovic´, M. Ho¨lbl, K. Kosic, M. Hericko, and A. Kamisalic, "Eductx: A blockchain-based higher education credit platform", *IEEE Access,* vol. 6, pp. 5112-5127, 2018. [http://dx.doi.org/10.1109/ACCESS.2018.2789929]

[56] K. Peterson, R. Deeduvanu, P. Kanjamala, and K. Boles, "A blockchain-based approach to health information exchange networks", *Proceedings of NIST workshop blockchain healthcare,* vol. 1, pp. 1-10, 2016.

[57] M. Jun, "Blockchain government-a next form of infrastructure for the twenty-first century", *J. Open Innov. market and Complex.,* vol. 4, no. 1, p. 7, 2018. [http://dx.doi.org/10.1186/s40852-018-0086-3]

[58] V.V. Vishwarupe, and P.M. Joshi, "Intellert: a novel approach for content-priority based message filtering", *2016 IEEE Bombay Section Symposium (IBSS),* pp.1-6, 2016. [http://dx.doi.org/10.1109/IBSS.2016.7940206]

[59] A. Schmidt, F. Giannotti, W. Mackay, B. Shneiderman, and K. Väänänen, *Artificial Intelligence for Humankind: A Panel on How to Create Truly Interactive and Human-Centered AI for the Benefit of Individuals and Society.,* C. Ardito, Ed., vol. 12936. Springer: Cham, 2021. [http://dx.doi.org/10.1007/978-3-030-85607-6_32]

[60] V. Vishwarupe, P.M. Joshi, N. Mathias, S. Maheshwari, S. Mhaisalkar, and V. Pawar, "Explainable AI and Interpretable Machine Learning: A Case Study in Perspective", *Procedia Comput. Sci.,* vol. 204,

pp. 869-876, 2022.
[http://dx.doi.org/10.1016/j.procs.2022.08.105]

[61] V. Vishwarupe, M. Bedekar, M. Pande, V.P. Bhatkar, P. Joshi, S. Zahoor, and P. Kuklani, "Comparative Analysis of Machine Learning Algorithms for Analyzing NASA Kepler Mission Data", *Procedia Comput. Sci,* vol. 204, pp. 945-951, 2022.
[http://dx.doi.org/10.1016/j.procs.2022.08.115]

[62] M. Leming, and J. Suckling, "Matthew Leming, John Suckling, Deep learning for sex classification in resting-state and task functional brain networks from the UK Biobank", *NeuroImage,* vol. 241, 2021.
[http://dx.doi.org/10.1016/j.neuroimage.2021.118409]

[63] V. Vishwarupe, M. Bedekar, P.M. Joshi, M. Pande, V. Pawar, and P. Shingote, "Data Analytics in the Game of Cricket: A Novel Paradigm", *Procedia Comput. Sci.,* vol. 204, pp. 937-944, 2022.
[http://dx.doi.org/10.1016/j.procs.2022.08.114]

[64] S. Zahoor, M. Bedekar, and V. Vishwarupe, "A Framework to Infer Webpage Relevancy for a User", In: *Proceedings of First International Conference on Information and Communication Technology for Intelligent Systems,* S. Satapathy, S. Das, Eds., vol. Volume 1. vol. vol 50. Springer: Cham, 2016.
[http://dx.doi.org/10.1007/978-3-319-30933-0_16]

[65] V. Vishwarupe, M. Bedekar, M. Pande, and A. Hiwale, Intelligent Twitter Spam Detection: A Hybrid Approach.*Smart Trends in Systems, Security and Sustainability. Lecture Notes in Networks and Systems.,* X.S. Yang, A. Nagar, A. Joshi, Eds., vol. Vol. 18. Springer: Singapore, 2018.
[http://dx.doi.org/10.1007/978-981-10-6916-1_17]

[66] M. Bedekar, S. Zahoor, and V. Vishwarupe, "PeTelCoDS—Personalized Television Content Delivery System: A Leap into the Set-Top Box Revolution", In: *Proceedings of First International Conference on Information and Communication Technology for Intelligent Systems,* S. Satapathy, S. Das, Eds., vol. Volume 2. vol. vol 51. Springer: Cham, 2016.
[http://dx.doi.org/10.1007/978-3-319-30927-9_27]

[67] V. Vishwarupe, S. Maheshwari, A. Deshmukh, S. Mhaisalkar, P. M. Joshi, and N. Mathias, "Bringing Humans at the Epicenter of Artificial Intelligence: A Confluence of AI, HCI, and Human-Centered Computing", *Procedia Computer Science,,* vol. 204, pp. 914-921, 2022.
[http://dx.doi.org/10.1016/j.procs.2022.08.111]

[68] S. Zahoor, M. Bedekar, V. Mane, and V. Vishwarupe, Uniqueness in User Behavior While Using the Web. In: Satapathy, S., Bhatt, Y., Joshi, A., Mishra, D. (eds) *Proceedings of the International Congress on Information and Communication Technology.* Advances in Intelligent Systems and Computing, vol 438.
[http://dx.doi.org/10.1007/978-981-10-0767-5_24]

[69] V.V. Vishwarupe, and P.M. Joshi, "Intellert: a novel approach for content-priority based message filtering", *2016 IEEE Bombay Section Symposium (IBSS)* pp.1-6, 2016.
[http://dx.doi.org/10.1109/IBSS.2016.7940206]

[70] V. Vishwarupe, M. Bedekar, and S. Zahoor, "Zone specific weather monitoring system using crowdsourcing and telecom infrastructure", *2015 International Conference on Information Processing.,* ICIP, pp. 823-827, 2015.
[http://dx.doi.org/10.1109/INFOP.2015.7489495]

[71] Available from: https://patents.google.com/?inventor=Varad+Vishwarupe

[72] I. Goodfellow, J. Pouget-Abadie, M. Mirza, B. Xu, D. Warde-Farley, S. Ozair, and A. Courville, "Y. Bengio Generative adversarial nets", *Adv. Neural Inf. Process. Syst.,* p. 27, 2014.

[73] K. Kollnig, A. Shuba, R. Binns, M. Van Kleek, and N. Shadbolt, "Are iphones really better for privacy? a comparative study of ios and android apps", *Proceedings on Privacy Enhancing Technologies,* vol. 2022, no. 2, pp. 6-24, 2022.
[http://dx.doi.org/10.2478/popets-2022-0033]

[74] F. Alan, "Luke Church Fifty years of the psychology of programming", *Int J Human-Computer Studies*, vol. 131, pp. 52-63, 2019.

[75] F. Colarusso, P.C. Cheng, G. Garcia Garcia, A. Stockdill, D. Raggi, and M. Jamnik, "A novel interaction for competence assessment using micro-behaviors: Extending CACHET to graphs and charts", *Proceedings of the 2023 CHI Conference on Human Factors in Computing Systems,* pp.1-14, 2023.
[http://dx.doi.org/10.1145/3544548.3581519]

CHAPTER 2

Role of Blockchain Technology in Industry 4.0

Priya Shelke[1,*] and **Riddhi Mirajkar**[1]

[1] *Department of Information Technology, Vishwakarma Institute of Information Technology, Pune, Maharashtra, India*

Abstract: Challenges in the industrial world are evolving rapidly. The game-changing technologies for overcoming these challenges on the path to Industry 4.0 are digitization and automation. We can control and improve every area of supply chain and manufacturing processes with the aid of Industry 4.0 technologies. It offers access to the real-time data and insights we need to run a company more profitably and efficiently. As a result, one can make better, quicker business choices. Supply chains and manufacturing processes may be built with the use of Blockchain technology. In this chapter, the connection between Blockchain and Industry 4.0 is made clear. The nine pillars of Industry 4.0 are defined as the core value drivers of the manufacturing process. The next part provides a quick overview of the characteristics of Blockchain technology. The final section investigates the function of Blockchain in Industry 4.0 through the use of different applications.

Keywords: Blockchain, Supply chain, Manufacturing, Immutable, Transparent, Trust.

1. INTRODUCTION OF INDUSTRY 4.0

The fourth industrial revolution, also known as Industry 4.0 (Industry 4.0), is now underway, and as a result, new disruptive technologies are being explored for integration into the manufacturing environment. One of these approaches is the Blockchain, which handles financial transactions, interconnects heterogeneous systems, and promotes asset traceability in a transparent and secure way. As a result, this technology helps to build an efficient supply chain that might have an influence on the worldwide market. The intersection between Blockchain and Industry 4.0 is revealed in this chapter.

* **Corresponding author Priya Shelke:** Department of Information Technology, Vishwakarma Institute of Information Technology, Pune, India; Tel: +91 9403615809; E-mail: priya.shelke@viit.ac.in

Parikshit N. Mahalle, Gitanjali R. Shinde and Prachi M. Joshi (Eds.)

1.1. Core Value Drivers

Manufacturing businesses must identify and define their core value drivers enabled by digital technology in order to succeed in the upcoming industrial era. The core value drivers are depicted in Fig. (**1**). Industry 4.0 will boost prospects through innovation and custom solutions to raise customer value as well as operational efficiencies through Smart Factories and Smart Supply Chains. They will eventually result in whole new business models and service offerings enabled by digitalization [1].

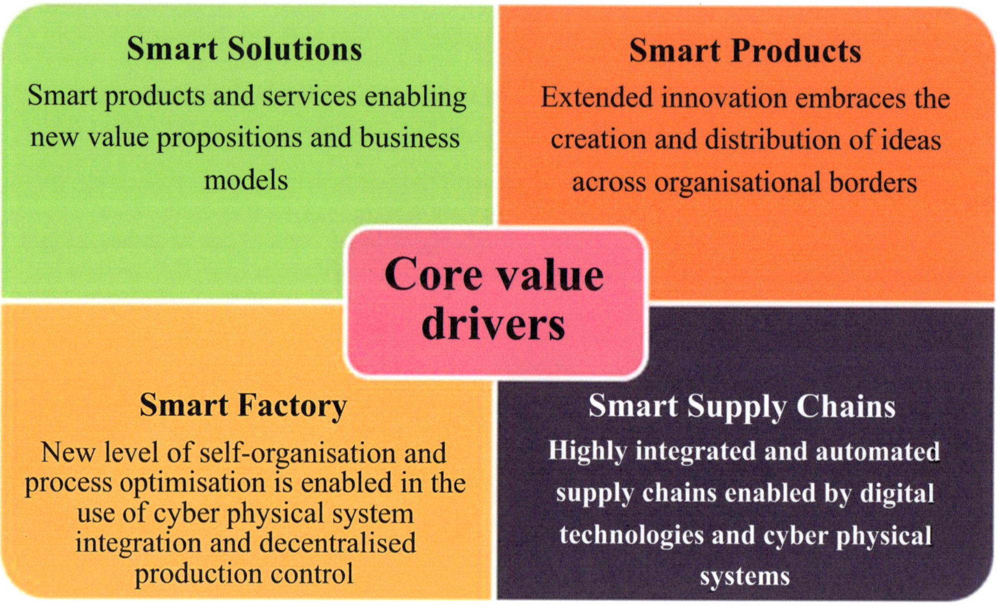

Fig. (1). Core value drivers.

1.2. The Nine Pillars of Industry 4.0

Industry 4.0 refers to a state of business that will be completely digitalized in terms of both production and financial flows. Every stage of the production process, in connection with the equipment, needs to be horizontally integrated. Machines communicate with one another in the globally networked environment of Industry 4.0 [2].

According to the Boston Consulting Group, Industry 4.0 is supported by nine technological pillars as shown in Fig. (**2**).

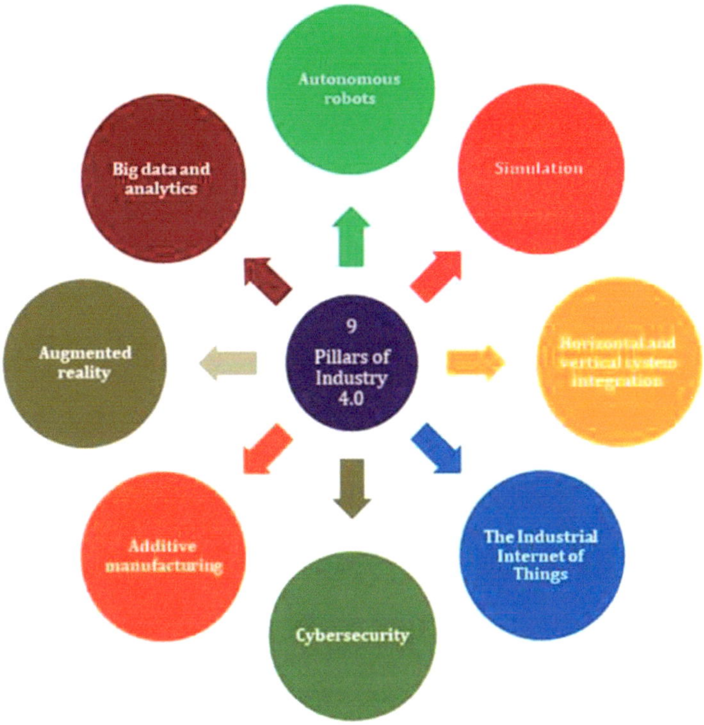

Fig. (2). 9 Pillars of Industry 4.0.

• Autonomous Robots

Robots have long been employed to complete complex jobs, and they now offer a greater range of services while also becoming more independent, adaptable, and collaborative. The term “robotics” is used to describe robots that assist operators in carrying out their responsibilities, and they will interact with one another and work safely with humans. They'll eventually be able to pick up knowledge from people. Robots have been employed by manufacturers across many industries to complete difficult tasks, but they are now becoming more useful. They are evolving toward increased adaptability, independence, and cooperation. They will consequently engage, collaborate, and learn from people in a safe manner. Compared to the current production robots, these analytic chatbots and robots will be more capable and affordable.

A company of robotic equipment in Europe named Kuka, for instance, provides communicative, autonomous robots. These robots are linked together so that they can cooperate and execute tasks that are automatically adjusted to the needs of the subsequent unfinished item in the production line. In-depth human collaboration is made possible by control systems and sophisticated sensors.

- **Simulation/Digital Twin**

There will be a significant increase in the 3D simulation of production processes, material development, and product development. It will make use of real-time data to create a virtual representation of the physical world that includes objects, people, and machines. For instance, operators will be able to test and improve machine settings for the upcoming product even before production begins, decreasing setup times and raising quality.

Based on data from the Internet of Things (IoT) sensors, a digital twin is a virtual representation of a real-world item, machine, system, or process. It enables firms to more thoroughly evaluate, comprehend, and enhance the performance and maintenance of goods and industrial systems. An asset operator might employ a digital twin to pinpoint a specific defective component, foresee foreseeable problems, and increase uptime.

Utilizing information from the physical machine, the German manufacturer of machine tools Siemens created a virtual machine that can replicate the milling of parts. By as much as 80%, this reduced the preparation time for the actual machining operation.

- **Horizontal and Vertical System Integration**

Information systems today are not entirely interconnected. Companies hardly ever communicate with their customers and suppliers. Rarely are engineering design departments inside a company directly connected to production. However, thanks to Industry 4.0, businesses will be connected to one another and to the rest of the organization.

The majority of IT systems now in use are not entirely interconnected. Businesses rarely have close relationships with their clients, suppliers, or customers. There is a lack of complete integration between organizational functions and full integration between factories, goods, and automation.

Organizations, functions, departments, and capacities will, however, become much more tenacious as Industry 4.0 develops and makes possible totally automated value chains thanks to cross-organizational, universal data-integration networks.

As an illustration, consider the collaboration platform that Boost Aerospace and Dassault Systems just introduced. This platform functions as a shared workspace for manufacturing and design collaboration and is accessible as a service on a private cloud. It handles all the challenging responsibilities involved in sharing product and manufacturing data with several partners.

- **The Industrial Internet of Things**

There are currently very few sensors and connections between machines. An increasing number of items will contain intelligence and connect *via* standardized protocols as a result of the Industrial Internet of Things. This will enable real-time reactions by decentralizing analytics and decision-making.

Currently, embedded computing is only used by a small portion of a manufacturer's machines and sensors that are networked. Industry 4.0 and the Industrial Internet of Things are synonymous because both concepts are so essential to it. Sensors are used by the majority of Industry 4.0's physical objects, including machines, robots, products, and equipment, to deliver real-time data about their functionality, state, or location.

Organizations can use this technology to manage their supply chains more efficiently, design and adapt products more quickly, monitor consumer preferences, stop equipment breakdowns, maintain inventories, and do a lot more.

A decentralized production and semi-automated process was installed in a valve manufacturing facility by a drive and control system supplier, Bosch Rexroth. The purpose was to determine which production processes must be carried out for each product and to adapt workstations that are used to identify products using identification codes, radio frequency, and workstations.

- **Cybersecurity**

Operational management systems that are cut off and disconnected no longer exist. Communication and connectivity protocols are becoming standard. It is becoming increasingly important to protect manufacturing processes and information systems from cybercrime attacks. Secure, dependable communications will be provided by sophisticated identity and machine access management systems.

Many businesses still rely on unconnected or closed production systems and management. Industry 4.0's growing connection and usage of common communications protocols have greatly enhanced the need to safeguard production lines and other crucial industrial systems from cybersecurity threats. As a result, maintaining trustworthy and secure connections as well as controlling user and machine access are essential.

Throughout the previous year, a number of suppliers of industrial equipment have partnered with or acquired cyber security firms.

- **Additive Manufacturing**

Companies are just now starting to use 3D printing for unit manufacturing and prototyping. These technologies will be used in Industry 4.0 because of their exceptional ability to produce customized goods in small numbers. Transport and inventory management expenses will go down with decentralized systems.

- **Augmented Reality**

The development of augmented reality tools is still in its infancy, but they are opening the door for new services. They will, for instance, give operators the real-time data they want for quicker decision-making and for streamlining work procedures.

- **Big Data and Analytics**

In the industrial sector, there are still enormous amounts of unused data. Their study will raise service standards, reduce energy consumption, and maximize production quality. Real-time decision-making is also desired in this instance.

The industrial industry has recently embraced analytics based on massive data sets, which optimizes production quality, enhances equipment maintenance, and reduces energy use. Big data analytics in Industry 4.0 refers to the practice that will soon be standard for supporting real-time decision-making: a thorough study and collecting of data from numerous sources, including industrial equipment, systems, organizations, and CMS.

By comparing single-chip data captured during the testing phase at the end of the production process with process data gathered during the wafer status phase in the early process, for instance, the semiconductor manufacturer Infineon Technologies has decreased product failures. Infineon was able to immediately spot patterns that let them discharge damaged chips early in the production process and enhance production quality thanks to Industry 4.0 analytics.

• Cloud Computing

Cloud computing is the "great enabler" of digital transformation. In the present scenario, cloud technology goes way beyond scalability, speed, cost efficiencies, and storage. It gives the foundation for the most advanced technologies – from AI and ML to the IoT – and provides organizations with a way to organize themselves. The data that power Industry 4.0 cloud computing technologies use in the cyber-physical systems and the cloud at the core of Industry 4.0, use the cloud to coordinate and communicate.

For digital transformation, cloud computing is the "great facilitator". The current state of cloud computing technology goes much beyond scalability, speed, cost-effectiveness, and storage. In addition to giving enterprises a method to be organized, it lays the groundwork for the most cutting-edge technologies, including the IoT and AI and ML. The cyber-physical systems and cloud at the Centre of Industry 4.0 use the cloud to coordinate and communicate the data that give power to such systems being installed there.

2. BLOCKCHAIN

One of the technologies identified as enabling this revolution in the context of Industry 4.0 is the Blockchain. In a variety of industries, including manufacturing and the supply chain environment, it has sparked a great deal of excitement and enthusiasm [3].

Blockchain, a ground-breaking technology that is reshaping several sectors, was mysteriously presented to the world with Bitcoin, as its first contemporary application. Bitcoin is nothing more than a type of virtual money known as a crypto currency that can be exchanged for fiat money. Since 2008, the growth of Bitcoin has been the primary example of a Blockchain application. This well-known cryptocurrency provides an efficient response to the problem of trust in a decentralized system. It has the ability to render transactions permanent, verifiable, and untraceable.

People frequently believe that Bitcoin and Blockchain are similar, however, this is not the case. For both small and large businesses, Blockchain may be used to enhance security, privacy, and data transparency. One of the uses for Blockchain technology is the creation of cryptocurrencies, and in addition to Bitcoin, there are many more uses for the technology that are currently being explored.

2.1. Features of Blockchain

The following features shown in Fig. (**3**) set the ground-breaking Blockchain technology:

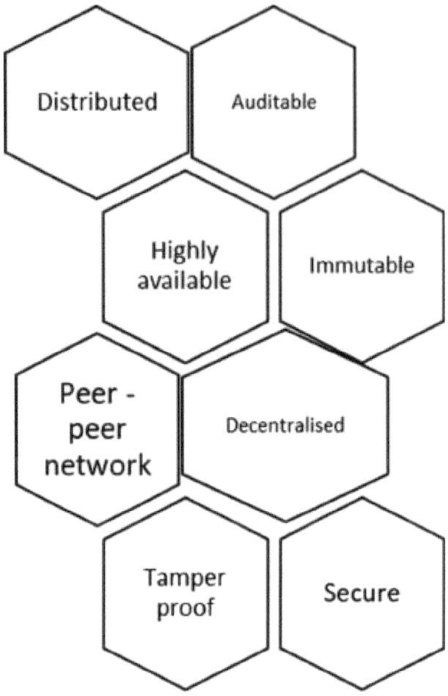

Fig. (3). Features of blockchain.

- **Distributed**

Collaboration is the only recurring concept in the blockchain. There must be several systems in place for collaboration to take place. Blockchain is a distributed system by nature since data is processed and stored by various parties. All network participants have access to the distributed ledger and its immutable record of transactions. With this shared ledger, transactions are recorded only once, eliminating the duplication of effort that's typical of traditional business networks.

- **Decentralized**

Blockchains are decentralized in nature meaning that no single person or group holds the authority of the overall network. While everybody in the network has a copy of the distributed ledger with them, no one can modify it on his or her own. This unique feature of Blockchain allows transparency and security while giving power to the users.

- **Peer-to-Peer Network**

The usage of Blockchain makes it simple to engage between two parties using a peer-to-peer architecture without the need for a middleman. Blockchain is a peer-to-peer protocol that enables each member of the network to have an exact copy of each transaction, enabling machine consensus for approval. For instance, with Blockchain, you may complete any transaction from one region of the world to another in a matter of seconds. Additionally, any delays or additional fees won't be subtracted from the transfer.

- **Immutable**

Any data that has been added to a blockchain cannot be modified after it has been sent , which is known as the immutability feature of a blockchain. Consider sending an email, as an illustration, to better grasp immutability. An email that has been sent to a large group of recipients cannot be canceled. You'll have to ask each receiver of your email to erase it, which is a laborious task. This is the operation of immutability. Data cannot be modified or altered once it has been processed. Because each block in a blockchain retains the hash of the one before it, if you try to modify the data of one block, you'll have to update the whole blockchain that follows it. Any changes to one hash will affect the remaining hashes as well. Since it takes a lot of processing power to modify all the hashes, it is quite difficult for someone to do so. As a result of immutability, data kept in a blockchain is immune to changes or hackers' assaults.

- **Tamper-Proof**

Because Blockchain is immutable, we cannot change the contents of the blocks. Nevertheless, if the content of a single block is changed, it can be quickly identified and remedied. As a result, Blockchain is also temper-proof. Hashes and blocks are the two main methods for spotting tampering. Each block-related hash function is distinct. It may be compared to a block's fingerprint. Any modification to the data will result in a modification to the hash function. A hacker would have to modify the hashes of all the blocks following that one in order to make any changes because the hash function of one block is connected to the next, which is a challenging task.

- **Auditable**

Blockchain does not only share the current state but the entire journey or log of how the state has arrived. The log is available for each node to inquire about. This makes activities happening on blockchain auditable.

- **Highly Available**

Distributed and decentralized nature of the blockchain network helps ensure consumers that the network always has a node available to serve the requests. This makes blockchain highly available.

2.2. Evolution of Blockchain

In 1991, Stuart Haber and W. Scott Stornetta dreamed of what many today call blockchain. Their initial project was creating a chain of blocks that was cryptographically secure such that document timestamps could not be altered.

The system was modified in 1992 to include Merkle trees, which increased performance and allowed for the accumulation of more documents on a single block. The evolution of blockchain technology is shown in Fig. (**4**).

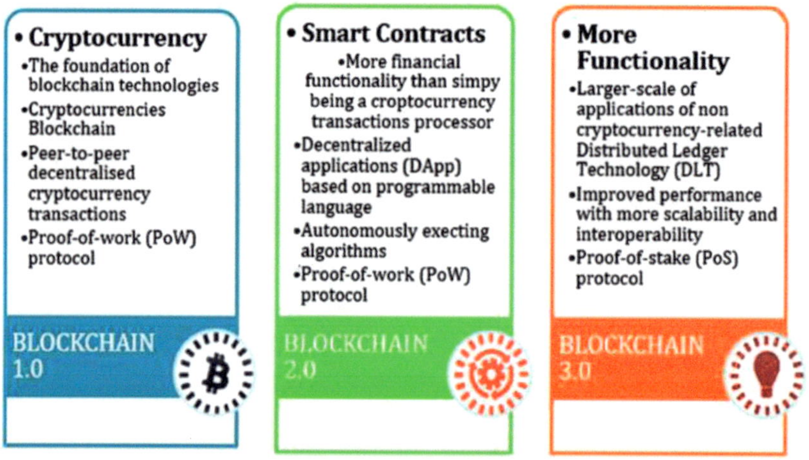

Fig. (4). Evolution of blockchain technology.

2.2.1. Blockchain 1.0

Blockchain technology is credited to Satoshi Nakamoto as its creator. There isn't much information available about Nakamoto, who is said to have worked on Bitcoin, the first use of the digital ledger technology.

In 2008, Nakamoto created the first blockchain, from which the technology developed and found use in a variety of applications outside cryptocurrencies. In 2009, Satoshi Nakamoto published the first whitepaper on the subject. He explained in the whitepaper how the decentralised feature of the technology meant that nobody would ever be in control of anything and that it was thus ideally suited to enhancing digital trust.

Since Satoshi Nakamoto left the scene and gave control of the development of Bitcoin to other core developers. The technology of digital ledgers has developed, giving rise to new applications that make up the block chain's history.

A Bitcoin user may now deal digitally with another user without the need for a single, centralized middleman (like a bank) to approve the transaction. Previous digital transaction systems have failed to reach this achievement. However, Bitcoin requires a tremendous amount of electricity on high-powered computers. This makes the process not just highly unsustainable, but also unsalable.

Numerous applications have emerged since the advent of Bitcoin, all of which aim to make use of the capabilities and guiding principles of the digital ledger technology. As a result, there are a vast number of uses for blockchain technology that have emerged over the course of history.

2.2.2. Blockchain 2.0

As one of the first contributors to the Bitcoin codebase and in a world where innovation is the norm, Vitalik Buterin is among a growing number of developers who believe that Bitcoin has not yet fully used the potential of blockchain technology.

Because of the limits of Bitcoin, Buterin began developing what he thought would be a flexible blockchain that could serve a variety of purposes in addition to serving as a peer-to-peer network. A crucial turning point in the history of the blockchain came when Ethereum was introduced as a brand-new public blockchain in 2013 with more features than Bitcoin.

By making it possible to store additional assets in addition to contracts, such as slogans, Buterin created Ethereum apart from the Bitcoin Blockchain. With the addition of the new functionality, Ethereum's capabilities were increased beyond those of a cryptocurrency to those of a platform for the creation of decentralised apps.

Given its capacity to enable smart contracts that are used to carry out various functions, the Ethereum blockchain, which was formally introduced in 2015, has developed into one of the most significant implementations of blockchain technology. The blockchain technology for Ethereum has also been successful in attracting a vibrant developer community, which has helped it build a real ecosystem.

Ethereum blockchain processes the most number of daily transactions thanks to its ability to support smart contracts and decentralized applications. Its market cap has also increased significantly in the cryptocurrency space.

2.2.3. Blockchain 3.0

Ethereum and Bitcoin are just the beginning of the Blockchain's history and evolution. Several initiatives have emerged in recent years that all make use of the potential of blockchain technology. In addition to developing new features utilizing blockchain technologies, additional initiatives have worked to fix some of the shortcomings of Bitcoin and Ethereum.

Blockchain 3.0 aims to address the primary problems with current blockchains: Scalability and interoperability, in order to make blockchain a significant competitor to conventional, centralized payment institutions.

Following Blockchain 2.0, Blockchain 3.0 is another stage of blockchain development. It intends to address current problems in the blockchain sector to promote acceptance by the general public.

Blockchain 3.0 is an improved version of Blockchain 2.0 that expands upon and improves the technological capabilities of its previous version. It eliminates block delays by enabling a unidirectional flow of information that cannot be returned to the sender using a directed acyclic graph (DAG) as its data structure. As a result, transactions may be handled at an amazing pace of 10,000 transactions per second, nearly instantly.

The introduction of Blockchain 3.0 aids in accelerating the adoption of blockchain technology with a quicker, more affordable, and more efficient strategy that can compete with that of current centralized financial institutions. It does this not only in the financial sector but also in a wide range of other industries, including healthcare, logistics, and even the implementation of transparent ledgers in voting systems to increase accessibility while enforcing security. Distributed ledger technology is also used to improve the security of information storage and transfer in the healthcare industry.

Blockchain 3.0 may not have achieved its objective of widespread adoption, but it has advanced beyond its original purpose of creating a decentralised financial system to enhance the storage and transit of sensitive data [3].

2.3. Consensus Mechanism in Blockchain Technology

Blockchain consensus is the process through which the network's peers come to an agreement on the current state of the data. Consensus algorithms do this by establishing reliability and trust in the Blockchain network. Transactions are verified consensus processes, which are often referred to as consensus protocols or consensus algorithms, and the underlying blockchain's security is maintained [4].

A blockchain is a digital ledger that is distributed, decentralised, and often public and used to record transactions. Each of these transactions is represented as a separate "block" of data that must first complete independent peer-to-peer network validation before being included in the chain. A collection of peers, or nodes, in a network decides which blockchain transactions are valid and which are not through a consensus process. The approaches used to arrive to this agreement are consensus mechanisms. It's these sets of rules that help to protect networks from malicious behavior and hacking attacks. Consensus methods like Proof of Work (PoW) are used by blockchain networks like Bitcoin and Ethereum to ensure that all users (or "nodes") concur on a single version of history.

Consensus mechanisms are available in different types as shown in Fig. (**5**), each with a unique set of advantages and disadvantages. The consensus process used by each blockchain network must be unique since various applications require different outcomes. While they differ in their energy usage, security, and scalability, they all share one purpose: to ensure that records are true and honest. Two of the most popular consensus mechanisms are proof of work (PoW) and proof of stake (PoS) [4].

Proof-of-Work: With proof-of-work, miners (also known as nodes) compete with one another to validate the next transaction block. Through trial and error, they attempt to resolve challenging mathematical puzzles. After solving mathematical puzzles, a miner receives a block as a reward if they are the first one to find the solution. Although it requires a lot of energy, this consensus method fosters a high level of trust.

Proof-of-Stake (PoS): This randomized method relies on the biggest holders of the network's currency to propose new blocks. It provides incentives for validators to keep the blockchain network running. In comparison to Proof of Work, Proof of Stake uses less energy [5].

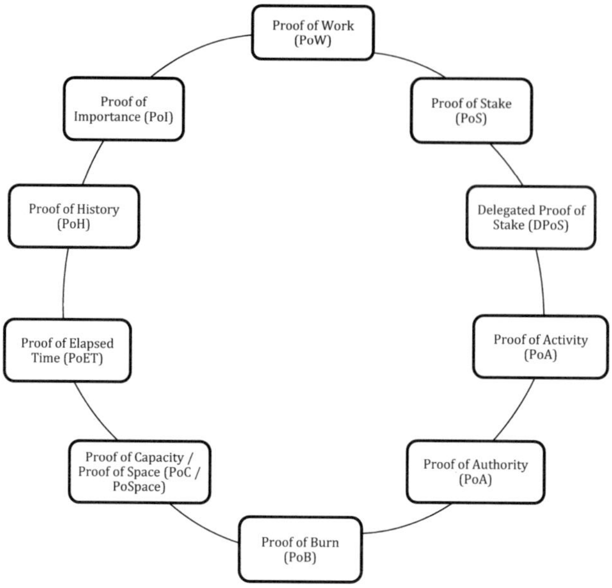

Fig. (5). Consensus mechanisms in blockchain.

3. ROLE OF BLOCKCHAIN IN INDUSTRY 4.0

The foundation of the fourth industrial revolution will be secure, interconnected networks that remove the need for middlemen. Blockchain will be the driving force behind whole new manufacturing business models by "distributing trust" across players. Blockchain's transparent consensus mechanism enables users to confirm the validity of transactions and the changes or additions made to data during the process. Blockchain's disruptive properties have already been experimented with and tested in the financial industry, where tools can swiftly and securely validate information without involving a human. Although the financial industry was the primary emphasis of Blockchain technology, manufacturing, agriculture, healthcare, supply chains, and logistics are showing far greater promise. Blockchain technology supports new organizational structures, work processes, and business models. It is changing the paradigm from hierarchical organizations to self-organizing economies. Blockchain has created a wide range of new opportunities for the simple and reliable direct transfer of value between participants. Workflow execution will be used with smart contracts to automate regulatory procedures. It will be simpler than ever to report and monitor the necessary data, verify compliances, and complete the approval processes. The following section describes how blockchain technology can be adapted in various domains, the issues involved in it and the benefits incurred.

3.1. Healthcare

Blockchain may be very helpful in the healthcare industry for identification verification, managing the pharmaceutical and medical supply chain, keeping patients' medical information private, and secure and updating patient data across several facilities and locations in real time. Blockchain technology adoption in the healthcare sector is rare at the national level. Examples from certain nations, like Estonia and Malta, demonstrate how blockchain technology may provide practical features like data security protection and patient consent management [6].

For the health sector to function effectively, accurate and verifiable identification of people (such as patients and providers) as well as organisations (such as hospitals, pharmacies, academic institutions, and other research institutes) is essential. Secure identification is made possible by a blockchain, which can enhance integrity and transparency while preventing differential versioning of IDs. As more information starts to flood in from wearable medical devices and the Internet of Things (IoT), this will become more and more crucial so that, for instance, the data can be appropriately linked with people's electronic medical records.

In order for patients to find healthcare providers, accreditation organisations to identify them, and payers to properly reimburse them, healthcare providers - both individual and organizational - must offer accurate and up to date information about their location and service availability. The veracity and accuracy of the pertinent information may be enhanced by a blockchain. A blockchain can provide an immutable log of each access to or modification of a data record. The management of product supply chains is the most typical use of blockchain across sectors. Blockchains are starting to be utilized in the healthcare industry to manage the supply chains for medicines, clinical supplies, blood products, and medical equipment. Trust concerns result from the failure of supply chains with professional medical equipment providers. Issues concerning new vendors include standard compliance, certification for customs, promptness of delivery of products, and fraud. The need for advance payment from suppliers exacerbates these trust problems. A blockchain is a potential tool for tracking goods and ensuring the reliability of suppliers. The supply chains for pharmaceuticals also have trust issues. They include concerns about quality assurance, intellectual property protection, copying, and the sale of illegal drugs.

Supply chains for medical devices face comparable concerns. These can include problems with efficacy and safety as well as high-risk devices having a history of security vulnerabilities. A blockchain might improve the security, transparency, and legitimacy of these initiatives if agreed-upon standards and protocols are in place. Blockchain may be a helpful option in situations where there are trust issues or limited information exchange capabilities.

Individuals can use blockchain to create a transparent, auditable method for allowing other parties to access their personal health data by using their unique credentials and encryption key. This includes allowing access to their medical records and other information for the purposes of direct healthcare provision or to allow research, statistical analysis, or other secondary uses of their data for other key parties (such as researchers and social care providers).

If someone chooses to alter the terms of their permission or consent, the modified terms can be added as a new block that overrides the earlier instructions on the chain. Blockchain may be employed as a safe approach to manage the flow of personal data while enrolling participants in clinical studies. Both the person, who may keep their data secret until an agreement is made and the research team, which can trust that it is obtaining meaningful and legitimate data, may have their interests protected by a Blockchain.

3.1.1. Issues in the Adaption of Blockchain in Healthcare

The promise of Blockchain technology in the health industry is overhyped, and its value may be exaggerated. Blockchain cannot eliminate the need for health data governance or the most difficult barriers to the digital transformation of the healthcare industry, such as a lack of data interoperability.

Blockchain can store data without a central authority, but they do not remove the need for any kind of authority. As a result of the nature of the health industry and the fact that its data is frequently sensitive and personalized, Blockchain applications will be dependent on standards, protocols, and supervision in addition to legislation. There will always be a need for a trustworthy body to set the rules. This might be the government or a reputable organisation or agency. For policy makers, the cost of developing and implementing new technology is crucial. Stakeholder engagement is crucial for the effective implementation of the technology since Blockchain represents a significant departure from the conventional ideas of data management and storage. To guarantee its effective and efficient usage, the health workers would need to be trained and educated. Successful adoption will depend on public input and education of patients on how to use the technology and their rights and obligations when the technology is introduced to allow patients to have more control over and access to their data. The immutability of Blockchains can be a doubled-edged sword. While the data included in Blockchain-based ledgers is intrinsically secure and tamper-proof, this does not guarantee that the data inputted are accurate or of acceptable quality.

Malicious actors might potentially influence people's decisions on consent and permissions to use their data, in addition to human error. With an increase in the number of people who are physically and cognitively vulnerable in older populations, this risk is especially significant. Only governance, legislation, and enforcement are capable of controlling this risk; blockchain cannot [7].

3.1.2. Current Application of Blockchain in Healthcare

Hashed health leverages blockchain to create a free and public community where medical experts may collaborate and debate Blockchain's potential applications. In order to assist healthcare institutions in understanding how blockchain might be incorporated into current systems, the company also offers an advising branch. Finally, the company involves a lab where it hopes to create novel blockchain technology solutions for issues that have confounded the healthcare sector. Another healthcare company with a blockchain emphasis is MedRec. Providers can easily trace files and information because of MedRec's transparent peer-to-peer ledger. Additionally, the programme makes it simpler to communicate directly with patients. A single platform connects clinics, facilities, and massive systems, enabling the most effective transmission of information. DYNOSTICS, yet another blockchain-based company, which caters to individual users, offers quick feedback and a centralized location for all data, assisting people in determining their current level of fitness. Data security and privacy are important to DYNOSTICS as well [7].

3.2. Agriculture

Blockchain technology has four classes of applications in the agricultural and food sectors: agricultural insurance, smart farming, food supply chain, and transactions of agricultural products [8].

3.2.1. Crop Insurance

The production of crops and livestock is impacted by weather extremes. Weather-related threats are traditionally managed through agricultural insurance schemes. They differ in terms of how losses are determined and, as a result, how payouts are initiated. While indemnity-based insurances (where damage assessment was made by an expert on the farm) can precisely cover losses, they are vulnerable to issues brought on by asymmetric information problems. Farmers and insurers are given disproportionate access to information about how risky agricultural output and production methods are. For instance, farmers shouldn't choose riskier crops just because they have insurance; rather, they should choose insurance products based on their risks. If the insurer lacks appropriate knowledge of the insurance plan, both scenarios result in market failure. Index-based insurance was developed as a solution to indemnity-based-insurances.

In this case, a quantifiable measure, such as rainfall at a nearby weather station, rather than the loss itself, triggers the payout.

In two ways, blockchain can help to improve index insurance. On the basis of meteorological information that initiates the payout as specified in a smart contract, payments can first be paid promptly and automatically. Second, a smart oracle may automatically integrate weather data and other data sources, such as plant growth data or data gathered by farm machines, to improve basis risk reduction and speed up the index determination and payout process.

Using blockchain technology, Etherisc, a Swiss company, offers decentralised crop insurance with reimbursements depending on meteorological information. A New York City-based insurance company called WorldCover, offers index insurance contracts to smallholder farmers in Ghana. It develops a smart contract that runs on the Ethereum blockchain. As a result, payouts would be made in the cryptocurrency Ether. A farmer may propose a contract that contains the premium payment, a payout, and a weather event that triggers the payout at Using Arbol, another clever crop insurance provider. After that, a counterparty acting as an investor might accept that suggested contract. Ether is used for both the initial and final settlement.

There are two significant flaws in this sector. The first is that payouts are done in cryptocurrency, which is still not widely utilized. And second, farmers might not have access to the necessary technical infrastructure, particularly in developing nations.

3.2.2. Smart Agriculture

According to their needs and capabilities, various actors and stakeholders develop and manage data and information as products move from inputs to output through multiple value-adding stages. ICT, the Internet of Things (IoT), and other modern data collecting and analysis technologies are features of smart agriculture. The implementation of a comprehensive security system that supports data utilization and administration is a critical component of developing smart agriculture. Traditional methods manage data in a centralized manner and are vulnerable to cyberattacks, faulty data, data distortion, and abuse. Using blockchain technology, data and information are stored. It makes sure that all recorded data is immutable and that the data and information are transparent to the involved actors and stakeholders. Instead of relying on the "security of obscurity" that traditional technologies rely on, blockchain technology provides security through decentralization. Data loss and tampering are less likely to occur when data is distributed to stakeholders' PCs as opposed to being stored on servers that are centrally controlled by administrators. The blockchain also solves the problem of developing a comprehensive, secure IoT infrastructure and integrating various ICT e-agriculture technologies.

Numerous IoT and blockchain-based smart farming models have been suggested and put into practice, for example, a blockchain-based ICT e-agriculture model and a blockchain-based architecture for smart greenhouse farms. Smart agriculture with blockchain does not lower, if not raise, the technological barrier for farmers to participate. Importantly, collecting reliable data from major farms rather than smallholders to upload it to the blockchain is better. Large farmers are more likely to participate in and gain from blockchain-based smart agriculture. Thus, this may contribute to or exacerbate the gap between large and small farmers.

3.2.3. Food Supply Chain

The traceability of food from the farm to the supermarket might be accelerated by blockchain technology.

Blockchain technology offers greater efficiency for the agricultural supply chain through improved data management, lower transaction costs, streamlined logistics, more rigorous traceability, and improved food safety measures. Leading technology firms are forming alliances with major retailers and logistics providers to create blockchain applications for the effective tracking and delivery of agricultural products.

The adoption of blockchain in agriculture will probably hasten the drive toward increased transparency and traceability from the farm to the fork and table. This will present farmers and the rest of the supply chain with opportunities and tools to prevent food fraud and provide consumers with verified products.

Following are startups based on blockchain that are transforming the agricultural sector.

- **AgriChain** is a blockchain startup that aims to eliminate intermediaries by enabling peer-to-peer agriculture processing and transactions.
- **AgriDigital** is a comprehensive, blockchain-based system for managing commodities for the global grains market. Through the use of smart contracts,

the platform assists in processing complicated agricultural transactions.

- **AgriLedger** is a social entrepreneurship initiative from the UK that helps farmers track down the source of their food, gain better access to funding, and save transaction data.

Demeter is a central hub that allows users to rent and grow micro fields anywhere in the globe without the need for middlemen, complexity, or high overhead.

A blockchain firm called Etherisc provides farmers with crop insurance through its decentralised insurance applications.

Ripe - The firm uses high-quality food data to build the Blockchain of Food, which charts the journey of food, by establishing a transparent digital food supply chain.

With the use of identifying technologies, TE-FOOD tracks fresh food parcels, livestock, and transporters along the whole supply chain.

The crop insurance company Worldcovr uses satellites to track rainfall and automatically initiate reimbursements in order to safeguard against yield loss.

3.3. Manufacturing

"Businesses in the industrial sector are demonstrating that blockchain technology is more than just cryptocurrencies".

Manufacturers are working on blockchain technologies that might improve operational efficiency, supply chain visibility, and the ability to track assets with unmatched accuracy. Blockchain technology has the ability to completely change how manufacturers develop, engineer, produce, and scale their goods [9].

3.3.1. Commercial Impact of Blockchain

Blockchain can improve transparency and trust at every point in the industrial value chain, from sourcing raw materials to delivering the finished product. It could alleviate the following problems:

- Supply-chain oversight should increase transparency
- Materials sourcing and fakes detection
- Engineering for high-complexity, long-lasting products
- Managing identities
- asset monitoring

- assurance of quality
- Observing regulations

In addition to providing tremendous value for industrial enterprises, blockchain-powered solutions can assist other cutting-edge technologies like augmented reality, IoT, and 3D printing to reach their full potential.

Utilizing this potent technology, producers are improving goods all along the product's lifecycle. Industrial firms demonstrate that blockchain technology is more diverse than just cryptocurrency. Manufacturers are working on blockchain technologies that might improve operational efficiency, supply chain visibility, and the ability to track assets with unmatched accuracy. Blockchain technology has the ability to completely change how manufacturers develop, engineer, produce, and scale their goods. Additionally, it is changing the way businesses engage by having the ability to build trust among rivals who yet need to work together in similar ecosystems.

3.3.2. Automating Across Boundaries while Enabling Trust

Manufacturing is frequently spread out across the globe to take advantage of the most affordable consumer markets, labor, capital, and raw material availability. Because businesses are closely linked by extensive, global supply and demand chains, a single weak link can put the operation's resilience to the test. Following are some examples of blockchain in manufacturing solutions.

- **Supply Chain Openness**

Using IBM Blockchain Transparent Supply, you can construct your own blockchain ecosystem to share data with dependable supply chain partners.

- **Supplier Management**

This blockchain network offers permission access to pre-verified supplier information, which speeds up supplier onboarding, to increase supply chain agility by modernizing procurement operations.

- **Logistics for Containers**

Through TradeLens, the open and impartial supply chain platform supported by blockchain technology, more than 150 exporters, importers, freight forwarders, customs authorities, and others currently collaborate to manage container logistics globally.

3.3.3. Blockchain's Case Studies in Manufacturing

At every level of the industrial value chain, from acquiring raw materials to delivering the finished product, blockchain can boost transparency and trust. The problems that it could alleviate include: Monitoring the supply chain for more transparency.

- **Materials provenance and counterfeiting detection**

Engineering design is for complex, long-lasting product management, asset management, quality control, and regulation observance. In addition to providing tremendous value for industrial enterprises, blockchain-powered solutions can help realize the full potential of other cutting-edge technologies like augmented reality, IoT, and 3D printing. Millions of pieces make a commercial aircraft. It might still be nearly impossible to determine which parts are on which plane, when they were last maintained, and by whom, despite advancements in sensor technology, data analytics, and cloud computing. The answer could come from blockchain technology, which would improve safety, aftermarket values, and asset use.

- **Automotive track and trace**

Auto manufacturers oversee extensive and sophisticated supplier lines. Moreover, the reliability and safety of a company's automobiles are ultimately up to the authorities and consumers. The origin of the vehicle's parts and their route from the mine to the showroom floor are frequently not sufficiently transparent. To trace every step of that journey into all supply chain tiers, automakers would benefit from a blockchain-enabled solution. The management of inventories may also benefit from this improved recall response.

- **Reliable data sharing and workflow automation**

Crossing organizational and international barriers, it enables reliable data sharing and workflow automation. Tracing the origins of raw materials and produced items encourages more ethical purchasing and helps to stabilize weak supply chains and commercial connections devastated by the pandemic.

- **Discover reliable supply chain provenance**

The immutable asset register of Blockchain is used to learn the origin of each component part of a product. The process can be audited more easily, fake goods can be found and eliminated more easily, and improperly acquired raw materials may be removed.

- **Enhance cooperation with trading partners**

Distributed supply ecosystems are managed efficiently by improving visibility, addressing concerns related to cost and complexity in supplier connections, and expanding connectivity. By using fewer manual approval processes and paper-based certificates, you may speed up the onboarding of new suppliers.

- **Reduce financial friction**

Data visibility is increased to quickly spot discrepancies and disagreements between business partners. By using smart contracts to automate business rules, we can drastically cut the time it takes to reconcile and arrive at an agreement almost instantly.

3.3.4. Best Practices for Blockchain Solutions

There are numerous ways for blockchain solutions to benefit industrial businesses. However, that does not imply that it is a workable answer for all businesses or all industrial manufacturing sectors. Companies can put themselves on a path toward effective execution by concentrating on four critical areas early on in their blockchain activities.

- **Make the business case:** Make a commitment to new approaches, outline the issue and the solution, start small, then go big.
- **Build an ecosystem:** Work across the value chain, expand your network, and concentrate on a cooperative few.
- **Design deliberately:** Face concerns early, think about privacy applications, and spend money on data and procedures.
- **Navigate regulatory uncertainty:** Influencing the use of trusted technology, keeping an eye on changing regulations, and using those regulations as a guide.

3.4. Government

74% of leaders like you concur that the conventional company models cannot survive in the face of tremendous upheaval. Technology is largely to blame for this upheaval, but in the case of blockchain, it can also offer a solution. Blockchain eliminates the traditional friction between systems and releases the value long locked inside fortified corporate silos by automating duplicate procedures and exchanging data across permissioned network members in a decentralized manner. As a result, there is an unprecedented level of confidence and openness in the food supply, supply chains, financial services, energy, identification, and many other areas. Additionally, IBM is collaborating with organizations at all levels in the public sector to demonstrate the potential of blockchain in advancing the government's digital transformation [10].

3.4.1. Building Trust in Government

Discover how blockchain may ease financial strains, facilitate transactions and asset management, and provide access to and analysis of data for more effective service delivery to residents. Greater trust, transparency, and accountability can be achieved by enabling safe data sharing between organizations and individuals *via* blockchain technology [11].

3.4.2. Benefits of Solving the Problems Unique to Government with Blockchain

- **Reducing the Risk of Data Leaks**

By offering an unalterable and transparent audit trail for statutory compliance, contract management, identity management, and citizen services, blockchains can decrease the time, expense, and dangers associated with maintaining sensitive information.

- **Removing Barriers to Innovation**

Friction can be a problem in any process. Blockchains assist in overcoming inefficiencies caused by incomplete information, stringent regulations, institutional inertia, and unforeseen dangers, such as cybersecurity problems and the disruption of innovative business models.

3.4.3. Case Studies

- **Accelerating the Drive to Net-Zero Emissions**

Blockchain is essential to the current energy shift. This case study outlines how firms are utilizing innovation to facilitate the transition while highlighting key process insights.

- **How the Centre for Disease Centre (CDC) is exploring Blockchain for Public Health**

By enhancing its data collecting and upholding rigorous data access policies, the National Center for Health Statistics at the CDC is utilizing the power of blockchain to safeguard the health of the American people [11].

- **Nuarca Transforms Proxy Voting using Blockchain**

In order to enable opposing beneficial owners and their votes to be directly represented within the proxy voting cycle, Nuarca collaborated with IBM to build a blockchain voting network solution based on the IBM Blockchain Platform.

- **International Mail Tracking and Remittance**

IBM, the USPS, and many airlines worked together on a successful blockchain pilot that records foreign mail and assures proper restitution back to the airlines while minimizing manual effort in payments and mail management.

- **Seamless Employee Record Management**

Records frequently do not follow government workers when they switch agencies. IBM is providing the Office of Personnel Management with a blockchain solution to manage cross-agency HR tasks, protect data privacy and security, and promote data exchange.

- **Blockchain for Defense Supply Chains**

The Department of Defense (DOD) and IBM are looking into how blockchain might assist assure secure, timely acquisition of commodities, boost confidence in supplier and vendor selections, speed up data sharing for precise analytics, offer more exact inventory insights, and provide auditability of important supply chain steps.

3.5. Education

Blockchain is now largely used by universities that have adopted it to store and share academic information and credentials. But according to academics, technology has the potential to transform education in a variety of ways, including by expanding chances for lifelong learning, improving educator efficiency through smart contracts, and giving students ownership of their academic records, among other advantages. Despite the intriguing potential, data security, scalability, and cost are all problems that prevent blockchain from being widely used in the education industry. Blockchain is probably going to become more important in the sphere of education as technology develops [12].

Teachers and administrators can save time when it comes to things like transfers across schools or states by using blockchain to reduce much of the overhead involved with this process and streamline verification procedures. A school accepting a transfer student may quickly and easily verify their academic history using blockchain, as well as the courses they had taken. With information on attendance, courses studied, and even the outcomes of particular tests or papers, a digital transcript can be incredibly detailed. Anybody who has access to a student's transcript, such as prospective employers or other educational institutions, can examine how they did on particular tests.

Information in blockchain is systematically recorded, saved, and added to the chain with a precise time stamp. An educational certificate, for example, that has already been entered onto the chain cannot be changed; only corrected by adding a new block. This makes it difficult to alter a transcript or fabricate an academic record. Blockchain's immutability can be a double-edged sword, too, as it makes it impossible to change a student's record for proper reasons.

3.5.1. Benefits for Students

Students can own and manage their academic achievements by storing them on a blockchain, giving them the freedom to share them whenever and wherever they want. Students have always had to rely on institutions to access and share their academic histories and accomplishments since colleges have historically owned and controlled student records.

Blockchain enables students to take control of their academic identities by giving them ownership of their personal information. For graduates looking for work, for instance, this makes verifying the integrity of the credentials listed on their resumes much easier and offers them greater control over what an employer can access.

3.5.2. Benefits for Institutions

Higher education institutions can save time and money by streamlining the verification process of previous academic records of students with Blockchain. For example, as Blockchain issued diploma certificates are tamper-proof, their verification and validation at graduate schools are simpler.

3.5.3. Benefits for Employers

During the hiring process, verification and validation of Blockchain-based academic certificates are simple. Employers merely require a link to a digital copy of a candidate's certificates; they don't need the issuing institution to certify a paper copy. Employers may be assured that new hires have the knowledge and skills essential to succeed in the workplace because it is more difficult for candidates to fake their academic credentials thanks to the enhanced security that comes with storing information on a blockchain.

3.5.4. Using Blockchain for University Curricula

Beyond only storing records, blockchain has a significant impact on schooling. Additionally, the management of university curricula may be transformed by technology. One benefit of blockchain is the ability to securely store electronic course materials and syllabuses. Hard discs are used by institutions for this, however, there is a chance that they could be harmed or corrupted. Another choice is cloud storage, which some organisations might find to be too pricey.

By using smart contracts, blockchain technology may also simplify the work of educators. A smart contract is made up of lines of code that are encoded into a blockchain and are executed automatically when specific criteria are met. As an illustration, a teacher may programme lessons and courses into a blockchain, assigning tasks to students. The Blockchain's smart contract would automatically check that each work was completed before assigning the next one, and so on until all tasks were completed.

The same smart contract technology might be utilized by teachers to aid in grading assignments. Teachers might encode full exams, complete with questions, solutions, and scoring criteria, into a blockchain and allow students to take them on computers or tablets.

The student's grade then becomes a part of their permanent academic record, recorded securely on the blockchain, freeing up teachers' time to work on other academic projects. Through the enhancement of the accreditation procedure, blockchain can also raise the caliber of online education. Online students may be at risk if unaccredited or uncertified colleges periodically compete with reputable institutions on an even playing field due to the convenience of online learning. Blockchain-based accreditation recording offers security and transparency. As a decentralized platform, blockchain may also be used by organisations to exchange details about online courses and programmes, as well as by students to rate what is offered online. This will aid in the discovery of accredited programmes that will help other students improve their education.

3.5.5. Blockchain's Role in Lowering Education Costs

By creating new, more accessible learning avenues and upending the current dynamic between schools and students, blockchain has the potential to completely alter the landscape of education. Tuition management is a time-consuming procedure that involves many stakeholders, including students, parents, scholarship foundations, private lending businesses, federal and state agencies, and the frequently overburdened finance offices of universities. Blockchain can simplify this process, saving administrative costs and perhaps even bringing down tuition prices.

By using smart contracts and accepting cryptocurrencies as payment, the technology has already been applied to pay-as-you-go courses and other open learning scenarios. (Many universities in the United States and overseas now accept cryptocurrencies as a form of tuition payment.) According to the Federal Reserve, there are currently more than $1.7 trillion in student loan debt in the United States, therefore choices that make a college education more accessible and cheap may be of interest to millions of people.

Blockchain technology has the ability to support lifelong learning by making open educational resources widely accessible. Open educational resources are textbooks, podcasts, and films that are in the public domain and are free to use and share. Blockchain makes it possible for these resources to be inexpensively and securely shared in a public network.

CONCLUSION

Blockchain technology has the potential to play a critical role in Industry 4.0, which is defined by the convergence of physical and digital systems. Blockchain technology is a distributed ledger that securely and transparently records transactions without the use of intermediaries. Despite blockchain technology's initial focus on the financial sector, other sectors such as manufacturing, agriculture, healthcare, supply chains, and logistics are demonstrating much greater promise. The healthcare sector may benefit greatly from blockchain in areas such as identity verification, managing the pharmaceutical and medical supply chain, maintaining the confidentiality of dynamic patient medical information, and securely updating patient data across numerous facilities and locations in real-time. Significant areas of the agriculture industry where blockchain can be used include agricultural insurance, smart farming, the food supply chain, and transactions involving agricultural products. Blockchain technologies are being developed by manufacturers with the goal of enhancing operational effectiveness, supply chain visibility, and the capacity to track assets with unparalleled accuracy. Blockchain technology has the potential to fundamentally alter how producers design, engineer, manufacture, and scale their products.

In order to increase public trust and ensure transparent government, governments can use blockchain technology in a variety of applications including the energy industry, public health, voting, employee record management, and the military supply chain. By increasing opportunities for lifelong learning, enhancing educators' efficiency through smart contracts, and granting students ownership of their academic records in addition to just storing, saving, and tracking academic records on blocks, blockchain technology has the potential to transform the education sector in a number of ways.

Overall, blockchain technology has the potential to revolutionize Industry 4.0 by improving transparency, security, and efficiency across a range of industries.

ACKNOWLEDGMENTS

We would like to thank our colleagues at Vishwakarma Institute of Information Technology for helping us through the paper and providing us with their insights and valued opinions.

We would also like to take a moment to thank our reviewers for giving their valuable time to go through the paper. The generosity and expertise provided by them have helped in improving the quality of the paper.

REFERENCES

[1] M. Javaid, A. Haleem, R.P. Singh, S. Khan, and R. Suman, "Blockchain technology applications for Industry 4.0: A literature-based review", *Blockchain: Research and Applications,* vol. 2, no. 4, p. 100027, 2021.

[2] A. Gilchrist, and A. Gilchrist, "Introducing Industry 4.0", Industry 4.0: The industrial internet of things, pp. 195-215, 2016.

[3] U. Bodkhe, S. Tanwar, K. Parekh, P. Khanpara, S. Tyagi, N. Kumar, and M. Alazab, "Blockchain for industry 4.0: A comprehensive review", *IEEE Access,* vol. 8, pp. 79764-79800, 2020.

[http://dx.doi.org/10.1109/ACCESS.2020.2988579]

[4] S.M.H. Bamakan, A. Motavali, and A. Babaei Bondarti, "A survey of blockchain consensus algorithms performance evaluation criteria", *Expert Systems with Applications,* vol. 154, p. 113385, 2020.
[http://dx.doi.org/10.1016/j.eswa.2020.113385]

[5] C. Lepore, M. Ceria, A. Visconti, U.P. Rao, K.A. Shah, and L. Zanolini, "A survey on blockchain consensus with a performance comparison of PoW, PoS and pure PoS", *Mathematics,* vol. 8, no. 10, p. 1782, 2020.
[http://dx.doi.org/10.3390/math8101782]

[6] V. Dhillon, D. Metcalf, M. Hooper, "Blockchain in healthcare", In: Blockchain enabled applications, understand the blockchain ecosystem and how to make it work for you, pp. 201-220.

[7] X. Hang, D. Tobias, W. Puqing, and H. Jiajin, "Blockchain technology for agriculture: Applications and rationale", *Frontiers in Blockchain*, pp. 4-5, 2021.

[8] J. Leng, G. Ruan, P. Jiang, K. Xu, Q. Liu, X. Zhou, and C. Liu, ""Blockchain-empowered sustainable manufacturing and product lifecycle management in industry 4.0: A survey",", *Renewable and Sustainable Energy Reviews,* vol. 132, p. 110112, 2020.

[9] S. Verma, and A. Sheel, "Blockchain for government organizations: past, present and future", *J. Global Operations and Strategic Sourcing,* vol. 15, no. 3, pp. 406-430, 2022.
[http://dx.doi.org/10.1108/JGOSS-08-2021-0063]

[10] J.E. Kasten, "Engineering and manufacturing on the blockchain: A systematic review", *IEEE Engineering Management Review,* vol. 48, no. 1, pp. 31-47, 2020.
[http://dx.doi.org/10.1108/JGOSS-08-2021-0063]

[11] A. Alketbi, Q. Nasir, and M.A. Talib, "Blockchain for government services—Use cases, security benefits and challenges", In 2018 15th Learning and Technology Conference, pp. 112-119, 2018.

[12] H. Yumna, M.M. Khan, M. Ikram, and S. Ilyas, "Use of blockchain in education: a systematic literature review", In Intelligent Information and Database Systems: 11th Asian Conference, ACIIDS 2019, Yogyakarta, Indonesia, Proceedings, Part II 11 (pp. 191-202). Springer International Publishing.

CHAPTER 3

Adoption of Industry 4.0 in Remotely Located Industries

Pratap Pandurang Halkarnikar[1,*] and **Hriday Pandurang Khandagale**[2]

[1] *Dr. D.Y. Patil Institute of Engineering, Management and Research, Nigdi Pradhikaran, Akurdi, Pune, India*

[2] *Department of Technology, Shivaji University, Vidyanagar, Kolhapur, India*

Abstract: The manufacturing industry is revolutionized by introducing information and communication technology for productivity, flexibility, and agility. This Industry 4.0 has revolutionized the way companies manufacture, update and distribute their products. Manufacturers are integrating new technologies, like the Internet of Things (IoT), cloud computing, data analytics, and AI, into their production facilities and business operations. This digitization of manufacturing has increased the productivity of plants, reduced the dependency on human resources and improved logistics. This led to a better return on investment in the manufacturing sector and started blooming again. Many start-ups are coming up with new business ideas based on new technologies. These ideas are now easy to integrate with Industry 4.0-ready facilities. Now it is challenging to take advantage of this wave of new business opportunities for the traditional manufacturing industry. These industries strive to implement this technology for their plants, which are also located geographically remote. To sustain these older plants to new generation competition and expectations, it is necessary to shift and adopt the technology of Industry 4.0. Transition business models need to be developed for shifting to a "new business model" of the company, along with the "old business model" that is slowly "decommissioned". In this chapter, we will discuss the need, challenges, and advantages of integrating new technology into old manufacturing processes for the sustainability of a business. Organizations that wish to shift to a new paradigm face many challenges. The most challenging aspects include the skills and qualifications of their human resource, the ability of their machines to connect and communicate with each other, and the adoption of various new technologies.

Keywords: Cloud computing, Industry 4.0, IoT.

* **Corresponding author Pratap Pandurang Halkarnikar:** Dr. D.Y. Patil Institute of Engineering, Management and Research, Nigdi Pradhikaran, Akurdi, Pune, India; E-mail: pp_halkarnikar@rediffmail.com

Parikshit N. Mahalle, Gitanjali R. Shinde and Prachi M. Joshi (Eds.)

1. INTRODUCTION

Global competitions, unpredictable markets, and demand of highly customized products become important factors for the manufacturing industry for survival in the market. Digitalization and new affordable technology are playing a vital role in changing the market trend. (Kumar *et al.*, 2018). The manufacturing industry is now in the age of Industry 4.0. This Fourth Industrial Revolution, with its high data connectivity and scale, allows you to take a more data-driven approach to industrial operations. The data is pulled from available resources; value addition is done and used for more intelligent decisions. We can integrate more assets into business workflows with technologies like 5G, edge computing, and AI. Real-time production planning is possible in Industry 4.0 with dynamic optimization [1, 2]. Industry 4.0 enables the implementation of processes that are autonomously controlled and dynamic. The value chains are optimized and could combine with the integration of information and communication technologies. Modern information and communication technologies could be implemented in manufacturing machines, production workers, and logistics. This set better communication among all participants in the product manufacturing process. The data collected is continuously analyzed according to defined algorithms, and production flow is controlled for continuous improvement. In order to have process competitiveness along the value chain, it is necessary to design productive, efficient, and flexible methods. These production processes need to be personalized to cater to the need of a customer. Therefore the volume of products manufactured in a plant is limited. To cater to this need for production, Industry 4.0 provides fast communication and autonomous, flexible manufacturing processes. Business houses can take advantage of the new age revolution using technology like 5G, Industrial IoT(IIoT), AI, and other advanced technologies. Transparency in the processes increases the understanding of business [3]. This gives the right information to the right person, who can make the right decision. The main goals of Industry 4.0 are personalized production, servicing, as well as real-time usage by customer interaction and avoiding the inefficiencies, irrelevance in design, and costs of intermediaries in a digital supply chain model. This customer-centric approach who demands cost efficiencies, value-added innovative services and speed of delivery.

The organizations that have an old plant with earlier manufacturing processes now want to shift to new paradigms of Industry 4.0. The challenges faced by them are many. Affordable new technologies like fast communication, high data transfer, Internet of Things (IoT), machine learning, and cloud computing, help these organizations for adopting new manufacturing processes. Other issues of firms are related to innovation, technological components, digital transformation, and interconnectivity developments between various resources that play an essential role [4]. Industry 4.0 consists of providing a new way of manufacturing and depends upon end-to-end digitization of all physical assets and integration into digital ecosystems of all value chain partners. This evolution from old manufacturing processes to new manufacturing processes needs insulation of the upcoming business model from old behaviors, metrics, processes, and reporting norms. It is challenging to develop a new business model with full access to existing core competencies, expertise, and networks. Adopting Industry 4.0 leads to diverse technological challenges to implement in existing manufacturing setups. Therefore it is required to develop a strategy for all stack holders involved in the entire value chain, to reach a common agreement on security issues and the allied architecture before implementation begins. To take the old manufacturing setup to a new digitized plant, it is necessary to define new metrics, technical solutions, and value propositions to tackle the issues. Human resource plays an important role in digitization. Proper awareness about new technology, advantages, and roles should be provided. Once the benefit of digitization in making working simple and controlled is well explained, people support the transition.

The convergence of 5G, IoT, and cloud computing technologies is the main facilitator and accelerators of Industry 4.0. The emergence of high-speed networks and data transfer helps in shifting computing from local sites to the cloud. The cloud also brings the advantage of low cost of computing without the setup of a costly hardware platform at the local site [5]. High-performance computing using cloud setup improves the decision from end-to-end digitization of value chain processes. The predictive demand will help to control inventory, thereby reducing the cost of production. Similarly, as the whole chain of production is monitored by collecting data from various points, it is easy to apply predictive maintenance to reduce downtime of plant or machinery.

In this chapter, we discuss the conversion of an old manufacturing unit into a digitized manufacturing unit. For this, a leather manufacturing unit is considered. The leather-producing unit is considered as polluting manufacturing, hence located in a rural area or outskirts of an urban area. Such units do not have the advantages of technology and communication. Converting such units into modern, flexible manufacturing has many challenges. This chapter discusses the issues and solution of such conversion with respect to leather manufacturing units.

2. COMPONENTS OF INDUSTRY 4.0

Manufacturing in today's era has changed from mass production to customized production. Innovation, flexibility, and real-time response are challenges in today's production processes to keep the challenges of modern business requirements. The end-to-end digitalization and virtualization of processes ensure and procure more opportunities for manufacturers to create new value addition and innovation to achieve competitive success in their business domain. In order to sustain competition due to globalization, innovation in product and manufacturing processes is the need of time. The production system is characterized by adaptability, flexibility, and agility. Optimization of resources by way of communication throughout the production cycle leads to get more productivity. Industry 4.0 is the ultimate path for this total automation of production plants. The Digital Enterprise brings together business processes that previously had separate traditional communication channels. It breaks down traditional silos and bridges the gaps between Information Technology and Operation Technology, software and hardware, shop floor, and top management. This optimizes resources to include the latest technology, like artificial intelligence, for precise production monitoring, predictive maintenance, and improved product quality. It focuses on individual customer service and satisfaction. Optimization takes place not only through the value chain within the factory but also through the entire supply chain of the company as an industry. Industry 4.0 focuses on creating new concepts, and new business models, creating synergy within a business [6]. The main technologies and concepts involved in Industry 4.0 consist of various sensors, IIoT (Industrial Internet of Things), autonomous robots, wired or wireless networks, virtual reality, augmented reality, Big Data analytics, and cloud computing. The main component is IoT which keeps the machine connected to the entire network. The data collected from sensors is transferred by this IoT hardware using the network to a processing station, which may be an edge computing or cloud computing type facility [7]. The following sections discuss the main components of Industry 4.0.

2.1. Internet of Things (IoT)

IoT stands for Internet of Things, a concept that refers to connections between physical sensors or machines and the Internet. IoT plays an important role in the digitization of manufacturing plants and supply chains. A major issue of inefficiency in the manufacturing sector was the gap or isolation of Information Technology & operation Technology (IT–OT). This gap created issues like lack of Plant Visibility, Quality of product, and Inefficiency in Inventory management and production Scheduling as per demand, scheduled maintenance, *etc*. IoT supports in filling this gap between IT and OT systems by connecting to sensors, hardware systems, control Systems, machines, PLCs and enabling bidirectional data transfer to ERP and Cloud. The main blocks of IoT are shown in Fig. (**1**).

IIoT stands for the Industrial Internet of Things, a concept that refers to the connections between people, data, and machines related to manufacturing. It helps in increasing production efficiency, quality of product, innovation, and timely supply. Sensor inputs to IoT are of varied types like analog, digital, video, and audio, as well as output of varied types, which are transferred over the network. IoT is capable of connecting to various types of networks, like wired, wireless, CAN, *etc*. There is a broad range of emerging IoT applications for health care, traffic control, vehicle safety, energy, agriculture, and manufacturing to name a few.

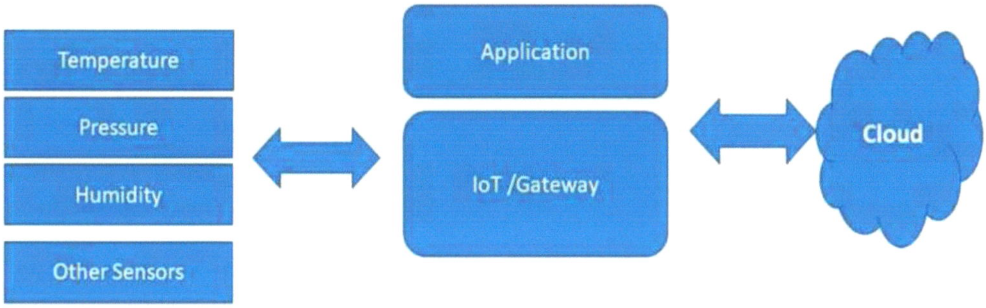

Fig. (1). IoT architecture.

2.2. Autonomous Robots

Autonomous robots can gain information about their environments and can work without human intervention. These self-reliant robots can move throughout the operation space without human assistance. They can avoid situations that are harmful to people, property, or themselves. Autonomous robots can adapt to changes in surroundings [8]. An autonomous robot can perform precisely autonomous production methods and work in places where the use of human workers is harmful. Autonomous robots can complete given tasks precisely within the given time limit. They can work with safety, flexibility, versatility, and collaboratively [9].

Autonomous robots are widely used for loading and unloading warehouses, which are the places where goods are stored systematically. Fig. (**2**) shows the present use of autonomous robots for carrying goods to a specified location and loading it properly as decided by optimization software for proper utilization of space in a warehouse.

Fig. (2). Autonomous robots in warehouse.

2.3. Big Data

Big Data is the term used for any technology which handles Big Data better. It covers data capture, network, storage, computing, and analytic methods. The characteristics of Big Data are the: data volume, data velocity with which it is captured, variety of types of data involved, and value of data. Any technique to handle such a larger amount of data, process it faster or robust to handle heterogeneous data, is called as a Big Data technique [10]. In manufacturing processes, the data analysis of previously recorded data is done and used to find out the threats that occurred in various processes earlier in the industry and also forecast the new issues that may occur, as well as the various solutions to stop that [11]. For example, a company incurs unnecessary costs if maintenance activities are carried out frequently. A smart factory, however, can use anomalies to predict the failure of assets and schedule maintenance only when it's needed. That means you can reduce both downtime and costs. The beauty of Big Data analysis lies in its ability to find those hidden anomalies while the system is behaving in a seemingly normal fashion. If say, two parameters are under consideration. Both of them might be within their thresholds and then will not send out alerts or notifications that something is going wrong. However, data analysis allows us to see that if "param1" is on the upper end but within range and "param2" is on the lower end, but within range, then there's a potential threat. Similarly, if hundreds of parameters exist with their complex relationship, then finding anomalies is possible by Big Data analytics only. It also uses machine learning algorithms to find the solution under different situations in plants. AI is an advanced stage of this data analysis, which can govern the whole possible situation by itself. Big Data classifies the information collected from different sources and IoT. Use this information to draw relevant conclusions which help to improve companies' operations in the following ways:

a. Better warehouse processes: portable devices and sensors are used to improve operational efficiency by finding human errors, performing quality controls, and adopting optimal production or assembly routes.
b. Bottlenecks are eliminated: Big Data identifies variables that can affect the performance of processes and guide manufacturers in identifying the problem.
c. Demand Prediction: More accurate and meaningful predictions are drawn using the visualization of activity through internal analysis (customer preferences) and external analysis (trends and external events) beyond historical data. This information is collected from internal as well as external sources. The external sources may include government agencies, as a change in the policy of the government may affect the manufacturing process. This allows the company to optimize its production processes.
d. Predictive maintenance: Data collected from sensors identify possible failures in the operation of machinery before it becomes a breakdown by analysing breakdown patterns. The system sends an alert so that it can handle this situation in time. The early detection of possible deterioration of sensors or parts prevents the catastrophic condition of failures. This reduces breakdown and loss of production.

Big Data helps to integrate all systems within companies that were previously isolated and helps to obtain a complete visualization of the manufacturing processes [12]. As shown in Fig. (**3**), it automates data collection and analysis, also facilitating a better understanding of the status of each system together or separately.

Big Data can apply business strategies directly in manufacturing process systems such as:

a. Enterprise Resource Planning (ERP)
b. Supplier Relationship Management Systems (SRMS)
c. Product Life Cycle Management Systems (PLMS)
d. More Environmentally Responsible Systems (ERS)

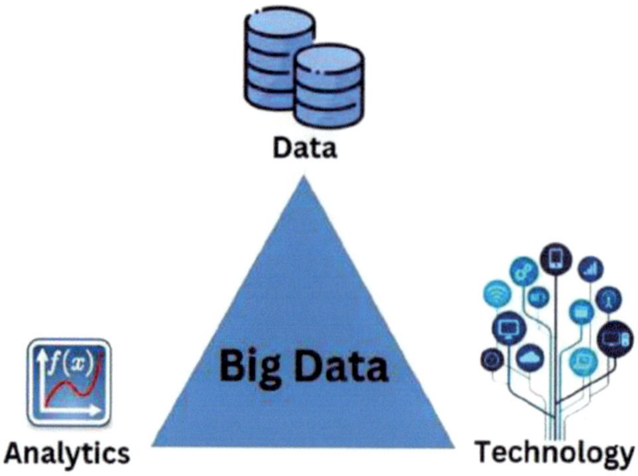

Fig. (3). Big Data in Industry 4.0.

2.4. Simulation

Simulation is a key technology in the digitization of the manufacturing process. Simulation helps in the optimization of resources for a better and more competitive product. It is the main backbone of flexible manufacturing, which is a key characteristic of Industry 4.0. Using dedicated simulation and analysis software, the system structure can be designed for any client-specific product can be designed. Simulation helps to study the behavior of any manufacturing processes and systems before they are deployed for actual production [13]. The simulation aims to increase production capacity in the view of diversifying production, increasing competitiveness, and short life cycle of products. It helps in the smooth integration of industrial robots and intelligent machine tools for flexible production systems. It also helps in monitoring and controlling the production beforehand. Simulation methods for manufacturing can give enormous benefits as the commissioning of new manufacturing facilities or production lines and processes is often costly and capital-intensive. For testing and studying new production processes before deploying them, Industry 4.0 uses key technologies like Virtual reality (VR) and augmented reality (AR) simulations [14].

2.4.1. Benefits of Simulation Software

a. Identifying possible manufacturing bottlenecks.
b. Finding opportunities to increase throughput.
c. Identifying cost savings opportunities such as optimization of direct and indirect labor.
d. Validating the expected performance of new or existing production facilities.

Fig. (**4**) depicts the simulation software used for the design of the whole production line. It gives a real-time view of plants with the interrelation of different processes [15]. The simulation technique can graphically model manufacturing processes with asynchronous/synchronous concurrent events in real-time. The simulation model presents a description of the alternative manufacturing systems possible for the optimization of processes [16]. In virtual reality (VR), a computer-generated video is superimposed on the real-world video to give the impression that the computer-generated objects have fixed locations in the real world. Manufacturing using VR would be limiting because of the obstruction that may take place at the time of real-world interaction. Augmented Reality (AR), combines the real world with virtual worlds generated by the computer. AR starts with capturing a real image that gets infused or augmented with different layers of digital information. It becomes possible using AR to have a seamless and natural perception of employee movement. The technology has proven useful in the manufacturing process in terms of measuring time changes, envisioning the end product, and seeking out dangerous working conditions [17].

Fig. (4). Plant simulation in siemens tecnomatix.

2.5. Cloud Computing

Cloud technology has unlimited computing, storage, and networking capabilities. Cloud platform technology is a secure way for any company to store, process and analyze data from their industrial devices. Looking at these advantages, cloud is becoming the backbone of the Industry 4.0 revolution. Cloud helps to optimize business processes, enable a more efficient supply chain, and provide predictive maintenance. Cloud Computing allows the storage of large amounts of data. This capacity is mainly important to store the data generated during a whole production process, as the machines and sensors produce more data continuously. All this data generated is connected by a virtual private network to all the concerned. Cloud computing reduces investment in technological resources, allowing the storage space and processing capacity to be contracted on demand, which provides flexibility, agility, and adaptability [18]. The main advantage of adopting cloud computing in Industry 4.0 is the investment cost of IT infrastructure is reduced as it is available on demand and as per its utilization. These cloud services are available from different third-party vendors on rental bases. Innovative new applications on integrated cloud platform services are adaptable to individual needs. Infinite storage capabilities of Cloud computing gather more information that is properly organized in order to make that information accessible and actionable. Cloud technology is flexible, scalable, and agile, which helps to create new avenues for cost-effective software delivery and development [19]. Software as a Service (SaaS) is one of the most in-demand methods used for leveraging cloud computing. The scalable structure of the cloud allows the consumption of resources on request. This reduces costs by avoiding purchasing servers, and licenses, and hiring specialized personnel for maintenance. It also saves the energy of an organization as the computing platform is of third-party providers [20].

Cloud provides the following services:

a. Infrastructure as a Service (IaaS): virtual computing infrastructure, like virtual CPUs or network components,
b. Platform as a Service (PaaS): virtual infrastructure with a software platform on top, like Virtual Machines (VMs) including an Operating System (OS),
c. Software as a Service (SaaS): ready-to-use applications, like cloud storage applications or a cloud-based Enterprise Resource Planning (ERP) system.

As depicted in Fig. (**5**), the cloud provides ease of access to storage from different geographical points, and different access points, regardless of the platform and connecting devices. Cloud facilitates the collaboration between customers and suppliers to create transparent manufacturing ecosystems. In particular, the customer can participate in all stages of the production process, increasing the satisfaction of the customer. There are also some drawbacks with the cloud. The large volumes of data processed in the cloud and the speed of the internet, lead to an increase in latency time which affects the performance of the production process. To overcome this drawback, edge computing or fog computing solutions are employed. Security is also a major concern while adopting the cloud. This also overcomes by the proper selection of gateways and firewalls. Private cloud, hybrid cloud, and public cloud are the variants of cloud computing based on security and data protection.

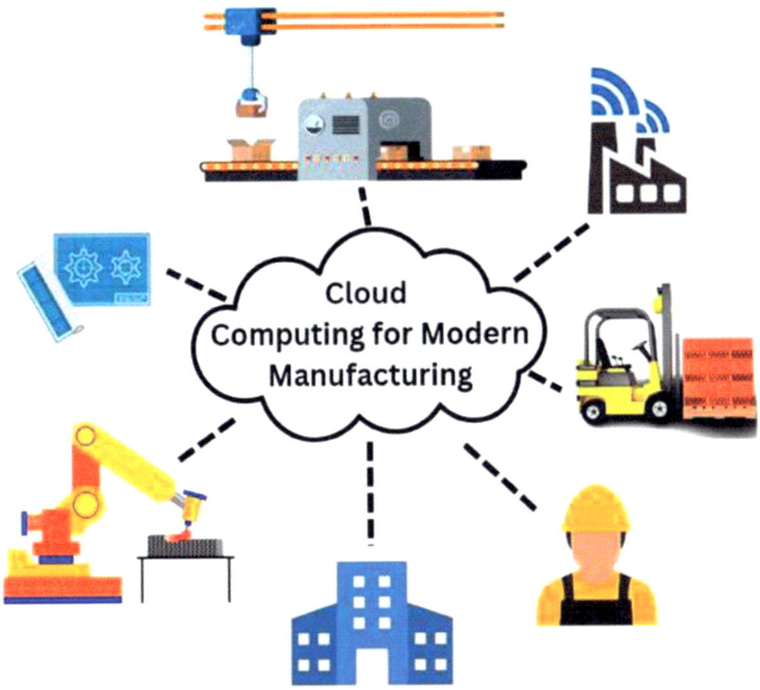

Fig. (5). Cloud Computing for Industry 4.0.

3. BENEFITS OF INDUSTRY 4.0

Industry 4.0 is the digitization of the industrial process of the life cycle of a product [21]. It is an end-to-end value chain digitization that provides the following benefits to a modern manufacturing plant.

a. Increased Efficiency in Production: With increased automation and capacity for continuous improvement, smart factories will be able to increase their efficiency to levels previously thought impossible. Every resource will be optimized automatically for minimum wastage.
b. More Potential for Innovation: Industry 4.0 is all about innovation. Through data gathered from connected devices such as the Internet of Things, design teams will know what works and what doesn't. This data will fuel their innovation for new and improved products and systems.
c. Accelerated Response to Customer Needs: Customer needs are changing faster

than many industries can keep up with. They want new designs, new technology, and new features every few months. Industry 4.0 is built for agility so that you can respond to market dynamics faster than the competition.

d. Quality Assurance: Industry 4.0 gives you the capability to perfect product quality. You will also be able to assure excellence beyond the factory through product tracking during delivery. By eliminating that elusive 1% or so of defective products, you can also keep your costs to a minimum.

e. Reduced Costs and Higher Profit Margins: You will achieve lower operating costs overall through better uses of resources, less wastage, reduced quality issues, and less downtime. Despite a large initial investment, you will have significantly higher profit margins to enable you to get an ROI within a few years. The maintenance of machinery can be scheduled using history instead of a total breakdown of the machine leading to the ceasing of the production process.

4. IMPLEMENTING INDUSTRY 4.0: CHALLENGES, ISSUES, AND SOLUTIONS

Looking at the advantages of Industry 4.0 it is need of the time to implement this in different industry sectors. Logistic companies have adopted and implemented it in many parts of warehousing, transport, and tracking. But the manufacturing industry is reluctant to adopt it. The following issues are observed in the Indian industry to adopt Industry 4.0 [22].

1. Technology involved. Digitization, automation, and the increased use of Information and Communications Technology (ICT) are the main concepts of the Industrial Revolution 4.0. To achieve this help of Big Data, autonomous robot, cloud computing, and high-speed internet is the backbone of implementation. These technologies are not understandable by management and people working at a plant. Proper training of the workforce can overcome this hurdle of technology.

2. Lack of skills. The biggest barrier to digital transformation is access to required skills at local sites. It is difficult to train and re-skill staff in the areas of the user interface, software development, data science, and machine-level controls for flexible manufacturing. Adoption of an optimized manufacturing process or design of a complete plant for effective production requires skilled and trained persons. Continued training, awareness, and new skill upgradation is the solution of this hurdle in the implementation of industry 4.0 [23].

3. New business models. With the advancement of digital technologies, new business models are evolving, requiring companies to restructure the way they do business. To overcome these internal fundamental changes business strategy must

be changed even at the top level. Recruitment of the right people to drive this change is required for the success of the new business model.

4. Capital investment. Depending upon new paradigm change in the behaviour, Industry 4.0 adoption sometimes involves high infrastructure costs. However, in Industry 4.0 a large investment is not required to transform the business as technology is available at an affordable rate and with a variety of options. To shift to a new business model, start with a simple, scalable solution. Increasing confidence and partial automation help to adopt a new culture of operation. A huge investment is not necessary to make a significant step toward Industry 4.0. Due to this low-cost solution and scope for scalability Industry 4.0 can be adopted not by large firms but also by medium and small-scale industries. (MSME).

5. IT security. Online connectivity and data transfer across the organization will increase the vulnerability of companies to cyber threats. Also, IT issues like misconfiguration, software failure, and the erroneous command will also become constraints. The IT infrastructure must be developed to handle the additional connectivity necessary for information and communication transportation. An organization should also analyze system vulnerabilities and machine-level operational failure risks. Companies should hire IT and data security solution providers to overcome these issues.

6. Government policies. End-to-end digitization of the supply chain in industry 4.0, needs support from the government. The flexible manufacturing and introduction of autonomous robots lead to the unemployment of a lower-skilled workforce. The government laws and policies may not fit to this work culture. Indian government set up new initiative to adopt Industry 4.0. by starting the Samarth Udayog policy. In 2018, the World Economic Forum set up its Centre for Industry 4.0 in India to work in collaboration with the government of India. The National Institute for Transforming India (NITI) Aayog is the designated nodal agency to interact with the World Economic Forum for elaborating the new policy frameworks for emerging technologies. The government of India has already made the enabling policy framework and set up incentives for infrastructure development on a Public Private Partnership (PPP) model. Smart Advanced Manufacturing and Rapid Transformation Hubs *i.e.* Samarth Udyog Bharat 4.0, under the Ministry of Heavy Industries & Public Enterprises [24]. This is India's initiative to push for Industry 4.0 implementation to make the manufacturing sector ready for global competition. National Manufacturing Policy (NMP) is declared for the industry, academia and international cooperation in the field of technologies related to Industry 4.0 in India.

5. CASE STUDY: LEATHER MANUFACTURING UNIT

For the implementation of digitization, a leather manufacturing unit located at Uchagaon, Kolhapur is selected for the study. Leather manufacturing units are located on the outskirt of an urban area or in rural areas, as these firms are classified as the most polluting industry. The digitization of machinery used in leather manufacturing units is already well-established. Many sensors and controllers are used for the quality produce of the units. The manpower used is a majority of low-skilled but trained to use digital readouts and controllers. Many manufacturing firms are now loss-making production units due to a lack of current information about market trends. These units are still producing leather as per their capacity, not considering clients' requirements and choices. The flexibility in production is not present. Producing high-quality products as per customer demand is becoming increasingly difficult and less efficient at the factory due to outdated automation. Production quantity and demand are mismatched due to less use of information and communication technology. Even if the quality of the product is high, it does not get fit to customer trends and demand. Modernizing the old, remotely located plant is a challenge. Industry revolution 4.0 with technology like IoT, Bigdata, and cloud computing with interconnection using 5G, these firms can also take advantage of flexible manufacturing and can get more returns from the business. Considering the issue of investment for the modernization of the plant, a phased transformation approach can be recommended. In a phased manner, the full digitization of the total manufacturing facility can be achieved in steps. The management can invest in steps and will gain the confidence of technology in their manufacturing unit. This stepped approach will give time to train the manpower to the required level of use. When the full conversion of the plant will take place the unit may turn into a profitable firm. Value addition of complete product chain logistics will help to get full advantage of the new revolution.

5.1. IoT-Based Area Measuring Machine

To start with the digitization of the leather manufacturing unit located at a geographically remote site, a phased transformation approach is used. This gives confidence to management about the new transformation and advantages of technology by own experience. Leather measuring machine used in the tannery industry is a key component of leather processing as price and production are decided on the quality and area of leather. This machine is at the end of manufacturing processing, which gives information about the production, quality, and quantity available. If this machine is made of IoT technology, then it can communicate to the internet to help other cloud based applications. Such applications will help to monitor the production and thereby provide live inventory to the market in real time. The availability of produced items will get notified to the buyers, thereby adjusting the production as per the demand of the market. The information of the trends in the market will be notified back to the manufacturing unit, so that it will change its product as per demand in the market. This two-way information exchange will optimise the production process. This will help to increase the production of the tannery and profit thereafter. The logistic chain of input inventory and output production can be decided from the real time data produced by measuring machines. Production became more stable and reliable with an increased yield and optimizing the production scheduling process. The cost of inventory in produced items will be reduced as it is matching with the requirement in the market. The accounting process has become easy and transparent to management and other stack holders.

CONCLUSION

The industry revolution 4.0 has changed manufacturing industry by introduction of information and communication technology for productivity, flexibility and agility. This total digitization of supply chain has revolutionized the way companies manufacture, update and distribute their products. Manufacturing is integrating new technologies, like Internet of Things (IoT), cloud computing, data analytics, and AI into their production facilities and also in their manufacturing processes. This digitization of manufacturing has increased productivity of plants, reduced the dependency on human resource, down time of machines and improved logistics. Innovative product and manufacturing processes are possible by taking advantage of flexible production possible in Industry 4.0. Implementing this new technology in Indian firms is a challenging task. This chapter discusses the issues and solutions for the adoption of this new technology. To sustain these older plants to new generation competition and expectations, it is necessary to shift and adopt the technology of Industry 4.0. A transition business model is discussed in this chapter for the development of confidence and skills to use this technology. The main advantage of this revolution is the capital requirements for change are not huge. The new IoT-based machines or autonomous robots are required but a phased replacement policy will reduce this burden of investment. In this chapter, we discussed a case study of a leather industry which is facing global competition. The replacement of a single machine with an Iot based machine can connect the production information to the cloud. This information can be used for the satisfaction of customer demands. The transparency provided by this change can bring automation in terms of logistics also. The single machine transformation to IoT-based machine will start the digitization of the whole plant. This can provide the full benefit of Industry 4.0. The integration of plant vertical and horizontal is possible by adopting this digitization.

REFERENCES

[1] Shashank Kumar, Balkrishna Narkhede, and Karuna Jain, "Industry 4.0: Literature Review and Future Research Directions", *Research Gate,* 2018.

[2] G. Pereira Andreia, M. Lima Tânia, and Charrua-Santos Fernando, "Industry 4.0 and Society 5.0: Opportunities and Threats"", *International Journal of Recent Technology and Engineering (IJRTE),* vol. 8, no. 5, pp. 3305-3308, 2020. [http://dx.doi.org/10.35940/ijrte.D8764.018520]

[3] S.N. Deshpande, and R.M. Jogdand, "A survey on Internet of Things (IoT), Industrial IoT (IIoT) and Industry 4.0", *Int. J. Comp. Apps*, vol 175, no. 27, pp 20-27, 2020.

[4] M. Mohamed, "Challenges and Benefits of Industry 4.0: an overview", *International Journal of Supply and Operations Management,* vol. 5, no. 3, pp. 256-265, 2018. [http://dx.doi.org/10.22034/2018.3.7]

[5] K. Chhaya, "Convergence of 5G, AI and IoT holds the promise of industry 4.0", *Telecom Business Review*, vol. 13, no. 1, pp 60-64, 2020.

[6] R. Ortt, C. Stolwijk, and M. Punter, "Implementing Industry 4.0: assessing the current state", *Journal of Manufacturing Technology Management,* vol. 31, no. 5, pp. 825-836, 2020. [http://dx.doi.org/10.1108/JMTM-07-2020-0284]

[7] G. Lampropoulos, K. Siakas, and T. Anastasiadis, "Internet of Things in the Context of Industry 4.0: An Overview", *International Journal of Entrepreneurial Knowledge,* vol. 7, no. 1, pp. 4-19, 2019. [http://dx.doi.org/10.37335/ijek.v7i1.84]

[8] S. Vaidyaa, P. Ambadb, and S. Bhosle, "Industry 4.0- A Glimpse", *2nd International Conference on Materials Manufacturing and Design Engineering*, Procedia Manufacturing, pp.233-238, 2018.

[9] I.H. Khan, and M. Javaid, "Role of Internet of Things (IoT) in Adoption of Industry 4.0", *Journal of Industrial Integration and Management,* vol. 6, no. 2, pp. 1-19, 2021.

[10] L. Duan, and L. Da Xu, "Data Analytics in Industry 4.0: A Survey", *Information Systems Frontiers,* pp. 1-17, 2021. [http://dx.doi.org/10.1007/s10796-021-10190-0] [PMID: 34456613]

[11] G.S. Aujla, R. Prodan, and D.B. Rawat, "Big data analytics in Industry 4.0 ecosystems", *Software Practice and Experience,* vol. 52, no. 3, pp. 639-641, 2022. [http://dx.doi.org/10.1002/spe.3008]

[12] Y. Lu, "Industry 4.0: A survey on technologies, applications and open research issues", *Journal of Industrial Information Integration,* vol. 6, pp. 1-10, 2017. [http://dx.doi.org/10.1016/j.jii.2017.04.005]

[13] A. Florescu, and S.A. Barabas, "Modeling and Simulation of a Flexible Manufacturing System—A Basic Component of Industry 4.0", *Appl. Sci.,* vol. 10, no. 22, p. 8300, 2020. [http://dx.doi.org/10.3390/app10228300]

[14] A. Ibrahim, "Industry 4.0: Eyeing The Future *via* Simulation", *IOP Conference Series: Materials Science and Engineering,* 2020. [http://dx.doi.org/10.1088/1757-899X/769/1/012001]

[15] A. Ibrahim, "Industry 4.0: eyeing the future via simulation", *IOP Conference Series Materials Science and Engineering,* vol. 769, 2020no. 1, p. 012001. [http://dx.doi.org/10.1088/1757-899X/769/1/012001]

[16] El Abdellaoui Mahdi El Alaoui, Bricard. Emmanuel, Grimaud Fred´ eric , Gianessi Paolo, and Delorme Xavier, "Scalable, Reconfigurable Simulation Models in Industry 4.0-Oriented Enterprise Modeling", *Conference: 2020 Winter Simulation Conference (WSC),* 2020 [http://dx.doi.org/10.1109/WSC48552.2020.9383973]

[17] B. Khaled, E. Chawki, C. Quentin, B. Abdel-Hakim, W. Peterr, B. Idir, L. Stéphane, G. Nooshin, and A. Amézian, "Development of an advanced MES for the simulation and optimization of industry 4.0 process", *International Journal of Simulation and Multidisciplinary Design Optimization,* vol. 12, p. 23, 2021.

[18] N. Velásquez, E. Estevez, and P. Pesado, "Cloud Computing, Big Data and the Industry 4.0 Reference Architectures", *Journal of Computer Science and Technology,* vol. 18, no. 3, p. e29, 2018. [http://dx.doi.org/10.24215/16666038.18.e29]

[19] L. Thames, and D. Schaefer, "Software-defined cloud manufacturing for industry 4.0", *Procedia CIRP,* vol. 52, pp. 12-17, 2016. [http://dx.doi.org/10.1016/j.procir.2016.07.041]

[20] G. Gil, D. Corujo, and P. Pedreiras, "Cloud native computing for industry 4.0: challenges and opportunities", *26th IEEE International Conference on Emerging Technologies and Factory Automation (ETFA).* pp.1-4, 2021. [http://dx.doi.org/10.1109/ETFA45728.2021.9613386]

[21] W.S. Alaloul, M.S. Liew, N.A.W.A. Zawawi, and I.B. Kennedy, "Industrial Revolution 4.0 in the construction industry: Challenges and opportunities for stakeholders", *Ain Shams Engineering Journal,* vol. 11, no. 1, pp. 225-230, 2020. [http://dx.doi.org/10.1016/j.asej.2019.08.010]

[22] B S Sagar, and D Praveen, "A study on impact of Industry 4.0 in India International Advanced Research Journal in Science", *Engineering and Technology,* vol. 4, no. 7, pp. 24-28, 2017.

[23] A.R. Bakhtari, V. Kumar, M.M. Waris, C. Sanin, and E. Szczerbicki, "Industry 4.0 Implementation Challenges in Manufacturing Industries: an Interpretive Structural Modelling Approach", *Procedia Computer Science,* vol. 176, pp. 2384-2393, 2020. [http://dx.doi.org/10.1016/j.procs.2020.09.306]

[24] K. Arun, and S. Kumar, "Industry 4.0: Overview, Components, and Initiatives of Indian Government", *International Journal of Research in Business Studies,* vol. 6, pp. 2455-2992, 2021.

CHAPTER 4

Predictive Analytics Algorithm for Early Prevention of Brain Tumor using Explainable Artificial Intelligence (XAI): A Systematic Review of the State-of-the-Art

Prasad Raghunath Mutkule[1,*], **Nilesh P. Sable**[2], **Parikshit N. Mahalle**[1] and **Gitanjali R. Shinde**[1]

[1] *Vishwakarma Institute of Information Technology, Pune, Maharashtra, India*

[2] *Department of Information Technology, Bansilal Ramnath Agarwal Charitable Trust's, Vishwakarma Institute of Information Technology, Pune, India*

Abstract: Advancement in the medical field promotes the diagnosis of disease through automation methods and prediction of the brain tumor also plays an important role due to the fact that millions of people are affected by brain tumor and the rate of affected people is increasing every year randomly. Hence, in saving the lives of many individuals, the early detection of the disease plays an important role. Using the MRI Images, it's easy to find the location and existence of the tumor. Expert manual diagnosis is playing a vital role in detecting the information about the tumor and its type. Though there are various models that can detect tumor location with the help of ML models in the medical field, somewhere there is a lag in the success of these models. Deep learning is one of the widely used approaches for the same. But the black-box nature of these machine-learning models has somewhat limited their clinical use. Explanations are essential for users to know, trust, and well manage these models. The chapter proposes dual-weighted deep CNN classifiers for early prediction of the presence of brain tumor along with the explanation-driven DL models such as Local Interpretable Model-agnostic Explanations (LIME) and SHapley Additive explanation (SHAP). The performance and accuracy of the planned model are assessed and relate with the existing models and it is expected that it will produce high sensitivity as well as specificity. It is also expected to perform well by means of precision and accuracy.

Keywords: Deep Learning, Dual weighted deep CNN classifier, Explainable artificial intelligence, LIME, Machine learning, SHAP.

* **Corresponding author Prasad Raghunath Mutkule:** Vishwakarma Institute of Information Technology, Pune, Maharashtra, India; E-mail: Mutkuleprasad000@gmail.com

1. INTRODUCTION

In order to produce an action, a complex network of fiber tissues and nerves that stimulate nerve impulses all over the body comes into play. There are two types of nervous systems: peripheral and central. As the central component of the nervous system, the human brain coordinates the functions of the various parts of the body in order to control it [1]. The activities of the brainstem are controlled by the various components of the brain, such as the movement of the muscles, the sense of touch, and the perception of things. The brain tumor consists of irregular cells that develop a structure in the form of a mass [2]. Any expansion within this region, which is only a small area, will trigger severe problems.

Non-malignant and benign brain tumors can be of different types. When these tumors grow, the pressure within the skull increases, which can lead to permanent brain injury [3]. Most brain tumors cause headaches, changes in mood, and difficulties speaking. Other symptoms such as vomiting and high blood pressure can also be caused by these types of tumors [4, 5]. Brain cancer is a benign or malignant development of anomalous cells in the brain that can be cancerous or non-cancerous. Benign tumors have a uniform structure but no active cells, whereas malignant tumors have aggressive cancerous cells and a non-uniform structure [6].

These cancers are categorized as either primary or metastatic. However, in tumors, cancer cells have expanded into the brain from another afflicted body area [7] and the cells in initial brain tumors are essentially brain cells. Early identification and categorization of brain tumors is a heavily researched subject in the medical imaging field, as it aids in determining the much more suitable treatment options to save patients' lives [8]. Brain and other cancers killed more people than any other type of neurological illness. It is the 10th largest cause of death for women and men. According to brain tumor estimations, "it is predicted that 23,890 individuals (13,590 men and 10,300 women) in America would be clinically tested with the cancer of the brain and spinal cord in the present year." Furthermore, primary malignant brain and CNS tumors are estimated to kill 18,020 individuals (10,190 men and 7830 women) in 2020. Furthermore, "the survivability percentage for persons along with malignant brain or CNS tumor is about 36% for 5 years and 31% for 10 years" [9]. The implementation of deep learning algorithms to identify brain tumors with greater accuracy and reliability has been an area of substantial possibility and interest [12]. Brain tumors affect 700,000 people in America, with that number predicted to rise to more than 79,000 by the end of 2020. 25,000 of them may have malignant tumors, with the rest having non-malignant tumors [15]. The most frequent category of brain tumor is Glioma and it is classified as low and high-rank brain tumors, with high rank being more deadly than low-grade [16].

Researchers have recently researched brain tumor categorization using machine learning algorithms, particularly in recent spans. The advancement of AI and DL-based technological advances has had a significant influence on medical image processing, particularly in illness detection. Because it provides extensive information, brain MRI is commonly used to diagnose malignancies. Some tumors, such as gliomas and glioblastomas, are extremely hard to locate in MRI, whereas meningiomas are quite simple. Despite X-ray and computed tomography (CT) scan pictures, the measure of cluster values in MRI is not uniform. While some brain segmentation approaches use handmade characteristics. Deep Neural Networks (DNNs) for feature extraction have recently been used. The identification, segmentation, and tracing of brain tumors over time are critical for detection, treatment planning, patient care, and tracking and for prediction as well. For radiologists, tumor segmentation is time-consuming as per as the traditional process is concerned, and also laborious, and prone to human error in practice. Because of the tumor's unexpected appearance, penetration into adjacent tissue, intensity, heterogeneity, size, shape, and position fluctuation, and longitudinal brain tumor segmentation is a significant chore [17]. However, computer-aided medical image processing tools are increasingly assisting clinicians in identifying brain cancers [20]. Because of their complicated anatomical structure and importance in studying human behaviour, there has been an extensive variety of applications in computer-aided medical image study and diagnosis, and segmentation in MRI brain images.

1.1. Explainable AI

XAI (Explainable AI) incorporate strategies and procedures in the field of AI technology that allow humans to understand the outcomes can be understandable to the humans. Fig. (**1**) illustrates the idea of the XAI.

Explainable Artificial Intelligence is an edge that focuses on creating a collection of ML methods that 1) guarantee a high level of learning performance by creating more explainable models (*e.g.* accuracy of prediction); and 2) facilitate humans to grasp, and adequately believe in the next generation of artificially intelligent stakeholders.The goall of such an initiative is to prevent explainable AI from reducing the efficiency of today's AI systems.

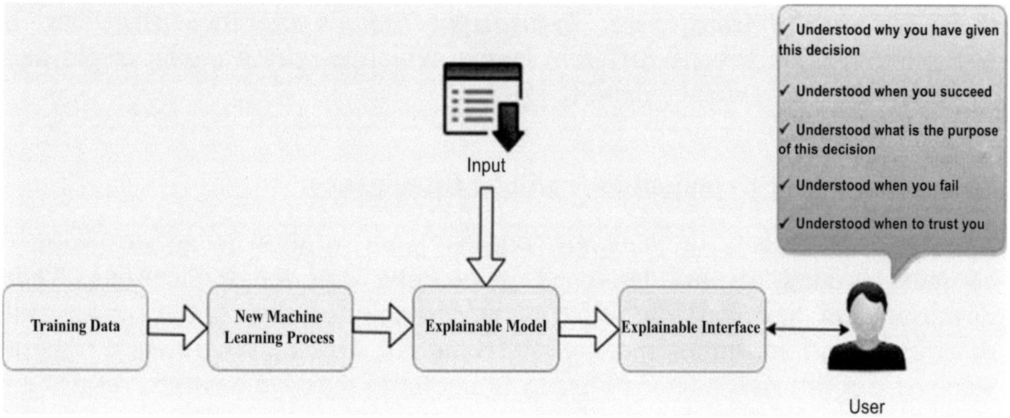

Fig. (1). Explainable Artificial Intelligence.

1.2. Some Key Concepts Related to XAI

- ***Explainability:*** Explainability is linked to the idea of description with a human involvement that would be both a genuine alternative for the decision maker to think. Explainability is linked to the concept of description as a human-t--human interface.
- ***Understandability:*** It is the capacity of a model to assist a human in comprehending its usefulness and how it performs, without the need to define the structural qualities of the model or the algorithmic procedures by which the model utilizes the information from inside [18].
- ***Comprehensibility:*** When applied to machine learning models, comprehensibility tells the capacity of a learning algorithm to describe the obtained facts in a manner that is accessible by humans [19 - 21]. This idea originates from Michalski's [22] postulates, which state that "the results of computer understanding must be conceptual summaries of given phenomena," which are "semantically and structurally similar to those that an analyst would construct seeing the same entities." This idea then goes on to suggest that "the outcomes of computer thinking should be conceptual depictions of given phenomena." Elements of these depictions must be understood as individual 'chunks' of data, quickly interpretable in everyday language, and must integrate quantitative as well as qualitative conceptions. Comprehensibility is often related to the assessment of model complexity [17], given the difficulties in defining comprehensibility itself.
- ***Interpretability:*** The capacity to describe anything to a human being or to provide one with significance in a manner that is understandable to that human.

- ***Transparency:*** When a model can be understood without any outside input then it is said to be transparent. Transparent models are those that can be comprehended on several different levels, which is why a model might have multiple levels of understandability [5].

1.3. Significance of Explainable Artificial Intelligence

- Stately achievements in machine learning have resulted in an explosion of computer vision, natural language processing, and AI applications. These developments have led to self-contained machines that sense, understand, determine, and act autonomously. Whereas AI, uses massive neural network stochastic optimization approaches to fit similarly massive datasets, resulting in complicated behaviour that is difficult for humans to explain. One major barrier to the implementation of AI-based systems is their lack of transparency.
- While the black-box feature of these systems allows for impressive predictions, they cannot be explained clearly. The machine's existing incapacity to explain its own judgments and actions to human users restricts the use of these systems. To be able to have confidence in system behaviour, exploitability must be there, either by utilizing intrinsically interpretable models or by establishing new ways for describing and managing otherwise excessively complicated decisions through local approximation and collaborative discussion.
- For this purpose, novel or improved machine-learning approaches that yield additional explainable models will be developed. These models will be matched with cutting-edge human-computer interface approaches able to convert them into clear and valuable explanatory dialogues for the end user.
- In order to make more explainable models, XAI focuses on building a collection of ML techniques whereas preserving a better level of learning performance, aiding human users to acquire, aptly trust, and effectively manage the next generation of artificially intelligent companions. New machine-learning systems will be able to describe their intellect, identify their advantages as well as deficiencies, and so give an insight into the future of XAI.

1.4. LIME (Locally Interpretable Model Agnostic Explanations)

A model with Local Interpretability Agnostic Interpretations is a prototype posthoc explanatory approach that seeks to mimic any black box machine learning model with a local, easily understandable model in order to explain each particular prediction. Because LIME is independent of the original classifier, it may be used to explain any classifier, regardless of the algorithm used for predictions. Finally, LIME operates locally, which means it is experience specific, and it, like SHAP, will offer reasons for the prediction in relation to each experience. LIME attempts to fit a local model using sample data points that are comparable to the observation under consideration. The local model can be of the interpretable model type, such as linear models, decision trees, and so on.

1.5. SHAP (SHapley Additive exPlanation)

Shapley values are returned by the Shapley Additive exPlanation, which represent model predictions as linear combinations of binary variables that indicate whether or not each subset of features is included in the model. In other words, the goal of this technique is to compute the influence of each characteristic to the forecast in order to explain the estimate of an instance.

2. MOTIVATION

Advancement in the medical field promotes the diagnosis of disease through automation methods and prediction of the brain tumor also has an important role since millions of people are affected by brain tumor and the rate of affected people is increased every year randomly. Hence, early detection of the disease performs a significant role in saving the lives of many individuals.

3. RELATED WORKS

Research is now being conducted to improve standalone brain tumor prevention methods that can help doctors diagnose brain tumors. As a consequence, survey and questionnaire have been made to advance the field's study and review methods for segmenting and classifying brain tumors.

Gokay Karayegen *et al.* [2] designed a convolutional neural network model to acquire precise tumor area and parameters such as height, breadth, and depth. Additionally, the scans were presented in various planes, including sagittal, coronal, and axial. The YOLOv2-inceptionv3 model is stated by Muhammad Irfan Sharif *et al.* [3]. The main advantage of this model is that using this model, tumors are classified as well as localized. As far as the segmentation issues are concerned, Sourodip Ghosh *et al.* [4] introduced a novel approach to tackling many other medical picture segmentation issues. Emrah Irmak [5] well presented a Grid search optimizer -convolutional neural network method in which using grid search, all hyper-parameters are automatically tuned with high robustness. Md Khairul Islam *et al.* [6] presented a TK algorithm (Template-based K-means algorithm) which is proved as a useful algorithm to reduce the dimensionality and the complexity of the system.

The basic aim of the study presented by Javaria Amin *et al.* [8] is to come up with a model called SSAE model (Stacked sparse autoencoder model). Using this model, the chance of error is reduced very efficiently. In addition to this, Muhammad Sharif *et al.* [9] presented a brain surface extraction (BSE) method. The main characteristic of this method is that it accurately segments complete tumor region only. Linmin Pei *et al.* [10] nicely presented a Lattice-Boltzmann method. The main aim of this method is to offer improved texture-based brain tumor segmentation. Marcin Wozniak *et al.* [11] well stated a novel CLM (correlation learning mechanism) that assists CNN to discover the most acceptable filers for pooling and convolution layers. The advantage of this mechanism is that the duration taken for training is small as compared to other mechanisms. Javaria Amin *et al.* [12] stated a LSTM (Long short-term memory) model that aims to classify both high and low-grade tumor.

All the studies discussed above are centric towards the classification of tumor based on the availability of the data. In view of all these methods and models discussed, a prediction algorithm needs to be developed by means of an explainable artificial intelligence technique. Table **1** lists both modern and historical literary works. Their advantages and disadvantages are also examined in detail.

Table 1. Review of existing works.

Authors	Method	Advantages	Limitations
Gokay Karayegen and Mehmet Feyzi Aksahin [2]	Convolutional neural network	In addition to obtaining the precise tumor location and parameters such as height, breadth, and depth, the images were shown in sagittal, coronal, and axial planes.	The storage capability of the system needs improvement for effective functioning.
Muhammad Irfan Sharif *et al.* [3]	YOLOv2-inceptionv3 model	Tumors are classified as well as localized.	Computational complexity of the system is reliably high.
Sourodip Ghosh *et al.* [4]	U-Net with VGG-16	Introduced a novel approach to tackling many other medical picture segmentation issues.	Due to either an irregular picture background or the computing power of the model, there may be a sudden randomization in the learnable parameters.
Emrah Irmak [5]	Grid search optimizer - convolutional neural network	Using grid search, all hyper-parameters are quickly and robustly adjusted.	The position and orientation of the attributes are not described.

(Table 1) cont.....

Authors	Method	Advantages	Limitations
Md Khairul Islam *et al.* [6]	TK (Template-based K-means algorithm)	The dimensionality as well as the complexity of the system is reduced.	Only a small number of data is utilized and there is a need in the improvement of accuracy.
Javaria Amin *et al.* [8]	Stacked sparse autoencoder (SSAE) model.	Occurrence of error is reduced.	Misclassification of the attributes may occur.
Muhammad Sharif *et al.* [9]	Brain surface extraction (BSE) method.	Accurately segment complete tumor region only.	All the regions in the brain are not interpreted in a distinct manner.
Linmin Pei *et al.* [10]	Lattice-Boltzmann method	Improves texture-based segmentation of brain tumors.	Few patients with lateral tumor development are available. For all forms of defective tissue the performance of segmentation prediction is poor.
Marcin Wozniak *et al.* [11]	A unique method for correlation learning (CLM)	This will enable CNN in identifying the best suitable filters for aggregating and convolution layers with little training time required.	The weights of the filters is not enabled and interpreted.
Javaria Amin *et al.* [12]	LSTM (Long short-term memory model)	Classifies high and low grade tumor	Sub-tumor region is not identified.

4. GAP ANALYSIS

Although extensive work on tumor detection and classification has been done, reliable tumor prediction remains a difficult problem with opportunity for improvement. While many efforts have been taken into feature extraction and reduction for the prediction of brain tumors, finding the best features to extract and choose is difficult since the number of features enhances correlation. Segmentation of the tumour region from the brain image also possess various challenges due to the complexity and sensitivity of the brain image.

5. PROPOSED METHODOLOGY

Predicting brain tumor in a more efficient way is the primary intention of this research. Initially, the data will be collected from the BRAT's18 dataset [15] and in the pre-processing stage, the noise and redundant data from the image are removed. The necessary region for the segmentation of the brain tumor is detected through the Region of Interest (RoI) and then the brain tumor is segmented from the image using the methods such as clustering by K-means, FCM (Fuzzy-C-means) and Bayesian c-means clustering. The k-means clustering is enabled because faster convergence is guaranteed in large datasets. Similarly, the FCM provides better results even if the data is overlapped and the Bayesian clustering analysis helps in assessing the statistical properties of the given data. The combined characteristics of these techniques pave the way for an efficient segmentation process [10, 11]. After segmentation using the clustering techniques, the similar region obtained from the techniques is extracted by the ensemble clustering that provides the segmented tumor and non-tumor region. After segmentation, the necessary features from the tumor and non-tumor region are extracted in the feature extraction stage for reducing the complexities. The obtained features are subjected to the dual-weighted deep CNN classifier, where the classifier is optimally tuned using the optimization algorithms such as PSO (Particle Swarm Optimization [13] and SSO (Salp Swarm Optimization) [14]. The effectiveness of the optimization techniques helps in the efficient tuning of the weights and bias in the classifier that helps in determining the desired output. The same CNN model was further imposed on LIME and SHAP. The representation of the proposed method is shown in Fig (**2**).

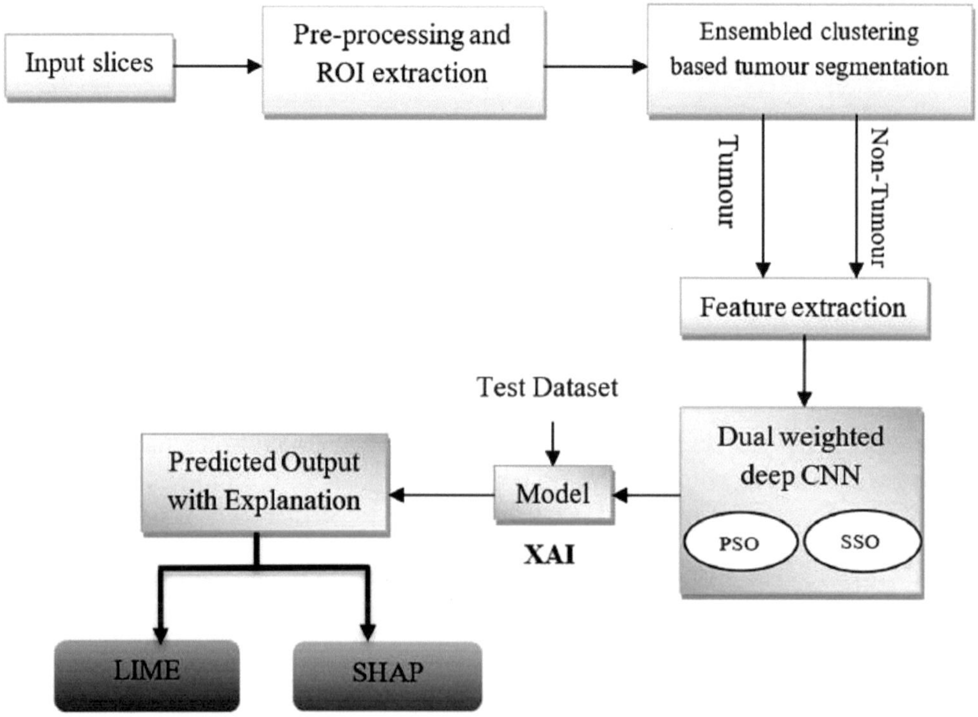

Fig. (2). Schematic representation of the proposed brain tumor prediction model with XAI.

6. ALGORITHMS FOR THE PROPOSED SYSTEM

6.1. PSO (Particle Swarm Optimization)

PSO (Particle Swarm Optimization) is a strong meta-heuristic optimization method that draws inspiration from swarm behaviour seen in nature, such as fish and bird swarming. PSO is a prototype of a streamlined social system. The primary goal of the PSO algorithm was to visually represent the artistic yet unpredictable dancing of a group of birds. Any bird's observation range in nature is constrained. However, having several birds in a swarm enables all of the birds to be aware of the wider surface of a fitness function. Nature has served as a source of motivation for ages, and there is still plenty to learn and explore about it. Swarm Intelligence (SI), a significant subfield of machine learning, is based on the intelligent group behavior of social swarming in nature, among many other things. The PSO method, one of the most well-liked SI paradigms, is introduced in this study. Since PSO's debut in the middle of the 1990s, several modifications have been implemented. Practitioners and researchers have created new applications, created new variations, and released theoretical concepts on the possible impact of various algorithmic settings and characteristics since they first learned about the technique.

The stepwise representation of PSO is given in Fig. (**3**).

6.2. SSO (Salp Swarm Optimization)

A salp is a type of aquatic creature that is a member of the Salpidae family. Its cylindrical shape with apertures at the tail, that allow water to flow over its jellylike body to move and provender through internal feeding filters, strongly resembles that of jellyfishes. Fig. (**4**) depicts the salp's form. The swarming habit is one of the behaviours shared by aquatic species, as was already noted. For instance, it is referred to as the classroom of fish for fish and the salp chain for salps as shown in Fig. (**4**). The biological experts are of the opinion that this behaviour aids the salps in accomplishing greater movement and foraging, despite the fact that their dwelling surroundings are quite challenging to reach.

SSA is recognized as one of the most effective modern meta-heuristic optimization algorithms, which has been effectively used to solve a variety of optimization issues in a variety of domains, including ML, engineering and design, wireless connectivity, processing of images, and electricity energy.

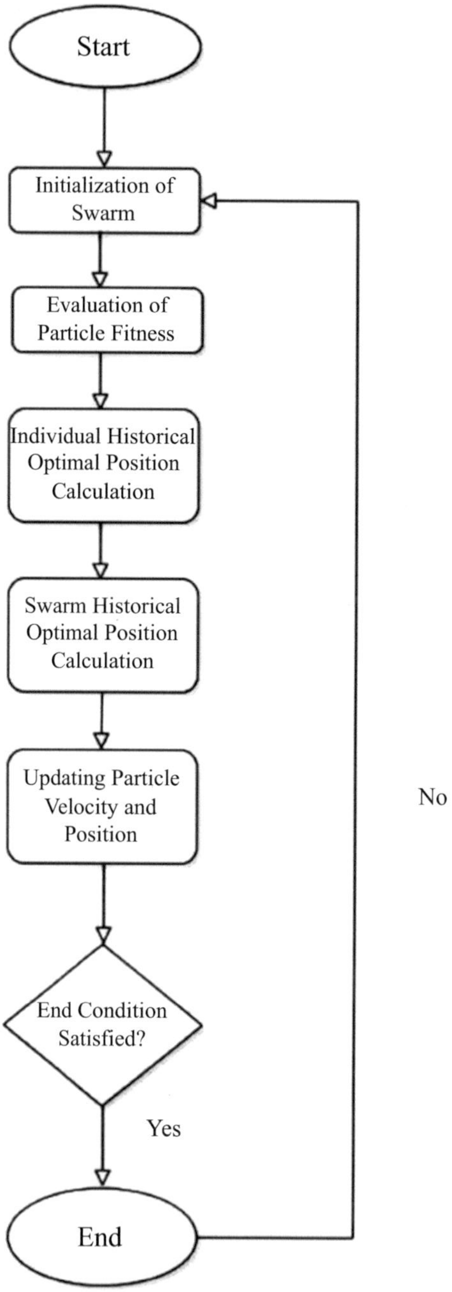

Fig. (3). Flowchart of particle swarm optimization algorithm.

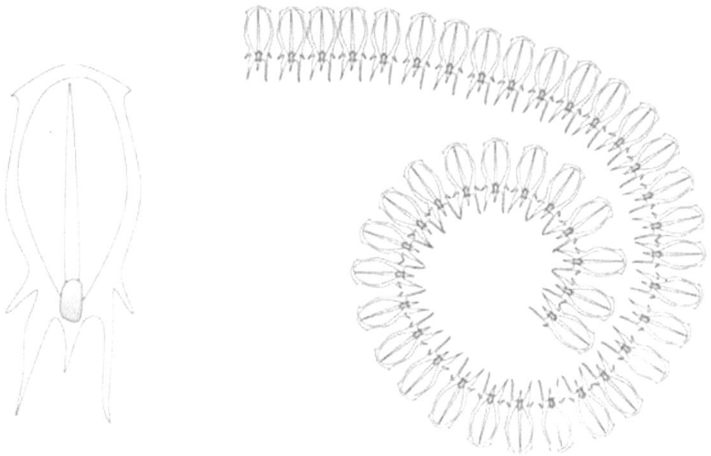

Fig. (4). Single *vs*. chain of salp.

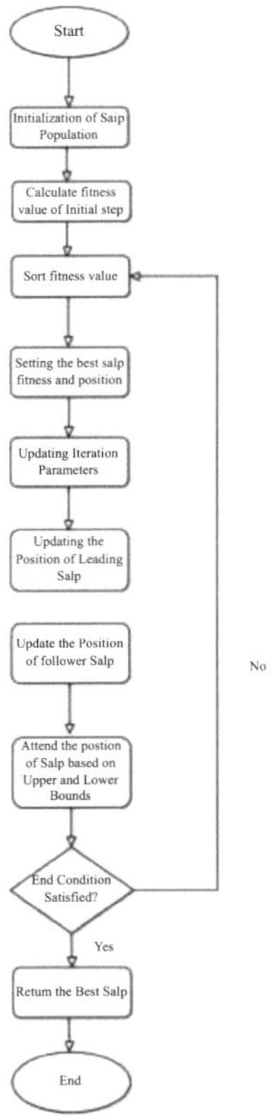

Fig. (5). Flowchart of salp swarm optimization algorithm.

Mirjalili *et al.* [22] introduced the SSA (Salp Swarm Algorithm), an optimization technique based on population. By figuring the SSA's behaviour while it searches for the best food sources, its behaviour may be shown. In SSA, people are classified either as leaders or followers according to where they are in the chain (*i.e.*, salps). The chain begins with a leader, and the chain serves as a direction for the followers' motions. The major phases of the SSA's flowchart are depicted in Fig. (**5**).

7. DESIGN ISSUES AND CHALLENGES

- Prediction of brain tumor is a crucial job because of the tumor's, intrusion to nearby areas, size, shape, tissue, heterogeneity, intensity and location discrepancy.
- Tumor finding is a big task due to complex brain construction. The prediction of tumor within a stipulated time and utility of optimal memory is also a challenging task.
- In order to get good results, choosing training/testing samples is another difficulty.

CONCLUSION AND FUTURE WORK

Early prediction model of the brain tumor aims to save lives of many individuals by means of Deep Learning algorithms. The chapter consists of an approach of dual weighted deep CNN classifier for early prediction of the presence of brain tumor along with the explanation-driven DL models such as LIME and SHAP. It is expected that the proposed technique will outperform all the conventional techniques in terms of specificity, sensitivity and accuracy. In future, XAI may be forced to employ classification algorithms with higher accuracy and better optimization. The study might be repeated on other XAI algorithms, including GradCAM, to improve clinical problems.

ACKNOWLEDGEMENT

The authors wish to thank Vishwakarma Institute of Information Technology for their support and guidance.

REFERENCES

[1] M.S. Majib, M.M. Rahman, T.M.S. Sazzad, N.I. Khan, and S.K. Dey, "VGG-SCNet: A VGG Net-Based Deep Learning Framework for Brain Tumor Detection on MRI Images", *IEEE Access,* vol. 9, pp. 116942-116952, 2021.
[http://dx.doi.org/10.1109/ACCESS.2021.3105874]

[2] G. Karayegen, and M.F. Aksahin, "Brain tumor prediction on MR images with semantic segmentation

by using deep learning network and 3D imaging of tumor region", *Biomed. Signal Process. Control,* vol. 66, p. 102458, 2021.
[http://dx.doi.org/10.1016/j.bspc.2021.102458]

[3] M. Sharif, J. Li, J. Amin, and A. Sharif, "An improved framework for brain tumor analysis using MRI based on YOLOv2 and convolutional neural network", Complex &Intelligent Systems, vol. 7, pp. 2023–2036, 2021.
[http://dx.doi.org/10.1007/s40747-021-00310-3]

[4] S. Ghosh, A. Chaki, and K.C. Santosh, "Improved U-Net architecture with VGG-16 for brain tumor segmentation", *Physical and Engineering Sciences in Medicine,* vol. 44, no. 3, pp. 703-712, 2021.
[http://dx.doi.org/10.1007/s13246-021-01019-w] [PMID: 34047928]

[5] E. Irmak, "Multi-Classification of Brain Tumor MRI Images Using Deep Convolutional Neural Network with Fully Optimized Framework", *Iranian Journal of Science and Technology, Transactions of Electrical Engineering,* vol. 45, no. 3, pp. 1015-1036, 2021.
[http://dx.doi.org/10.1007/s40998-021-00426-9]

[6] M.K. Islam, M.S. Ali, M.S. Miah, M.M. Rahman, M.S. Alam, and M.A. Hossain, "Brain tumor detection in MR image using superpixels, principal component analysis and template based K-means clustering algorithm", *Machine Learning with Applications,* vol. 5, p. 100044, 2021.
[http://dx.doi.org/10.1016/j.mlwa.2021.100044]

[7] F.J. Díaz-Pernas, M. Martínez-Zarzuela, M. Antón-Rodríguez, and D. González-Ortega, "A deep learning approach for brain tumor classification and segmentation using a multiscale convolutional neural network", *Healthcare (Basel),* vol. 9, no. 2, p. 153, 2021.
[http://dx.doi.org/10.3390/healthcare9020153] [PMID: 33540873]

[8] J. Amin, M. Sharif, N. Gul, M. Raza, M.A. Anjum, M.W. Nisar, and S.A.C. Bukhari, "Brain tumor detection by using stacked autoencoders in deep learning", *J. Med. Syst.,* vol. 44, no. 2, p. 32, 2020.
[http://dx.doi.org/10.1007/s10916-019-1483-2] [PMID: 31848728]

[9] M. Sharif, J. Amin, M. Raza, M. Yasmin, and S.C. Satapathy, "An integrated design of particle swarm optimization (PSO) with fusion of features for detection of brain tumor", *Pattern Recognition Letters,* vol. 129, pp. 150-157, 2020.
[http://dx.doi.org/10.1016/j.patrec.2019.11.017]

[10] L. Pei, S. Bakas, A. Vossough, S.M.S. Reza, C. Davatzikos, and K.M. Iftekharuddin, "Longitudinal brain tumor segmentation prediction in MRI using feature and label fusion", *Biomedical Signal Processing and Control,* vol. 55, p. 101648, 2020.
[http://dx.doi.org/10.1016/j.bspc.2019.101648] [PMID: 34354762]

[11] M. Woźniak, J. Siłka, and M. Wieczorek, "Deep neural network correlation learning mechanism for CT brain tumor detection", *Neural Computing and Applications,* 2021.
[http://dx.doi.org/10.1007/s00521-021-05841-x]

[12] J. Amin, M. Sharif, M. Raza, T. Saba, R. Sial, and S.A. Shad, "Brain tumor detection: a long short-term memory (LSTM)-based learning model", *Neural Computing and Applications,* vol. 32, no. 20, pp. 15965-15973, 2020.
[http://dx.doi.org/10.1007/s00521-019-04650-7]

[13] F. Wang, H. Zhang, and A. Zhou, "A particle swarm optimization algorithm for mixed-variable optimization problems", *Swarm and Evolutionary Computation,* vol. 60, p. 100808, 2021.
[http://dx.doi.org/10.1016/j.swevo.2020.100808]

[14] M. Tubishat, S. Ja'afar, M. Alswaitti, S. Mirjalili, N. Idris, M.A. Ismail, and M.S. Omar, "Dynamic Salp swarm algorithm for feature selection", *Expert Systems with Applications,* vol. 164, p. 113873, 2021.
[http://dx.doi.org/10.1016/j.eswa.2020.113873]

[15] Available from: https://www.med.upenn.edu/sbia/brats2018/data.html

[16] L. Gaur, M. Bhandari, T. Razdan, S. Mallik, and Z. Zhao, "Explanation-driven deep learning model for prediction of brain tumour status using mri image data", *Front. Genet.,* vol. 13, p. 822666, 2022. [http://dx.doi.org/10.3389/fgene.2022.822666] [PMID: 35360838]

[17] M. Esmaeili, R. Vettukattil, H. Banitalebi, N.R. Krogh, and J.T. Geitung, "Explainable artificial intelligence for human-Machine interaction in brain tumor localization", *J. Personalized Med,,* vol. 11, no. 11, p. 1213, 2021.
[http://dx.doi.org/10.3390/jpm11111213] [PMID: 34834566]

[18] L. Gaur, M. Bhandari, T. Razdan, S. Mallik, and Z. Zhao, "Explanation-driven deep learning model for prediction of brain tumour status using MRI image data", *Frontiers In Genetics,* vol. 13, p. 822666, 2022.
[http://dx.doi.org/10.3389/fgene.2022.822666] [PMID: 35360838]

[19] M. Gupta, S.K. Sharma, R. Saxena, and S. Arora, "Analysis of machine learning algorithms in brain tumour prediction", *J. Phys. Conf. Series.,* vol. 2070, no. 1, p. 012090, 2021.
[http://dx.doi.org/10.1088/1742-6596/2070/1/012090]

[20] J.A. Cruz, and D.S. Wishart, "Applications of machine learning in cancer prediction and prognosis", *Cancer Informatics,* vol. 2, no. 1, 2006.
[http://dx.doi.org/10.1177/117693510600200030] [PMID: 19458758]

[21] B.H.M. van der Velden, H.J. Kuijf, K.G.A. Gilhuijs, and M.A. Viergever, "Explainable artificial intelligence (XAI) in deep learning-based medical image analysis", *Medical Image Analysis,* vol. 79, p. 102470, 2022.
[http://dx.doi.org/10.1016/j.media.2022.102470] [PMID: 35576821]

[22] S. Mirjalili, A.H. Gandomi, S.Z. Mirjalili, S. Saremi, H. Faris, and S.M. Mirjalili, "Salp Swarm Algorithm: A bio-inspired optimizer for engineering design problems", *Advances in Engineering Software,* vol. 114, pp. 163-191, 2017.
[http://dx.doi.org/10.1016/j.advengsoft.2017.07.002]

CHAPTER 5

Designing a Human-centered AI-based Cognitive Learning Model for Industry 4.0 Applications

Varad Vishwarupe[1,4,*], Saniya Zahoor[2], Ravesa Akhter[2], Vijay P. Bhatkar[3], Mangesh Bedekar[3,4], Milind Pande[3,4], Prachi M. Joshi[5], Avinash Patil[3,4], Vishal Pawar[3,4] and **Neha Mandora[4]**

[1] *Amazon Research and Development Centre, Bangalore, Karnataka, India*

[2] *National Institute of Technology Srinagar, Srinagar, Jammu and Kashmir, India*

[3] *Maharashtra Institute of Technology World Peace University, Pune, India*

[4] *Human Inspired AI Research Pvt. Ltd - HumInspAIRe, Pune, Maharashtra, India*

[5] *DES Pune University, Pune, Maharashtra, India*

Abstract: The aim of this chapter is to focus on the status of data mining approaches for e-learning and identify the gaps in them. It is seen that a predominant work has been done in e-learning through data mining techniques such as educational recommenders, association rules, clustering, profile-based approaches, personalization, prediction techniques, and decision support systems. However limited work is done on e-learning from a cognitive science perspective, which gives us the motivation to work in this field. The proposed work aims at proposing a cognitive model for e-learning systems using data mining for Industry 4.0 applications which shall usher in a new datum for e-learning in cyber-physical systems.

Keywords: Artificial intelligence, Cognitive learning model, Cognitive e-learning.

1. INTRODUCTION

The main objective is performance evaluation of e-learning systems in order to identify the learner's learning style and propose a cognitive e-learning model to improve students' experience. The main emphasis of this work is on delivering content based on their behavior while learning. Learning style differs with respect to multiple dimensions which are demographic features, social and economic content, emotional condition of the learner, and physiological and physiological elements. The learning style can also be predicted from the behavior of learners such as how people gain knowledge and preserve skills, ways of accessing information to help their progress, *etc*. The aim is to make e-learning similar to classroom learning.

* **Corresponding author Varad Vishwarupe:** Amazon Research and Development Centre, Bangalore, Karnataka, India; E-mail: varad44@gmail.com

Parikshit N. Mahalle, Gitanjali R. Shinde and Prachi M. Joshi (Eds.)

More specifically, the following are the main objectives and methodologies:

1. Encounter Cold-Start Problem in e-learning,

2. Explicit feedback from students and teachers for questionnaire collection and statistical analysis related to learning styles,

3. Determination of the cognitive factors that affect student's learning,

4. Identifying the constraints *(e.g.* time constraints) present in the e-learning system,

5. Weighting the cognitive factors and constraints,

6. Evaluation of the performance of learning of student according to these cognitive factors,

7. Designing a cognitive model for e-learning applications using data mining techniques,

8. Identification of patterns present in learning styles for students, and

9. Recommendations to the students *(e.g.* course preferences).

The proposed cognitive model for e-learning will assist in students' learning and provide teachers with the necessary feedback. The only crucial step in this model is weighting the cognitive and constrained factors of e-learning because the priority of each factor can differ from one university to another. The end results of the cognitive e-learning model will also provide significant information to teachers and decision-makers for improving e-learning programs in the future.

The work will be carried out by comparing our proposed model with the standard model in order to prove the efficiency of our model. Analysis of cognitive data will be carried out in MATLAB and data mining tools.

2. NATIONAL AND INTERNATIONAL STATUS

With the advancement in information technology, electronic learning (e-learning) has played a key role in teaching and learning which has become more and more important in colleges and schools nowadays [1]. Further, the COVID-19 pandemic has led to a rise in teaching and learning courses through online portals [2]. Various educational institutes have adopted video conferencing platforms such as Microsoft platform, Zoom and Webex Blackboard, and Google Classroom, leading to the enhancement of e-learning globally [3]. There are many advantages of e-learning which include no time and space constraints for learners to study courses, saving internal training costs, improving classroom teaching, *etc.* The design of e-learning objectives focuses on providing opportunities for students to learn through virtual experience the functional value of the material by working directly with the content. There has been a recent shift in attention toward web-based e-earning systems that provide us a virtual educational environment independent of any specific hardware platforms [4].

Research in e-learning systems has been focusing on various methodologies to keep learners as active learners for longer duration and how to deliver appropriate learning and learning material for them. Authors [5] developed a learning model using various research works on psychology and cognitive science. Learning is the process of retrieving the relevant information by integrating knowledge/behavior of the learners. Learning goals should be compatible with learner's background knowledge, their interest and learning style. Research on learning face challenges in terms of explicit issues such as indirect suggestions and implicit issues e.g. course recommendations [6]. Learner personalization characteristics play a vital role in e-learning. Authors [7] proposed that learning is a process to acquire knowledge that can be created through the transformation of experience. Some authors [8] define learning style as an instructional strategy which helps in improving cognition, based on the context and content of learning. Learning style can be predicted from the behavior of learners like how people gain knowledge and preserve skills, their way of accessing information to help in their progress, *etc.*

According to a study [9], the most important aspect in the design of active learning applications should be grounded in the principles of cognitive science. Cognitive e-learning focuses on best practices for designing an online course, organizing and presenting its content, helping students develop skills, deciding on teaching and assessment methods, incorporating social interaction and providing students with feedback [10]. Designing a cognitive model for a real-time e-learning application should clearly distinguish between two things whether the system is a rule-based system or a constraint-based model. The working principle of a rule-based model purely depends on the knowledge of the end-user and the constraint-based model expresses its requirement by raising queries. These queries should be resolved with the help of problem related e-learning [11].

The concept of cognitive e-learning has led to several technological developments in teaching which include intelligent tutoring systems that redirect the students to the next steps in learning; artificial intelligence that represents the mental learning processes; pre-determined learning outcomes based on different cognitive activities; and instructional design approaches that ensure the success of learning objectives [12]. These e-learning systems generate a large amount of information about students' behavior that helps teachers with possible improvements in their teaching methods. But such systems face major challenges in terms of voluminous data generated daily that becomes very difficult to manage manually. To address this, data mining is a promising area that plays an important role in managing this huge amount of data [13]. Various interest indicators are derived from the interaction of a student on an online course or examination through data mining that forms the basis for e-learning objectives. Fig. (**1**) shows the role of data mining in cognitive e-learning.

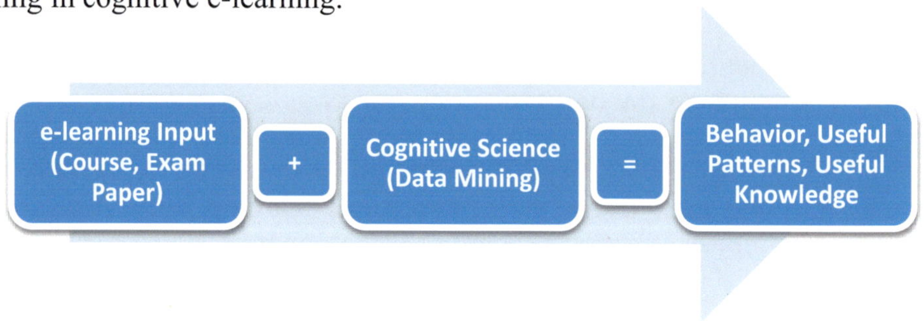

Fig. (1). Data mining in cognitive e-learning.

Data mining aims at mining useful patterns and knowledge from the educational activities in e-learning systems such as students' performance, registration, course selection, examination scores, *etc.* [14]. It aims at understanding lower-order and higher-order thinking skills of students in relation to the correlation analysis between brain dominance and multiple intelligence. Various computer-based learning tools help us collect and analyze students' data to discover patterns and make new discoveries about student cognition [15]. The aim of this proposal is to focus on the data mining approaches for e-learning to understand student's cognitive behavior based on the real-time data of the student's activities in e-learning systems.

Data mining is one of the most appropriate technologies suitable for giving supplementary study materials to the students, teachers and other educational staff and serving them for making enhanced decisions about their educational activities. This causes many advantages to the educational system such as making the best use of educational system competence, rising withholding rate, growing success rate, rise in learning outcomes of students, *etc.* [17]. In recent times, there has been research on finding various data mining methods to help teachers improve e-learning systems by allowing the discovery of new knowledge based on students' usage data, therefore, trying to understand the student's cognitive behavior [18]. Authors in [19] performed a study on student performance by selecting a sample of 300 students (225 males, 75 females) from a group of colleges and it was found by means of simple linear regression analysis that the factors like family income and mother's education of a student were highly correlated with his performance in academics. Similarly, data mining finds its applicability in analyzing the student's learning behavior to predict the results and to warn students at risk before their final exams [20].

Considerable work has been done in cognitive e-learning through data mining techniques such as educational recommenders, association rule, clustering, profile-based approach, personalization, prediction techniques, decision support system, *etc.* as shown in Fig. (**2**). Educational recommenders are widely used to provide recommendations to students or teachers who want to select preferred choices from a set of courses, subjects or any educational activities [21]. Modeling and analyzing the preferences of users is one the common methods used by educational recommenders that enable the educational data to be ranked and filtered out as per the user's preferences stored in his profile [22]. There has been predominant work done on educational recommenders used for cognitive e-learning that provide students with suggestions when having trouble choosing courses [23 - 25]. Considerable work in this domain includes personalized CAI courseware system that provides course recommendations based on the similarity of the learner's profile [26], course recommendation algorithm that selects courses based on the user's interests [27], an adaptive model for e-Learning recommender systems based on student's learning style [28], ontology-based recommender systems in e-learning [29], intelligent course recommendation during online lectures in e-learning system [30], novel predictive model for collaborative filtering recommenders, *etc.* Therefore, the learner's profile plays a crucial role in the recommendations to improve the e-learning process.

Clustering finds its application in cognitive e-learning. There has been work done on clustering for the evaluation of students in a tutorial supervisor system to deal with the questions' difficulty in the evaluation process. The Exception Maximization algorithm is one of the algorithms mostly used in e-learning applications to group students into clusters on the basis of their behaviors and actions on the web which is gathered and preprocessed using data mining techniques. This information is also used by the teachers to provide suggestions to the students belonging to each cluster. Considerable work has been done grouping similar course materials to help e-learning users find and organize distributed courses. These include the bisection K-Means algorithm to group similar learning materials, the SOM algorithm to cluster similar learning materials using semantic similarities in probabilistic learning to group data as per the student's behavior on an online course Generative Topographic Mapping (GTM) variant to rank the available data according to their groups of student.

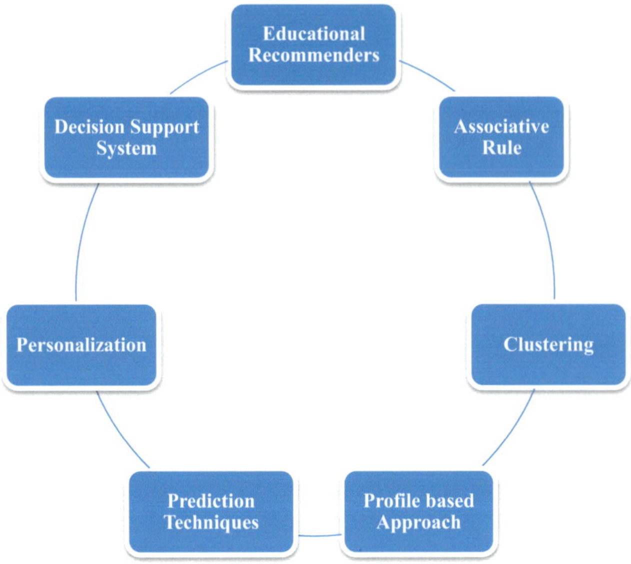

Fig. (2). Approach and methodology.

Understanding the behavior of end-users is one of the major challenges in e-learning systems. There has been a lot of research towards finding information about the user's interests by user profiling. User's interests can be very well inferred from their attitudes about e-learning systems and it will depend on how much information about the user is available with the profiling system. The profiling systems tend to learn fast but can add an overhead to student's activities especially when questions are asked to explicitly capture the user profile. The e-learning systems with explicit feedback force users to evaluate e-learning materials and indicate the relevancy of these using a rating scale. Such systems offer simplicity and high performance but require extra time and efforts. On the other hand, e-learning systems with implicit feedback obtain information by monitoring behavior of the students on the online course and thus, recommendations are automatically provided based on the data captured in their profiles

A lot of work has been done in the area of implicit user profiling but most of the papers focus on interest indicators which play an important role in user profiling. Hence, these concepts, to a large extent, can be used in the field of e-learning systems. For example, the time spent on a particular question during examination can tell a lot about the student's learning about the particular topic of the subject. Following are a few interest indicators that can play an important role in e-learning systems: time spent, mouse scrolling, mouse movements, mouse clicks,

Keyboard keys, keyboard shortcuts, *etc*. However, the user profile is initially empty in case of e-learning systems with implicit feedback and it becomes difficult to make recommendations in these systems due to a lack of information. This well-known problem is termed a "cold-start" problem. To address this, there has been a lot of research on how preferences can be given in user profiles to rank the set of educational items for necessary recommendations. This includes user profiles that can contain a vector value of user's interests qualitative preferences represented with fuzzy terms, numerical attributes ontology-based semantic information, *etc*. The user profile contains implicit information on the preferences of the user in these aspects.

Associative rule mining is one the most important techniques of data mining that help in extracting useful information mainly patterns that help the students and teachers to evaluate various educational activities such as assessment of learning material, course adaption according to behavior of the students, educational website evaluation, learning recommenders, *etc*. There has been research in associative rule mining that defined contrast rules to detect the pattern of performance evaluation among students. Similar work has been presented with the Concept Effect Relationship (CER) model to diagnose the learning problems of students and provide suggestions. Many e-learning frameworks based on associative rule mining have been proposed, which include a web usage framework, learning assessment framework, e-learning website models framework for predicting, interpreting, and improving learning outcomes, *etc*. All these frameworks aim at developing a support system for e-learning systems in reorganizing the course material and personalizing course materials as per the student's requirements.

Various prediction techniques of data mining are used to understand the behavior and performance of students in e-learning systems. Few evolutionary algorithms have been used in cognitive e-learning systems to understand useful patterns and relationships among the knowledge of students, time spent on e-learning courses and marks obtained. And to make future predictions based on the analysis of user's activities on online learning systems, prediction analysis methods such as regression techniques are used. To find the sources of error in the prediction of knowledge behavior of students, stepwise regression is applied to assess the metrics that explain the poor prediction of exam scores. One can also use linear regression to predict whether the next response of students is correct, and how long he or she will take to generate that response. Likewise, the other prediction techniques include Naïve Bayes, KNN, C4.5, Logistic Regression, and Support Vector Machines which are used for the detection of students' behavior. In cognitive e-learning, it is necessary to know and analyze the student's psychology of what he learns or likes to learn so that the teacher addresses the student's needs successfully. Personalization systems have the ability to tailor and suggest the e-learning material based on past or present interactions with that student. There has been research in personalized e-learning systems for many years. These include the PerLCol Framework for personalized user models consisting of useful attributes such as preferences, knowledge, *etc.* stored in a user profile. These intelligent personalized e-learning systems are used to predict the preferences of students for new items in e-learning applications. Authors proposed a personalized English learning system that uses the concept of clustering and associative rules to provide recommendations to the students. Similarly, a research work has been performed wherein course modeling is performed for personalized recommendation services using fuzzy-based Item Response Theory. To support decision-makers engaged in solving various problems related to e-learning material such as multiple objectives, a Decision Support System (DSS) is used. Users are often asked to provide their preferences either on alternatives and/or on the relative weights of attributes. Authors [12] present a prioritized decision-making model in which low-priority weights are given to each alternative depending on whether or not each alternative satisfies the high priority criteria requirements. Works on related areas examine learning strategies employed by DSSs to facilitate learning of organization.

The aim of this proposal is to focus on the national and international status of data mining approaches for e-learning. Predominant work has been done in the field of e-learning through data mining techniques such as educational recommenders, association rules, clustering, profile-based approach, personalization, prediction techniques and decision support systems. But limited work is done on e-learning from a cognitive science perspective. The proposed work aims at proposing a cognitive model for e-learning systems using data mining.

3. RESEARCH METHODOLOGY

The proposed cognitive model for e-learning will assist in student's learning and provide teachers with the necessary feedback. The only crucial step in this model is weighting the cognitive and constrained factors of e-learning because the priority of each factor can be different from one university to another. The end results of the cognitive e-learning model provide significant information to teachers and decision-makers for improving e-learning programs in the future. The work will be carried out by comparing our proposed model with the standard model in order to prove the efficiency of our model. Analysis of cognitive data will be carried out in MATLAB and data mining tools.

4. RESULTS

The proposed human-centered AI-based cognitive e-learning model has ushered in some significant leaps into the learning pedagogy by ushering in rapid and efficient student learning. This includes having developed an intelligent interactive system that is more user-friendly and works on experiential and instance-based cognitive e-learning. Using explainable AI frameworks such as SHAP and LIME, we were also able to provide outcomes as follows:

• Using a human-centered AI-based cognitive model helped us in understanding the cognitive behavior of a student on an online educational course.

• It also provided a correlation of cognitive factors with student's learning progress.

• Based on XAI and HCI, we were able to create relevant user profiles.

• Human-centered AI-based recommendation based on student's engagement in the e-course and providing constructive feedback from the learning model.

• This approach allowed us to understand the student's cognitive behavior.

• It also assisted in student's learning towards the course and

• Course-wise recommendations on which courses to choose based on a student's performance in e-learning activities such as exam scores.

• Improved feedback to teachers regarding the content and conduct of their teaching so that they incorporate improvements in their teaching style in online mode and comparison and suggestions as compared to offline teaching.

CONCLUSION

The aim of this research is to focus on developing a Human-Centered AI-based cognitive e-learning model that is supported by modalities in Explainable AI, HCI and Human-Centered Computing. The same has been reflected in the development of the cognitive e-learning model which, in contrary to the black-box nature of traditional AI models, provides a very holistic and complete overview of why the system recommended a certain teaching-learning paradigm for a student. It also facilitates the need for developing an intelligent interactive system that is not only intelligent in nature so that it can aid in the progress of a student's learning abilities but also interactive in nature so as to maximize the productivity of instructor's efficiency.

It has been observed that predominant work has been done in e-learning through data mining techniques such as educational recommenders, association rule, clustering, profile-based approach, personalization, prediction techniques, and decision support systems. However limited work is done on e-learning from a cognitive science perspective. The said work aims at proposing a cognitive model for e-learning systems using data mining. The said work will provide significant information to decision-makers for improving and incorporating e-learning programs in the future. Developing a human-centered AI-based approach to cognitive e-learning model design and development requires interdisciplinary collaboration and future work in this regard will involve deploying this model in more schools and educational institutions to measure real-world impact and usher in a new era of cognitive e-learning.

REFERENCES

[1] C. Kolski, A. B. Guy, M. Guy, O. Magalie, and V. Jean, "Cross-Fertilisation Between Human-Computer Interaction and Artificial Intelligence", In: Marquis Pierre, Papini Odile, and Prade Henri, *A Guided Tour of Artificial Intelligence Research* vol. III. Springer, Cham, 2020, pp. 365-388. [http://dx.doi.org/10.1007/978-3-030-06170-8_11]

[2] T. Hewett, R. Baecker, S. Card, T. Carey, J. Gasen, M. Mantei, G. Perlman, G. Strong, and W. Verplank, "ACM SIGCHI curricula for humancomputer interaction", In: *ACM*New York, NY, USA, 1992. [http://dx.doi.org/10.1145/2594128]

[3] N. Mhetre, A. Deshpande, and P. Mahalle, "Experience-Based Access Control in UbiComp: A New Paradigm", *J. Comput. Commun.,* 2022pp. 133-157. [http://dx.doi.org/10.4236/jcc.2022.101007]

[4] J. John, "Crowdsourcing Interface Feature Design with Bayesian Optimization", In: *Proceedings of the 2019 CHI Conference on Human Factors in Computing Systems (CHI '19).* vol. 252. Assoc. Comput. Mach.: New York, NY, USA, 2019, pp. 1-12.

[5] L. Hetzel, J. Dudley, A.M. Feit, and P.O. Kristensson, "Complex Interaction as Emergent Behaviour: Simulating Mid-Air Virtual Keyboard Typing using Reinforcement Learning", *IEEE Trans. Vis. Comput. Graph.,* vol. 27, no. 11, pp. 4140-4149, 2021. [http://dx.doi.org/10.1109/TVCG.2021.3106494] [PMID: 34449380]

[6] J. Shen, J. Dudley, and P.O. Kristensson, "Simulating Realistic Human Motion Trajectories of Mid-Air Gesture Typing", In: *2021 IEEE International Symposium on Mixed and Augmented Reality (ISMAR)* IEEE, 2021. [http://dx.doi.org/10.1109/ISMAR52148.2021.00056]

[7] S. Bobek, S.K. Tadeja, Ł. Struski, P. Stachura, T. Kipouros, J. Tabor, G.J. Nalepa, and P.O. Kristensson, "Virtual reality-based parallel coordinates plots enhanced with explainable ai and data-science analytics for decision-making processes", *Appl. Sci.,* vol. 12, no. 1, p. 331, 2021. [http://dx.doi.org/10.3390/app12010331]

[8] B. Mo George, J Dudley John, and Ola Kristensson Per, "Gesture Knitter: A Hand Gesture Design Tool for Head-Mounted Mixed Reality Applications", In: *Proceedings of the 2021 CHI Conference on Human Factors in Computing Systems (CHI '21)* vol. 291. Association for Computing Machinery: New York, NY, USA, 2021, pp. 1-13. [http://dx.doi.org/10.1145/3411764.3445766]

[9] T. Jason, and Kristensson Per Ola, Studying Programmer Behaviour at Scale: A Case Study using Amazon Mechanical Turk, Companion Proceedings of the 5th International Conference on the Art,

Science, and Engineering of Programming,,
[http://dx.doi.org/10.1145/3464432.3464436]

[10] Uzor Stephen, and Kristensson Per Ola, "An Exploration of Freehand Crossing Selection in Head-Mounted Augmented Reality", *ACM Trans. Comput.-Hum. Interact. 28, 5, Article 33 (October 2021),,* p. 27.
[http://dx.doi.org/10.1145/3462546]

[11] J. Shen, J. Dudley, G. Mo, and P.O. Kristensson, "Gesture Spotter: A Rapid Prototyping Tool for Key Gesture Spotting in Virtual and Augmented Reality Applications", *IEEE Trans. Vis. Comput. Graph.,* vol. 28, no. 11, pp. 3618-3628, 2022.
[http://dx.doi.org/10.1109/TVCG.2022.3203004] [PMID: 36048982]

[12] V.V. Vishwarupe, and P.M. Joshi, "Intellert: a novel approach for content-priority based message filtering", *IEEE Bombay Section Symposium (IBSS),* 2016. pp. 1-6,
[http://dx.doi.org/10.1109/IBSS.2016.7940206]

[13] A. Schmidt, F. Giannotti, W. Mackay, B. Shneiderman, and K. Väänänen, Artificial Intelligence for Humankind: A Panel on How to Create Truly Interactive and Human-Centered AI for the Benefit of Individuals and Society.*Human-Computer Interaction.,* C. Ardito, Ed., vol. 12936. Springer: Cham, 2021.
[http://dx.doi.org/10.1007/978-3-030-85607-6_32]

[14] V. Vishwarupe, P.M. Joshi, N. Mathias, S. Maheshwari, S. Mhaisalkar, and V. Pawar, "Explainable AI and Interpretable Machine Learning: A Case Study in Perspective", *Procedia Comput. Sci.,* vol. 204, pp. 869-876, 2022.
[http://dx.doi.org/10.1016/j.procs.2022.08.105]

[15] J.M. Gorriz, J. Suckling, J. Ramirez, C. Jimenez-Mesa, and F. Segovia, "A connection between pattern classification by machine learning and statistical inference with the General Linear Model", *IEEE Journal of Biomedical and Health Informatics.*
[http://dx.doi.org/10.1109/JBHI.2021.3101662]

[16] V. Vishwarupe, M. Bedekar, M. Pande, V.P. Bhatkar, P. Joshi, S. Zahoor, and P. Kuklani, "Comparative Analysis of Machine Learning Algorithms for Analyzing NASA Kepler Mission Data", *Procedia Comput. Sci.,* vol. 204, pp. 945-951, 2022.
[http://dx.doi.org/10.1016/j.procs.2022.08.115]

[17] M. Leming, and J. Suckling, "Deep learning for sex classification in resting-state and task functional brain networks from the UK Biobank", *NeuroImage.* Volume 241, 2021, 118409, ISSN 1053-8119
[http://dx.doi.org/10.1016/j.neuroimage.2021.118409]

[18] V. Vishwarupe, M. Bedekar, P.M. Joshi, M. Pande, V. Pawar, and P. Shingote, "Data Analytics in the Game of Cricket: A Novel Paradigm", *Procedia Comput. Sci.,* vol. 204, pp. 937-944, 2022.
[http://dx.doi.org/10.1016/j.procs.2022.08.114]

[19] S. Zahoor, M. Bedekar, and V. Vishwarupe, "A Framework to Infer Webpage Relevancy for a User", In: A Framework to Infer Webpage Relevancy for a User.*Proceedings of First International Conference on Information and Communication Technology for Intelligent Systems,* S. Satapathy, S. Das, Eds., Springer: Cham, 2016.Volume 1. Smart Innovation, Systems and Technologies, vol 50.,
[http://dx.doi.org/10.1007/978-3-319-30933-0_16]

[20] V. Vishwarupe, M. Bedekar, M. Pande, and A. Hiwale, Intelligent Twitter Spam Detection: A Hybrid Approach.*Smart Trends in Systems, Security and Sustainability. Lecture Notes in Networks and Systems.,* X.S. Yang, A. Nagar, A. Joshi, Eds., vol. Vol. 18. Springer: Singapore, 2018.
[http://dx.doi.org/10.1007/978-981-10-6916-1_17]

[21] M. Bedekar, S. Zahoor, and V. Vishwarupe, "PeTelCoDS—Personalized Television Content Delivery System: A Leap into the Set-Top Box Revolution", *Proceedings of First International Conference on Information and Communication Technology for Intelligent Systems,* 2016 Volume 2. Smart Innovation, Systems and Technologies, vol 51.,

[http://dx.doi.org/10.1007/978-3-319-30927-9_27]

[22] V. Vishwarupe, S. Maheshwari, A. Deshmukh, S. Mhaisalkar, P. M. Joshi, and N. Mathias, "Bringing Humans at the Epicenter of Artificial Intelligence: A Confluence of AI, HCI, and Human-Centered Computing", *Procedia Computer Science,* vol. 204, pp. 914-921. [http://dx.doi.org/10.1016/j.procs.2022.08.111]

[23] S. Zahoor, M. Bedekar, V. Mane, and V. Vishwarupe, "Uniqueness in User Behavior While Using the Web", In: *Proceedings of the International Congress on Information and Communication Technology. Advances in Intelligent Systems and Computing,* S. Satapathy, Y. Bhatt, A. Joshi, D. Mishra, Eds., vol. 438. Springer: Singapore, 2016. [http://dx.doi.org/10.1007/978-981-10-0767-5_24]

[24] V.V. Vishwarupe, and P.M. Joshi, "Intellert: a novel approach for content-priority based message filtering,", In: *2016 IEEE Bombay Section Symposium (IBSS)*, 2016, pp. 1-6.

[25] V. Vishwarupe, M. Bedekar, and S. Zahoor, "Zone specific weather monitoring system using crowdsourcing and telecom infrastructure,", In: *2015 International Conference on Information Processing.* ICIP, 2015, pp. 823-827.

[26] V. Vishwarupe, "All Things Policy: Synthetic Content Generation Using Artificial Intelligence", 2022/2/10, https://shows.ivmpodcasts.com/show/all-things-poli-y-Rx64RVpQImivrNQ8/episode/synthetic-content-generation-and-chinas-worries-ja9s-I7rfgZE3IhXRg2Fk?startTime=0

[27] V. Vishwarupe, "A zone-specific weather monitoring system", Australian Patent No. AU2021106275 Australian Government, IP Australia, https://patents.google.com/?inventor=Varad+Vishwarupe

[28] I. Goodfellow, J. Pouget-Abadie, M. Mirza, B. Xu, D. Warde-Farley, S. Ozair, and A. Courville, "Y. Bengio Generative adversarial nets", *Adv. Neural Inf. Process. Syst.,* p. 27, 2014.

[29] A. Mittal, K. Dahiya, S. Agrawal, D. Saini, S. Agarwal, and P. Kar, "DECAF: Deep extreme classification with label features", In: *Proceedings of the 14th ACM International Conference on Web Search and Data Mining*, 2021, pp. 49-57.

[30] K Kollnig, A Shuba, R Binns, M Van Kleek, and N Shadbolt, Are IPhones Really Better for Privacy?,

CHAPTER 6

Integrating Internet of Things (IoT), Machine Learning (ML), and the Cloud Infrastructure to Monitor Driving Behavior for Usage-based Insurance in the Indian Context

Pawan S. Wawage[1,*] and **Yogesh D. Deshpande**[1]

[1] *Vishwakarma University, Pune, Maharashtra, India*

Abstract: Although Usage-Based-Insurance has a wide range of applications, it is practically nonexistent in India. We have done research to help design a system that combines IoT, ML, and cloud to help us overcome this problem as a next step. The goal is to create a machine learning model for the cloud that will allow us to calculate driver and customer safety scores based on where and how the car has been driven. We were able to do this by evaluating information from our smartphone's sensors. Utilizing this data and classification system, problems like Usage-Based-Insurance can subsequently be resolved in the real world (UBI). Usage-based insurance has proven to be efficient and appealing to both insurers and the ones insured in a wide range of countries. The use of this method is sparse to nonexistent in India, but it is on the horizon. As a result, there is a lot of potential for our research and suggested works on UBI in India.

Keywords: Cloud, Driver Behavior, IoT, Machine Learning, Pay-as-you-drive, Smartphone, Sensors, Usage Based insurance.

1. INTRODUCTION

Having the appropriate kind of knowledge, but more importantly, data, is critical in today's world. It's not about how much information you can receive, but about what kind of information you can get and why you want to have it. That is why data is so crucial. Because the world is constructed on data, it makes sense to learn how to use the information to improve the world in a variety of ways.

* **Corresponding author Pawan S. Wawage:** Vishwakarma University, Pune, India; E-mail: pawan.wawage-026@vupune.ac.in

Parikshit N. Mahalle, Gitanjali R. Shinde and Prachi M. Joshi (Eds.)

As a result, the goal of our work is to collect driving data [1] and create a categorization system that will provide us with information about the driver's behavior and profile while driving. Utilizing this data and classification system, problems like Usage-Based-Insurance can subsequently be resolved in the real world (UBI).

Usage-based-insurance, also known as the Pay-As-You Drive (PAYD) model, is effective for giving cheaper insurance to consumers who have strong safety scores rather than relying solely on other statistical characteristics such as age and gender (age, gender, marital status *etc.*) [2]. This system will assist us in identifying driver behavior based on characteristics such as aggressive braking, sudden turns, speeding, and cornering, which will aid us in preventing vehicle accidents caused by road rage. The fundamental goal of UBI is to provide a more practical and equitable method for determining risk, with customers who have demonstrated aggressive driving behavior being required to pay a higher premium [3, 4].

Usage-based insurance, sometimes referred to as pay-as-you-drive insurance, is a type of auto insurance that, depending on the specific insurer's programme, can track how far, where, and how a vehicle is driven [5]. We plan to accomplish this by performing analysis on the data obtained from sensors on our Smartphone. The number of cell phones in use around the world continues to rise year after year, resulting in new signal processing applications.

The Smartphone is a ubiquitous gadget that comes pre-loaded with a variety of environmental sensing capabilities. Modern smart phones also have adequate processing power to clean data and run classification models [6]. Usage-based insurance has been shown to be efficient and desirable to both insurers and insured in a wide range of countries. The usage of this approach is sparse to nonexistent in India, but it is on the horizon. As a result, there is a lot of potential for our works' utilization in India.

On top of standard rating procedures, age, gender, marital status, credit and driving records, and insurance ratings, which have all been shown to be predictive over time, are the risk factors and variables that are being examined in the context of UBI. UBI broadens the range of pertinent data, enabling risk to be evaluated in light of actual driving behavior, propensities for safe or dangerous behaviors, trip specifics, vehicle condition, location of operation, weather circumstances, and more [7, 8]. When combined with standard rating criteria, UBI demonstrates a more accurate evaluation of risk, allowing insurers to give the best drivers the biggest discounts while yet maintaining a healthy profit margin.

2. BACKGROUND

The country's insurance regulator, Insurance Regulatory and Development Authority of India (IRDAI), has granted general insurance companies' permission to introduce tech-enabled concepts for the Motor Own Damage (OD) cover in order to provide customers with usage-based insurance covers as add-ons to the basic policies of Motor Own Damage. The regulator claims that the concept of auto insurance is always evolving. It is enabling general insurers to add complex add-ons to Motor Own Damage coverage, like "Pay as You Drive" and "Pay How You Drive," in an effort to facilitate technology-enabled policies. Additionally, the regulator has authorized insurers to design floater policies for two-wheelers and private vehicles owned by the same person.

Planning, labor, technology and equipment, logistics, and support all contribute to the efficient deployment of UBI and analytical tools to record and analyze driving data. However, the financial benefits of usage-based insurance often justify these costs:

- Recruiting low-risk drivers
- Increasing customer retention
- Lowering the cost of claims
- Annual increases in the number of potential touchpoints
- Providing insurance plans with individualized, revenue-generating value-added services in order to better satisfy consumer interests.

Telematics can assist insurance carriers in strengthening their market position through the addition of low-risk drivers to their customer base, the use of driving data to enhance pricing, enhancing the customer's perception of the business as more technologically advanced, and strengthening long-term relationships through improved communication [9]. The likelihood of success when creating a telematics programme can be increased by employing certain tactics such as rigorous planning and testing, the use of value-added services, the management of customer interactions, the pricing model, and efficient data analytics use within the programme. Overall, it is evident that the auto insurance sector is evolving quickly. Usage-based insurance programmes will give early adopters a substantial edge over those who wait and run the risk of losing important clients to more creative competitors.

The survey's findings [10] suggest that aggressive driving practices and episodes of road rage, such as speeding in congested areas, cutting lanes, and abrupt braking by drivers, need to be addressed. Attempts to identify the risk posed by aggressive driving by taking into account a driver's behavioral and emotional components would result in fewer traffic accidents and insurance claims. The findings of this study will assist auto insurance companies in measuring driving risk more precisely and in proposing a method for calculating customized rates based on driving behavior, with an emphasis on risk mitigation [11].

A number of machine learning models are used in the past for driver behavior analysis and usage-based insurance. According to the results of the survey, the random forests algorithm [12, 13] was deemed to be the best of the algorithms in terms of accuracy in prediction and classifying three distinct states as shown in Table **1**.

Table 1. Machine learning models and their accuracy.

Model Name	Accuracy	Purpose
Support Vector Machine [6].	< 70%	Tested on all types of driving events.
Bayesian Network [6].	< 70%	Tested on all types of driving events.
Random Forests [6].	Worst – 88%, Best – 97%	Consistently good results among all types of events; Classify 3 distinct states: normal, drowsy, aggressive & Best and most consistent model;
Multi-Layer Perception [3].	94% - 99% for two cases	Performs exceptionally well for aggressive lane change events & not consistent results among all events.
Simple RNN [3].	Max 70%	Tested on all types of events with accelerometer data.
Long Short-Term Memory (LSTM) [6].	Max 95%	Tested on all types of events with accelerometer data; Good model but only works efficiently with 10 neurons.
Gated Recurrent Unit (GRU) [9].	Max 95%	Tested on all types of events with accelerometer data
Naïve Bayes Classifier [9].	Max 90%	For Aggressive driving styles.
Gaussian Mixture Model [15].	< 80%	Good result on training data but very limited in real world.
Neural Networks [6].	Out-performs all	Very high computational power and load.

3. METHODOLOGY

Because none of the other systems had cloud connectivity, our goal was to interface our system with any of the cloud platforms [14]. After evaluating numerous platforms, we discovered that the Google Cloud Platform was the most efficient with our system. Google App Engine was the most cost-effective way to install the machine learning model on the cloud platform. Visual data analysis was also employed to observe data trends in existing vehicle data sets. On the supplied raw datasets, we applied Time-Series graphs and attempted to make sense of the resulting graphs. We used data from the smartphone's accelerometer and gyroscope sensors to compare the two.

This work seeks to create a system that includes multiple functionalities such as Smartphone sensors (accelerometer, gyroscope, and magnetometer) for data collection, driver behavior profiling (safe or aggressive), calculating safety score and more. For that excursion, assigning a safety score to the driver, using the above data for Usage Based Insurance premium on a monthly or quarterly basis, we used a Smartphone platform for data collection and cleaning. We deployed the model on an Android Smartphone and a cloud platform in order to handle large amounts of data, depending on the algorithm load.

3.1. Data Collection Environment

The goal was to capture sensor data from a smartphone as the driver engaged in specified driving maneuvers in a realistic traffic situation [15]. The next step is to create the experiment and its settings after the model driver (persona) has been chosen. The driver made two journeys each day during the testing, which lasted several days. Each one-way trip was around 4-5 kilometers long and took, on average, 5 to 10 minutes. In this experiment, data from smartphone sensors were recorded using an Android application (accelerometer, gyroscope, *etc.*). While the driver was performing driving-related tasks, the smartphone was mounted horizontally using a phone holder on the dashboard of the vehicle. The complete experimental set-up is shown in Table **2**.

Table 2. Experimental setup.

Number of Drivers	2
Phone model	Samsung Galaxy M20 and ONE Plus 8
Phone fitting	Dashboard phone holder/stand
Phone position	Horizontal
Video recording	Phone rear camera
Vehicle type	LMV
Vehicle model	Wagon-R, LXI
Road type	City
Traffic condition	Mild
Smartphone Sensors	Accelerometer and Gyroscope
Data recorded	Longitude, Latitude, Speed, Distance, Time, Heading.

3.2. Random Forests Algorithm

Machine learning algorithms have traditionally been employed in projects and datasets to forecast a goal value, attribute, or discover patterns. In these kinds of applications, data is used to help machines discover new patterns so they can make precise predictions based on freshly provided input data at various time intervals. Linear regression, decision trees, Support Vector Machines (SVMs), Naive Bayes, Neural Networks, and Ensemble approaches are some of the most widely used machine learning techniques [16]. To enable a training approach using the provided labelled training dataset, the current study uses supervised machine learning. The accuracy and loss of the provided model are used to evaluate the Random forests method.

A supervised machine learning method for addressing classification and regression problems is random forest. To create decision trees from different samples, it employs the average vote for regression and the majority vote for classification. One of the most crucial properties of the Random Forest technique is its capacity to handle datasets with both continuous and categorical variables, as in regression and classification. When it comes to classification issues, it performs better than the opposition.

A decision tree is a type of tree that can be found in a forest. Random forests build decision trees out of randomly chosen data samples, get predictions from each tree, then vote on the best option. With the model, Scikit-learn includes an extra variable that displays the relative importance or contribution of each attribute to the prediction. During the training phase, it calculates the relevance score of each feature automatically.

3.3. Proposed Architecture

The architecture shown in Fig (**1**) is followed in our system. As shown in Fig (**2**), the function is sent into the system *via* the mobile app. The data collection will be handled by the mobile app. In the mobile app, the safety score and driver behavior will be presented. The safety score is calculated on a cloud server using APIs, and the entire model is delivered using the flask application.

User: In order to use the system's services, users must first register in the app. Users have their own unique credentials to log in to further access facilities once they have registered. The user will have access to UBI data as well as all alerts and updates.

App: The sensor data will be collected by the app, which will then be sent to the cloud.

Cloud server: The safety score will be calculated and sent to the app using the cloud server's machine learning model.

Database: The database will be in charge of storing the user's real-time data as well as other UBI-related information.

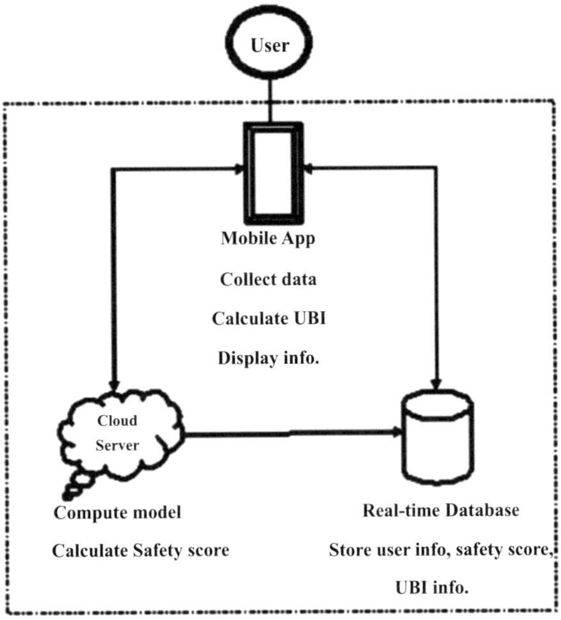

Fig. (1). System architecture.

3.4. Proposed UBI Strategy

Usage-based insurance, sometimes referred to as pay-as-you-drive insurance, is a type of auto insurance that, depending on the specific insurer's programme, can track how far, where, and how a vehicle is driven. The proposed usage-based insurance system determines the amount of insurance premium paid by the insured. The safety score of the drivers will be generated based on the smartphone sensor data collected throughout all of the excursions. The steps to determine the safety score are listed below, and Table **3** displays the real logic:

- Every instance starts with a 10 out of 10 safety score.
- We get a list of 0's (Normal) and 1's (Exceptional) for every 5 min interval of data (Aggressive).
- We calculate the number of 1's in the list as a percentage.
- We deduct a percentage of 1's from the safety score based on the percentage of 1's.

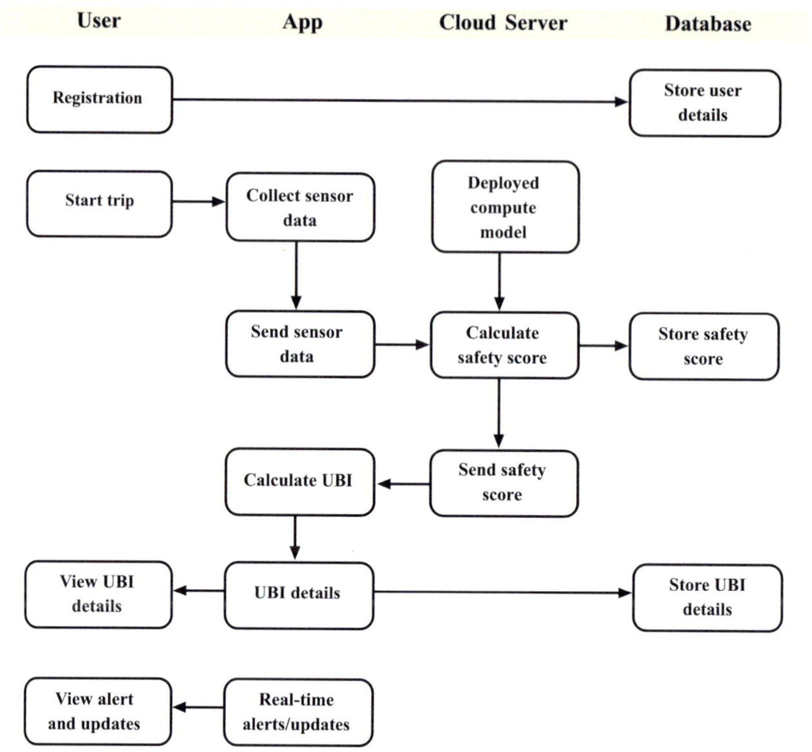

Fig. (2). System flow.

Table 3. Safety score logic.

Aggressive Instances (% of 1's)	Deduction from 10
> 20%	-1
> 25%	-2
> 30%	-3
> 35%	-4
> 40%	-5
> 50%	-6

Data is collected in 5-minute intervals from the start to the completion of the trip. During the first interval, the score was calculated using the prior scoring procedure. The score for the next interval is then calculated, followed by the average (for example, if the second period's score is 7, the overall score becomes 6+7/2 = 6.5). The average of the previous overall score and the current interval score is then calculated. (For example, if the third period's score is 8, the overall score is 6.5+8/2 = 7.25). The same method can be used to calculate the score for each trip. This number can be averaged over all of the trips made in a week or month to get the average safety score for that week or month. We can average the weekly or monthly scores to determine the overall score, depending on whether the insurance payment is paid monthly or annually. The proposed approach in Table **4** can be used to provide a discount on the premium for the consumer based on these scores.

Table 4. Safety score and discount logic.

Safety Score	Discount in Premium
6	5%
7	10%
8	12.5%
9	15%
10	20%

4. RESULTS AND DISCUSSION

The following metrics were used to assess the method: accuracy, F1-score, precision, recall, and support. The sum of the deviations between the predicted value and the actual value, which holds true for both the training and testing sets, constitutes the loss measure. The accuracy statistic is calculated as the proportion of accurate forecasts to all predictions made. Both the training and testing sets used the accuracy metric. The F1-score is computed using data on loss, accuracy, recall, precision, and precision-recall. The rate of true positives in actual and predicted positives is represented by precision and recall measurements, respectively. As a result, the harmonic mean of precision is the F1-score and is indicated in Tables **5** and **6** respectively. We were successfully able to develop a model that could classify a driver's behavior with high accuracy.

Table 5. Result metrics of the tested algorithm on the dataset.

-	Precision	Recall	F1-score	Support
-1	1.00	1.00	1.00	5
0	0.80	0.86	0.83	1826
1	0.85	0.79	0.82	1808
accuracy	-	-	0.83	3639
macro avg.	0.88	0.88	0.88	3639
weighted avg.	0.83	0.83	0.83	3639

Table 6. Result metrics of the tested algorithm on the dataset.

-	Precision	Recall	F1-score	Support
-1	1.00	1.00	1.00	4
0	0.90	0.90	0.90	1692
1	0.91	0.91	0.91	1945
accuracy			0.91	3641
macro avg.	0.94	0.94	0.94	3641
weighted avg.	0.91	0.91	0.91	3639

CONCLUSION

We have successfully implemented a classification model with high accuracy, efficiency, and scalability. We were able to create an end-to-end system that adhered to new technologies and trends by deploying on a cloud server and connecting it with an Android app. To improve the accuracy and efficiency of the classification model, Deep Learning or ensemble methods might be used. Different types of training data, such as data vectorization and increased hyperparameter tweaking, can be used to further investigate the model. New features, such as sleepiness monitoring and real-time notifications, can be added to the app.

REFERENCES

[1] A. Abdelrahman, H.S. Hassanein, and N. Abu-Ali, "A cloud-based environment-aware driver profiling framework using ensemble supervised learning", *IEEE International Conference on Communications (ICC),* pp.1-6, 2019.
[http://dx.doi.org/10.1109/ICC.2019.8761675]

[2] M. Ameksa, H. Mousannif, H. Al Moatassime, and Z. Elassad, "Toward flexible data collection of driving behavior", *International Archives of the Photogrammetry, Remote Sensing and Spatial Information Sciences - ISPRS Archives,* vol. Vol. 4, pp. 33-43, 2020.

[3] Y. Bian, Y. Chen, and J. Zhao, "A study of usage-based vehicle insurance models", *Transportation Research Part A: Policy and Practice,* p. 107, 2018.

[4] L. Eboli, G. Mazzulla, and G. Pungillo, "How to define the accident risk level of car drivers by combining objective and subjective measures of driving style", *Transportation Research Part F: Traffic Psychology and Behaviour,* vol. 49, pp. 29-38, 2017.
[http://dx.doi.org/10.1016/j.trf.2017.06.004]

[5] Eleni Mantouka, Emmanouil Barmpounakis, Eleni Vlahogianni, and John Golias, "Smartphone sensing for understanding driving behavior: current practice and challenges", *International Journal of Transportation Science and Technology,* pp. 266-282, 2021.
[http://dx.doi.org/10.1016/j.ijtst.2020.07.001]

[6] J. Ferreira, E. Carvalho, B.V. Ferreira, C. de Souza, Y. Suhara, A. Pentland, and G. Pessin, "Driver behavior profiling: An investigation with different smartphone sensors and machine learning", *PLoS One,* vol. 12, no. 4, pp. 1-16, 2017.
[http://dx.doi.org/10.1371/journal.pone.0174959] [PMID: 28394925]

[7] I. Skog, P. H'andel, M. Ohlsson, and J. Ohlsson, "Challenges in smartphone-Driven usage based insurance", *IEEE Global Conference on Signal and Information Processing* pp.1135, 2013. [http://dx.doi.org/10.1109/GlobalSIP.2013.6737098]

[8] P. Handel, J. Ohlsson, M. Ohlsson, I. Skog, and E. Nygren, "Smartphone-Based measurement systems for road vehicle traffic monitoring and usage-Based insurance", *IEEE Systems Journal,* vol. 8, no. 4, pp. 1238-1248, 2014. [http://dx.doi.org/10.1109/JSYST.2013.2292721]

[9] K. Stratis, C. Stavros, and Alexander Chroneos, "Smartphones as an integrated platform for monitoring driver behaviour: the role of sensor fusion and connectivity", *Transportation Research Part C: Emerging Technologies,* p. 95, 2018. [http://dx.doi.org/10.1016/j.trc.2018.03.023]

[10] E. Lattanzi, G. Castellucci, and V. Freschi, "Improving machine learning identification of unsafe driver behavior by means of sensor fusion", *Appl. Sci.,* vol. 10, no. 18, p. 6417, 2020. [http://dx.doi.org/10.3390/app10186417]

[11] T. Liu, Y. Guang, and S. Dong, "Construction of driving behavior scoring model based on OBD terminal data analysis", *5th International Conference on Information Science, Computer Technology and Transportation ISCTT,* pp.24-27, 2020. [http://dx.doi.org/10.1109/ISCTT51595.2020.00012]

[12] P. Ping, W. Qin, Y. Xu, C. Miyajima, and K. Takeda, "Impact of driver behavior on fuel consumption: classification, evaluation and prediction using machine learning", *IEEE Access,* vol. 7, pp. 78515-78532, 2019. [http://dx.doi.org/10.1109/ACCESS.2019.2920489]

[13] S. Kadhim Alluhaibi, M.S. Najim Al-Din, and A. Moyaid, "Driver behavior detection techniques: A survey", *Int. J. Appl.Eng. Res.,* vol. 13, no. 11, pp. 8856-8861, 2018.

[14] S. Arumugam, and R. Bhargavi, "A survey on driving behavior analysis in usage based insurance using big data", *J. Big Data,* vol. 6, no. 1, p. 86, 2019. [http://dx.doi.org/10.1186/s40537-019-0249-5]

[15] I. Vasconcelos, R.O. Vasconcelos, B. Olivieri, M. Roriz, M. Endler, and M.C. Junior, "Smartphone-based outlier detection: A complex event processing approach for driving behavior detection", *J. Int. Serv. Appl.,* vol. 8, no. 1, p. 13, 2017. [http://dx.doi.org/10.1186/s13174-017-0065-0]

[16] W. Josh, L. Jeff, and S. Vadi, "Clusters of driving behavior from observational smartphone data", *IEEE Intelligent Transportation Systems Magazine,* vol. 11, no. 3, pp. 171-180, 2019. [http://dx.doi.org/10.1109/MITS.2019.2919516]

CHAPTER 7

Academic Emotion Prediction in Online Learning Utilizing Deep Learning Approach

Snehal Rathi[1,*], Yogesh D. Deshpande[2], Pranali Chavhan[1] and **Priyanka More[1]**

[1] *Department of Computer Engineering, Vishwakarma Institute of Information Technology, Pune, Maharashtra, India*

[2] *Vishwakarma Institute of Information Technology, Pune, Maharashtra, India*

Abstract: As the world is progressing more towards new technology, more and more people are getting close to computers to perform their tasks. Computers have become an integral part of life. In recent years, web-based education has been perceived as a support tool for instructors as it gives the comfort of use at any time, and any place. In this situation, recognizing the user's engagement with the system is important to make human-computer interaction more effective. Recognizing user engagement and emotions can play a crucial role in several applications including advertising, healthcare, autonomous vehicles, and e-learning. We focus on understanding the academic emotions of students during an online learning process. Four academic emotions namely, confusion, boredom, engagement, and frustration are considered here. Based on the academic emotions of students, we can incrementally improve the learning experience. In this paper, we have developed a system for identifying and monitoring the emotions of the scholar in an online learning platform and supplying personalized feedback to reinforce the online learning process.

To achieve this, we have extracted images from the videos of the DAiSEE dataset and performed pre-processing steps like convert it into greyscale, detect a face from that image using OpenCV, change the size of the image, and then save it. Then labeling of the emotions is done and the model is trained using a convolution neural network (CNN) on the said images. In this way, the neural network is trained and can predict the emotion.

Keywords: Academic emotions, Convolution neural network (CNN), DAiSEE dataset, E-learning.

* **Corresponding author Snehal Rathi:** Department of Computer Engineering, Vishwakarma Institute of Information Technology, Pune, Maharashtra, India; E-mail: snehal.rathi@viit.ac.in

Parikshit N. Mahalle, Gitanjali R. Shinde and Prachi M. Joshi (Eds.)

1. INTRODUCTION

With the modern education paradigm shifting towards the online mode from conventional classroom teaching, a good online platform is needed in today's world for both the learner and the teacher. This online platform should take advantage of modern technology and research like machine learning and neural networks. In this modern world, we cannot rely on the sheer ability of the teacher to recognize the ability of students. We can take advantage of this new emerging and convenient technology of machine learning to better help our students to achieve their goals and help our teachers ease their tasks.

In the current scenario, many times students lack interest in the lecture due to distance learning. Hence even an important lecture becomes boring for them and all the efforts made by the faculty become ineffective. So, the need is to have more interactive lectures to recognize students' emotions during learning. Hence there is a necessity for a system that can recognize the state of mind of the student.

The improvement in online learning platforms has been made by researchers in the last few years. By understanding the emotions of students, faculty can change the teaching style or give more/less attention to particular students which might change the performance of the student. The academic emotion detection system is used to figure out the emotions of a student throughout his learning process. Thus giving the teacher feedback on the progress of the student. This system helps the teachers to take corrective action at a certain point for the students who are in states of confusion, boredom, and frustration, instead of waiting till the end of the course. Teachers may give an alarm to the students and ask for reasons for not concentrating on the course. In the same way, this system is really helpful to the students as they get an alarm from the teacher so they start concentrating on their studies to avoid further failure.

It is possible to implement such systems using approaches based on interaction log, the expressions, eye movements, head movements, and various sensors like Galvanic Skin Response (GSR), Electromyography (EMG) sensor, and Electrocardiogram (ECG), *etc.* while the student is watching the online lectures.

Some experiments predict emotions with the use of bio-heart rate sensors [1, 2]. The sensors would record variations in the autonomic nervous system (ANS) of the body. They also used a Support Vector Machine (SVM) algorithm for training data and predicting emotions [1, 3, 4]. But for making use of sensors, data need to be collected in a close environment.

If the video is captured through the student's webcam and the processing is done to know how much the student is concentrating and perceiving the contents, then this information can be viewed by the teacher to track the progress of the students and then he/she can make changes accordingly in either the curriculum or in the teaching method. In this work, we are using DAiSEE (Dataset for Affective States in E-Environments) dataset to train the machine learning model [5]. DAiSEE dataset is available to the community for research. We are focusing on academic emotions engagement, frustration, confusion, and boredom here, which are relevant to students' learning.

2. LITERATURE SURVEY

A literature survey was initiated to understand the role of academic emotions in learning. Many researchers have worked on eye movement [6]. By keeping track of the movement of the eyes, researchers have classified the state of mind. In a paper [6], the researcher measured the concentration level based on eye movement and head position. A person's body gesture is also taken into consideration to get the correct output [7]. Here authors have considered the upper portion of the body. Commercial sensors like Kinect are used to capture the data which helps identify gestures but they are of high cost. Few researchers have built a robust technique called field-programmable gate array (FPGA) with some algorithms for Regression Modeling.

It is estimated that a person's eye gaze performs an important role in understanding emotions [8]. Facial expressions, voice, and bio-potential signals also play an important role in predicting emotions [9]. For capturing data of signals, commercial sensors are required which are costly. For doing such an experiment, a close environment will be required due to the limitation of resources and it is a bit difficult to make use of them. As far as the interaction log is concerned, you need a platform where it is possible to collect data that is required for prediction. But as far as facial expressions are concerned, it is possible to capture video using a webcam while learning and then either extract frames from it or do processing on videos to predict various emotions.

Various tools and techniques are proposed to identify emotions [9, 10]. Gupta, A, and their team [11] developed DAISEE: Dataset for Affective States in E-Learning Environments, the first multi-label dataset having 9068 videos captured from 112 users. It has images of confusion, boredom, engagement, and frustration.

Researchers Brigham TJ and team [12] used a mix of various information sources – facial expressions, voice recognition, and gestures to predict the emotions of an individual. Authors [13] have recognized emotions using commercial sensors.

Kiavash Bahreinia along with his associates has experimented [5], which used the FILTWAM framework for predicting the feelings of learners. Data is captured through a FILTWAM framework by using a microphone and webcam. Then it is analyzed to predict the learner's feelings. This framework consists of the following layers.

1- Learner: It corresponds to the student, learning through video lectures.

2- Device: It consists of a user interface through which contents are presented.

3- Network: It consists of resources needed for live streaming and communicating the generated feedback to the learner.

4- Application: This is the most important layer. It is used to store, train and analyze the data. It is also used for generating feedback based on state.

5- Data: It consists of data needed for analysis.

Here authors predicted emotions in real-time with the help of a webcam and according to the predicted state, feedback is generated. To verify the accuracy of the developed module, the authors asked participants about the correctness of generated feedback and participants agreed with it [5].

As given in Fig. (**1**), Kort has built up a learning spiral model. It shows the interaction between effect and learning. It has four quadrants. The horizontal axis is the influence axis and the opposite is the learning pivot. As per Kort, the understudies begins with the first quadrant, and during learning, it might move towards the second and the third quadrant where their emotional condition is negative like disarray, disappointment, and so forth, and the state of learning is Un-learning. If the understudied students receive the right support at this moment, they might move towards the first quadrant through the fourth where their state may become cheerfulness [14]. It shows how significant the feelings are during learning. For distinguishing such feelings different modalities like log examination, looks (facial expressions), and sensors are utilized.

Facial expression recognition has a very important role in human-computer interfaces and many researchers have worked on it [15 - 17]. Facial analysis in videos and images has been a difficult task for machine learning models [18].

E-learning has developed very fast in the past few years and has become a development of education [19, 20]. For students' levels of assessment, an online learning system should be designed with the evaluation function [21] and the handiest method in distance education is online testing [21, 22]. Evaluating the learners based on only knowledge domain may not be appropriate. Therefore, online-learning courses should give equal importance to the affective domain along with the knowledge domain. Like face-to-face learning, it is difficult in E-Learning to recognize body language, facial expressions [22], and gestures of the learner. So it has been depicted as less emotional and more impersonal [23].

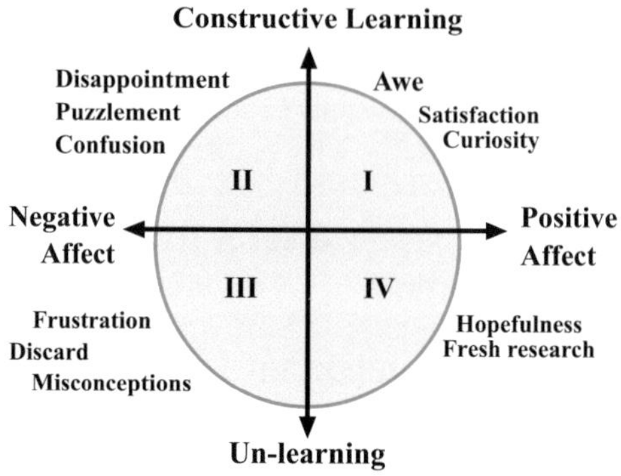

Fig. (1). Kort's Learning Spiral Model [14].

From this study, we have perceived the significance of affect prediction in E-learning and that is the reason there is a need to foster a framework that distinguishes affective state and gives criticism to the understudies to make a restorative move.

3. METHODOLOGY

The details of the proposed methodology consist of various steps. They are:

- Extracting the image from videos
- Adding Emotion Column in the Dataset
- Training the Convolution Neural Network

Images are extracted from the videos using the following steps:

- Convert the image to a grayscale
- Detect face in the image using OpenCV HAAR cascade
- Crop the image and set it to the size of 200 * 200
- Finally, save the image

3.1. Converting Image to Gray Scale

In the process of grayscale, the image from other color space *e.g.* RGB is converted to shades of Grey. The reason for doing this is dimension reduction. For example, in RGB, there are three channels and three dimensions. The grayscale has a single dimension. It also reduces model complexity because the RGB image will have thrice the input node compared to that of a grayscale image. Also, many algorithms are customized to work only on gray-scale images. Here we are using OpenCv which works with gray-scale images.

3.2. Detecting the Face in the Image Using OpenCV HAAR Cascade

In this approach, based on machine learning, a cascade function is trained from a lot of positive and negative samples. Based on the training, it is used to identify the object in other images. A lot of positive and negative sample images are given to the algorithm and then features are extracted from it. For this purpose, HAAR features like edge feature, line feature, and four-rectangle features are used. The image is divided into many windows and these features are applied to all these windows to see if it is a face region or not. This way we can easily detect a face in the image. As shown in Fig. (**2**), the face is detected from the original image.

Fig. (2). Detection of the face from an original input image. (The person in the photo has lent their image to the research).

3.3. Crop the Image of the Face and Resize it to 200 * 200

Once a face is detected in an image, a rectangle is drawn around the face. This is done by using the cv2.rectangle() function. The cv2.rectangle function has different parameters such as image start point, endpoint, color, and thickness. These parameters are passed accordingly and a rectangle is drawn around the face. Then we need to scale the image. For this purpose, we use the cv2.resize () function. This function uses three parameters. First is the path of an image then the width and the height. Here we are re-sizing the face image in 200 * 200 sizes.

3.4. Save the Image

We need to save this image to the desired location. For this, we use the cv2.imwrite function. This function takes two parameters. The first one is the filename and the second is the image that is to be saved. It returns true if the image is saved successfully.

The preprocessed images were given as input to the convolution neural network which predicts the emotions by avoiding all background constraints and color parameters and will help us lead the more accurate academic emotion output.

3.5. Adding Emotion Column in the Dataset

DAISEE is a multi-labeled dataset based on 4 academic emotion parameters *i.e.* Boredom, Engagement, Confusion, and Frustration. In this step, we added a new column named emotion to the dataset which contains an array of emotions that the image possesses. The sample multi-labeled dataset is shown in Table **1** and the sample multi-labeled dataset with an array of emotions is shown in Table **2**.

Table 1. Sample multi-labeled dataset.

-	Clip ID	Emotion			
-	-	**Boredom**	**Engagement**	**Confusion**	**Frustration**
1	1100011002.jpg	0	2	0	0
2	1100011003.jpg	0	2	0	0
3	1100011004.jpg	0	3	0	0
4	1100011005.jpg	0	3	0	0
5	1100011006.jpg	0	3	0	0
6	1100011007.jpg	1	2	0	0
7	1100011008.jpg	0	3	0	0
8	1100011009.jpg	0	2	1	0
9	1100011010.jpg	0	3	0	0
10	1100011011.jpg	0	3	0	0
11	1100011012.jpg	0	2	2	0
12	1100011013.jpg	0	3	0	0
13	1100011014.jpg	0	3	0	0
14	1100011015.jpg	0	3	0	0
15	1100011016.jpg	0	3	0	0

Table 2. Sample multi-labeled dataset with an array of emotion.

Sr. No.	Clip ID	Emotion
1	1100011003.jpg	['Engagement']
2	1100011004.jpg	['Engagement']
3	1100011005.jpg	['Engagement']
4	1100011006.jpg	['Engagement']
5	1100011007.jpg	['Boredom', 'Engagement']
6	1100011008.jpg	['Engagement']
7	1100011009.jpg	['Engagement', 'Confusion']
8	1100011010.jpg	['Engagement']
9	1100011011.jpg	['Engagement']
10	1100011012.jpg	['Engagement', 'Confusion']
11	1100011013.jpg	['Engagement']
12	1100011014.jpg	['Engagement']
13	1100011015.jpg	['Engagement']
14	1100011016.jpg	['Engagement']
15	1100011017.jpg	['Engagement']

3.6. Training the Convolution Neural Network

Convolution Neural Network (CNN) is a feed-forward neural network. CNN is a highly productive recognition algorithm that is widely used for recognizing patterns in image processing. It possesses various features like a simple structure, fewer training parameters, and adaptability. It has been a trending subject in speech analysis and image recognition.

To train the CNN, we are using the DAiSEE dataset which has videos. We have extracted images from it. Loading the whole data set into the memory makes the training speed of the model very slow which is very inefficient. So, we have made batches of the dataset and then trained the model.

We have created a Sequential CNN Model made up of the following layers:

Sequential Model:

The sequential model is suitable for layers in which every layer has just one input as well as one output. We cannot use this model for multiple inputs or outputs.

Conv 2D:

In this layer, we can generate a tensor of outputs from the convolution kernel. First Conv2D with a 3×3 convolution window is used to study our 16 filters. We are using ReLu (Rectified linear activation function) activation function which gives us the output based on the provided input.

Batch Normalization:

This function facilitates each layer in the network to identify by itself some more information independently. The output of previous activation layers is normalized in the batch normalization layer to extend the steadiness of the neural network. This is done by subtracting the batch mean and dividing it by the batch standard deviation. It transforms the mean output near 0 and therefore the output standard deviation near 1.

Max Pool 2D:

This layer is used to sample the input data. It is done by taking the highest value of the window defined by 2×2 pool size for every dimension around the feature axis.

Dropout:

This layer is used to prevent our model from overfitting. It is employed for setting outgoing edges of masked units to zero randomly while the training phase is going on at each update. The probability on which outputs are dropped out is given as output in this layer.

Flatten:

In this layer, a multi-dimensional array of data is converted into a single-dimensional array which will act as an input to the subsequent layer.

Dense:

The dense layer is a deeply connected neural network layer. For predicting the probability of 4 classes (Boredom, Engagement, Confusion & Frustration), we require a dense layer having 4 neurons. For predicting the binary output, the sigmoid function is used. The sigmoid function gives 0 or 1 as an output for all 4 classes hence resulting in which emotions are seen in the scholar.

Fig. (**3**) gives a summary of the model which will be trained.

BEProject.ipynb

File Edit View Insert Runtime Tools Help Last edited on 6 December

+ Code + Text

```
model. add (Dense(4, activation- 'sigmoid'))

model . summary ( )

Model: "sequential"
```

Layer (type)	Output Shape	Param #
conv2d (Conv2D)	(None, 198, 198, 16)	448
batch_normalization (BatchNo	(None, 198, 198, 16)	64
max_pooling2d (MaxPooling2D)	(None, 99, 99, 16)	0
dropout (Dropout)	(None, 99, 99, 16)	0
conv2d 1_(Conv2D)	(None, 97, 97, 32)	4640
batch_normalization_1 (Batch	(None, 97, 97, 32)	128
max_pooling2d_1 (MaxPooling2	(None, 48, 48, 32)	0
dropout_1 (Dropout)	(None, 48, 48, 32)	0
conv2d_2 (Conv2D)	(None, 46, 46, 64)	18496
batch_normalization_2 (Batch	(None, 46, 46, 64)	256
max_pooling2d_2 (MaxPooling2	(None, 23, 23, 64)	0
dropout_2 (Dropout)	(None, 23, 23, 64)	0
conv2d_3 (Conv2D)	(None, 21, 21, 128)	73856
batch_normalization 3 (Batch	(None, 21, 21, 128)	512
max_pooling2d_3 (MaxPooling2	(None, 10, 10, 128)	0
dropout_3 (Dropout)	(None, 10, 10, 128)	0
flatten (Flatten)	(None, 12800)	0
dense (Dense)	(None, 128)	1638528
batch_normalization_4 (Batch	(None, 128)	512
dropout_4 (Dropout)	(None, 128)	0
dense_1 (Dense)	(None, 128)	16512
batch_normalization_5 (Batch	(None, 128)	512
dropout_5(Dropout)	(None, 128)	0
dense_2 (Dense)	(None, 4)	516

Total params: 1,754,980
Trainable params: 1,753,988
Non-trainable params: 992

Fig. (3). Summary of trained model.

4. RESULT AND DISCUSSION

85% of the total images were trained with 25 epochs (for the 25 times data was iterated) and 15% remaining images were used for testing purposes.

The final accuracy of 78.62% was achieved after the testing. Model accuracy and model loss graphs are as follows in Fig. (**4**). Fig. (**4**) represents the accuracy of CNN for training and validation for 25 epochs respectively.

Fig. (**5**) represents binary cross entropy loss of CNN for training and validation for 25 epochs respectively.

The model is saved and it can be used to predict academic emotions by capturing the images of the learner from a webcam.

model. predict () will give us the probabilities for all 4 classes. We will sort the probabilities using np. argsort () and then select the classes having the top 2 probabilities.

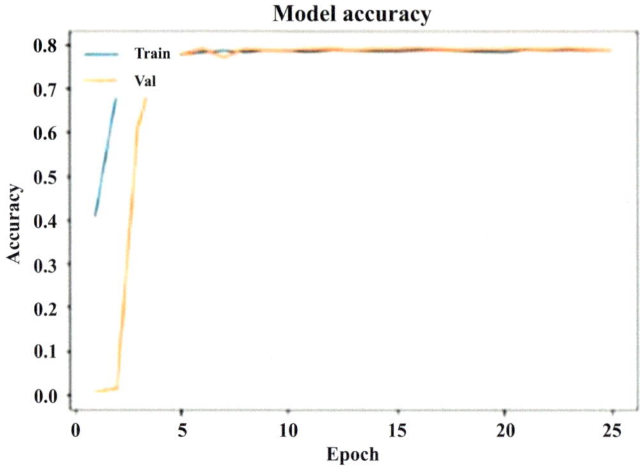

Fig. (4). Model accuracy.

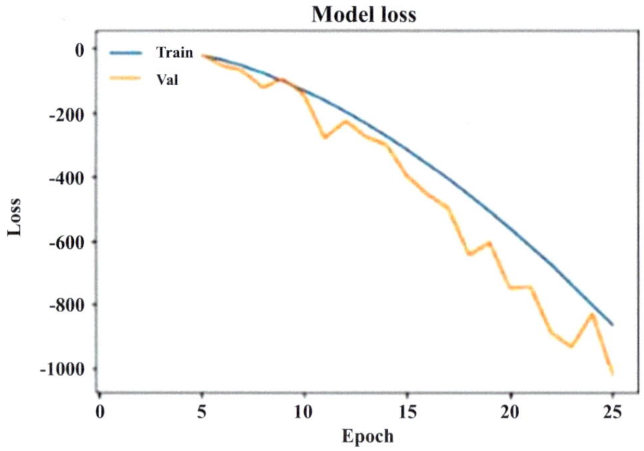

Fig. (5). Model loss.

For example, If we get output INDEX ([‘Boredom’, ‘Engagement’, ‘Confusion’, ‘Frustration’], dtype = ‘object’) for a certain image.

In such case, our system states that the image has high boredom and slight engagement from the order of the top two emotions detected from the trained model.

As shown in Fig. (**6**) system detects engagement for the Very High, High, and Low engagement levels. In this way, four different emotions Engagement, Boredom, Confusion, and Frustration are detected on the scale of Very High, High, and Low.

Very High Engagement **High Engagement** **Low Engagement**

Fig. (6). Engagement prediction. (The person in the photo has lent their image to the research).

CONCLUSION AND FUTURE WORK

We have developed a system to predict the emotions of the learners during learning. We utilize images/video captured in a webcam present on the laptop or computer of the learner during the learning process. This system utilizes the pictures captured by the camera and classifies them as per priority into four classes Boredom, Confusion, Frustration, and Engagement of emotions. This technique uses a multi-labeled dataset as input and also gives multiple emotions with severity as an output for specific images. The system proposed here was designed to give real-time emotion detection of a student. This may help to enhance the interface and make the training better for school and college students. By looking at students' emotions, it could help the teachers to vary the teaching style so that students can understand well. In the future, this technique can be often utilized to recommend topics consistent with the mood of students at run time. It is also possible to predict these emotions using other modalities like log files [24], questionnaires, and different sensors and use multimodal fusion instead of developing a unimodal technique.

REFERENCES

[1] H. Guo, Y. Huang, C. Lin, J. Chien, K. Haraikawa, and J. Shieh, "Heart rate variability signal features for emotion recognition by using principal component analysis and support vectors machine", *IEEE 16th International Conference on Bioinformatics and Bioengineering (BIBE),* pp. 77-274, 2016. [http://dx.doi.org/10.1109/BIBE.2016.40]

[2] H. Abdi, and L.J. Williams, "Principal component analysis", *Wiley Interdiscip. Rev. Comput. Stat.,* vol. 2, no. 4, pp. 433-459, 2010. [http://dx.doi.org/10.1002/wics.101]

[3] G. Rigas, C.D. Katsis, G. Ganiatsas, and D.I. Fotiadis, A User Independent, Biosignal Based, Emotion Recognition Method.*User Modeling,* C. Conati, K. McCoy, G. Paliouras, Eds., vol. 4511. Springer: Berlin, Heidelberg, 2007.

[http://dx.doi.org/10.1007/978-3-540-73078-1_36]

[4] C. Wang, and F. Wang, "An emotional analysis method based on heart rate variability", *Proceedings of 2012 IEEE-EMBS International Conference on Biomedical and Health Informatics,* pp. 04-107, 2012.
[http://dx.doi.org/10.1109/BHI.2012.6211518]

[5] Bahreini Kiavash, Nadolski Rob, and Westera Wim, "Towards multimodal emotion recognition in e-learning environments", In: *Interactive Learning Environments*, 2014.
[http://dx.doi.org/10.1080/10494820.2014.908927]

[6] L. Krithika, G.G. Lakshmi, L.B Krithika, and GG Lakshmi Priya, "Student Emotion Recognition System (SERS) for e-learning improvement based on learner concentration metric", *Procedia Comput. Sci.,* vol. 85, pp. 767-776, 2016.
[http://dx.doi.org/10.1016/j.procs.2016.05.264]

[7] T. Hachad, A. Sadiq, F. Ghanimi, and L. Hachad, "A Novel Architecture for Student's attention detection in classroom based on Facial and Body expressions", *International Journal of Advanced Trends in Computer Science and Engineering,* vol. 9, no. 5, pp. 7357-7366, 2020.
[http://dx.doi.org/10.30534/ijatcse/2020/68952020]

[8] J. Bidwell, and H. Fuchs, "Classroom digital twins with instrumentation-free gaze tracking", *In CHI Conference on Human Factors in Computing Systems (CHI '21),.* May 8–13, 2021, Yokohama, Japan. ACM, New York, NY, USA pp.9.
[http://dx.doi.org/10.13140/RG.2.1.4865.6242]

[9] A. Konar, *Aruna Chakraborty: Emotion Recognition: A Pattern Analysis Approach.* WILEY, 2015.

[10] C-H. Wu, Y-M. Huang, and J-P. Hwang, "Review of affective computing in education/learning: Trends and challenges", In: *British Journal of Educational Technology*, 2015.
[http://dx.doi.org/10.1111/bjet.12324]

[11] "DAISEE: Dataset for affective states in e-learning environments", *arXiv.,* pp. 1-22, 2016.

[12] T.J. Brigham, "Merging technology and emotions: Introduction to affective computing", *Med. Ref. Serv. Q.,* vol. 36, no. 4, pp. 399-407, 2017.
[http://dx.doi.org/10.1080/02763869.2017.1369289] [PMID: 29043945]

[13] R. Subramanian, J. Wache, M.K. Abadi, R.L. Vieriu, S. Winkler, and N. Sebe, "ASCERTAIN: Emotion and personality recognition using commercial sensors", *IEEE Trans. Affect. Comput.,* vol. 9, no. 2, pp. 147-160, 2018.
[http://dx.doi.org/10.1109/TAFFC.2016.2625250]

[14] B. Kort, R. Reilly, and R. Picard, "An affective model of the interplay between emotions and learning", *IEEE International Conference on Advanced Learning Technologies,* pp. 3-46, 2001.
[http://dx.doi.org/10.1109/ICALT.2001.943850]

[15] Saeed Turabzadeh, Hongying Meng, Rafiq M. Swash, Matus Pleva, and Jozef Juhar, "Facial expression emotion detection for real-time embedded systems", *Technologies,* vol. 6, p. 17, 2018.
[http://dx.doi.org/10.3390/technologies6010017]

[16] D.V. Sang, N. Van Dat, and D.P. Thuan, "Facial expression recognition using deep convolutional neural networks", *9th International Conference on Knowledge and Systems Engineering (KSE),* pp. 30-135, 2017.
[http://dx.doi.org/10.1109/KSE.2017.8119447]

[17] M. Mohammadpour, H. Khaliliardali, and S. Mohammad, "AlyanNezhadi: Facial Emotion Recognition Using Deep Convolutional Networks", *In: IEEE 4th International Conference on Knowledge-Based Engineering and Innovation (KBEI),.* pp. 0017-0021, 2017.
[http://dx.doi.org/10.1109/KBEI.2017.8324974.2017]

[18] N. Ronghe, S. Nakashe, A. Pawar, and S. Bobde, "Emotion recognition and reaction prediction in videos", *3rd International Conference on Research in Computational Intelligence and Communication*

Networks (ICRCICN), pp. 6-32, 2017.
[http://dx.doi.org/10.1109/ICRCICN.2017.8234476]

[19] A. Samadi, E.F. Hanaa, M. Qbadou, M. Youssfi, and F. Akef, "A syntactic and semantic multi-agent based question answering system for collaborative E-learning", *4th International Conference on Optimization and Applications (ICOA),,* 2018
[http://dx.doi.org/10.1109/ICOA.2018.8370588]

[20] R. Picard, *Affective Computing.* The MIT Press, 2000.
[http://dx.doi.org/10.7551/mitpress/1140.001.0001]

[21] S.K. D'Mello, S.D. Craig, A. Witherspoon, B. McDaniel, and A. Graesser, "Automatic detection of learner's affect from conversational cues", *User Model. User-adapt. Interact.,* vol. 18, no. 1-2, pp. 45-80, 2008.
[http://dx.doi.org/10.1007/s11257-007-9037-6]

[22] S.R. Rathi, and Y.D. Deshpande, "Embedding affect awareness into online learning environment using deep neural network", *2019 5th International Conference On Computing, Communication, Control And Automation (ICCUBEA),* Pune, India, pp.1-6, 2019.
[http://dx.doi.org/10.1109/ICCUBEA47591.2019.9128811]

[23] M. Cocea, and S. Weibelzahl, "Eliciting motivation knowledge from log files towards motivation diagnosis for adaptive systems", *UM '07: Proceedings of the 11th international conference on User Modeling,* pp. 97-206, 2007.
[http://dx.doi.org/10.1007/978-3-540-73078-1_23]

[24] S.R. Rathi, and Y.D. Deshpande, "Course complexity in engineering education using E-learner's affective-state prediction", *Kybernetes,* 2022.
[http://dx.doi.org/10.1108/K-09-2021-0806]

CHAPTER 8

Implementation of Fruit Quality Management and Grading System using Image Processing and ARM7 Platform

Yuvraj V. Parkale[1,*]

[1] *Department of Electronics and Telecommunication Engineering, SVPM's College of Engineering, Malegaon (BK), Baramati, Maharashtra, India*

Abstract: Throughout the history of the industry, producers and retailers have focused on fruit quality as a major concern. Over the past ten years, the market for high-quality fruit has expanded quickly, raising the price of the upscale item. However, the state-of-the-art methods have some major drawbacks such as the mechanical systems are bulky, require more manpower to operate the system, are less accurate, slow, expensive and with more chances of human mistakes. In this paper, we have addressed these drawbacks and proposed systems for the management of the fruit quality and grading of fruits in different categories. These fruits can be sorted automatically depending upon their different characteristics such as color, size, shape, weight, specific gravity, sugar contents, and ph. In this paper, we have selected three characteristics of fruit namely color, size, and weight for measuring the quality of fruit and grading them accordingly. The result shows that the proposed system has successfully implemented fruit quality management and grading. The system is automatic and results in lightweight, simple and inexpensive hardware, increased speed of operation and reduces manpower, and mistakes.

Keywords: ARM7, Fruit quality, Image processing.

1. INTRODUCTION

The field of electronics has made a tremendous revolution in almost all the fields in today's life such as communication, entertainment navigation, industrial environment, *etc.* The agriculture field is also not an exception to it. Since India is a horticultural country, the economy of India relies upon farming, and thus, there is a large scope of developments in the agriculture field.

* **Corresponding author Yuvraj V. Parkale:** Department of Electronics and Telecommunication Engineering, SVPM's College of Engineering, Malegaon (BK), Baramati, Maharashtra, India; E-mail: yuvrajparkale@gmail.com

Parikshit N. Mahalle, Gitanjali R. Shinde and Prachi M. Joshi (Eds.)

Throughout the history of the industry, producers and retailers have focused on fruit quality as a major concern. Over the past ten years, the market for high-quality fruit has expanded quickly, raising the price of the upscale item. In the event that the nature of the organic product is chosen physically, it has different hindrances, for example, the undesired method for taking care of the organic products, weariness, and absence of sight; quality criteria can differ from person to person. Thus, the sorting of good quality fruits becomes difficult.

2. LITERATURE REVIEW

Iqbal *et al.* [1], proposed an algorithm to categorize particular citrus fruits, for example, orange, lemon, and sweet-lime. The researchers, Nandi *et al.* [2], proposed a reviewing framework for mango natural products. Researchers Dubey and Jalal [3], proposed a texture feature for color images and validated it for fruit and vegetable sorting. The researcher Habib *et al.* [4], proposed recognition of papaya disease based on machine vision. The researchers Bhargava and Bansal [5] introduced a writing survey on PC vision-based quality assessment of fruits and vegetables. The researcher Dang *et al.* [6], proposed an image processing based fruit size detection and grading system. The researcher Njoroge *et al.* [7], proposed a picture handling based programmed natural product evaluation framework. Another researcher [8] proposed a computerized natural product reviewing framework in view of a picture acknowledgment procedure. Some of the major drawbacks of these state-of-the-art systems are as follows [8]:

- These mechanical components are substantial.
- Requires manpower to function machine.
- Less accuracy.
- Deteriorated area.
- No operation is entirely automatic.
- More probabilities of human error.
- Even when controlling is semi-automatic, accuracy suffers because it is done manually.
- Non-automatic systems are very high-priced.

Hence, we have proposed a system that overcomes all these drawbacks. The proposed system measures the quality of the fruits and sorts them into different categories automatically. The fruits can be sorted depending upon their different characteristics such as color, size, shape, weight, specific gravity, sugar contents, and ph.. In this paper, we have selected three characteristics of fruit namely color, size, and weight for measuring the quality of fruit and grading them accordingly.

The fruit quality management and grading of different circular fruits such as apple, tomato and orange, *etc*. can be achieved using the proposed system. These fruits can be graded in various classifications utilizing different reviewing standards of natural products, like products of a particular tone, products of a particular size, and products of explicit weight. In this paper, we have proposed the Tomato quality management and grading system. Fig. (**1**) shows the grading process of Tomato. Whereas, Table **1** shows different grading categories of fruits [8].

Table 1. Shows grading categories of fruit *e.g*. Tomato.

Grading Category of fruit *e.g*. Tomato		
Grade	Color and weight specification of fruit	Fruit Diameter
A	Tomatoes with Red color of more weight	Diameter 4cm
B	Tomatoes with Red color of less weight	Diameter 3cm
C	Tomatoes with Green color of more weight	Diameter 4cm
D	Tomatoes with Green color of less weight	Diameter 3cm

The proposed system has the following advantages:

- Fully automatic and smooth operation possible.
- The database of each fruit is created for quality analysis.
- Comparatively less expensive.
- The quality of fruit is decided without physical contact with fruit.
- Any damage to fruit is completely avoided.
- The scale of quality parameters can be changed.
- Completely user-friendly operation.
- Fruits are divided into three categories according to quality.

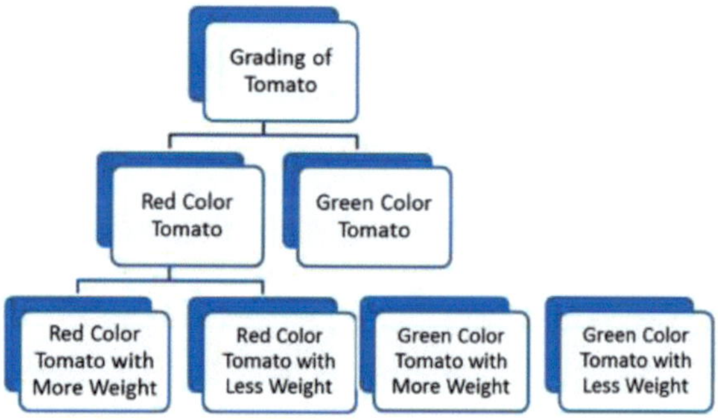

Fig. (1). Indicates the grading process of Tomato.

The paper is coordinated as follows: Section II discusses the proposed framework. Section III discusses the result and Section IV presents the conclusions.

3. PROPOSED SYSTEM

Fig. (**2**) shows the block chart of fruit quality grading and management system. It consists of the following blocks:

A. ARM PROCESSOR
B. IR Sensor
C. Web Camera
D. DC Motor
E. LCD Display
F. Load cell
G. Signal conditioning
H. Personal computer

The description of each block is given below.

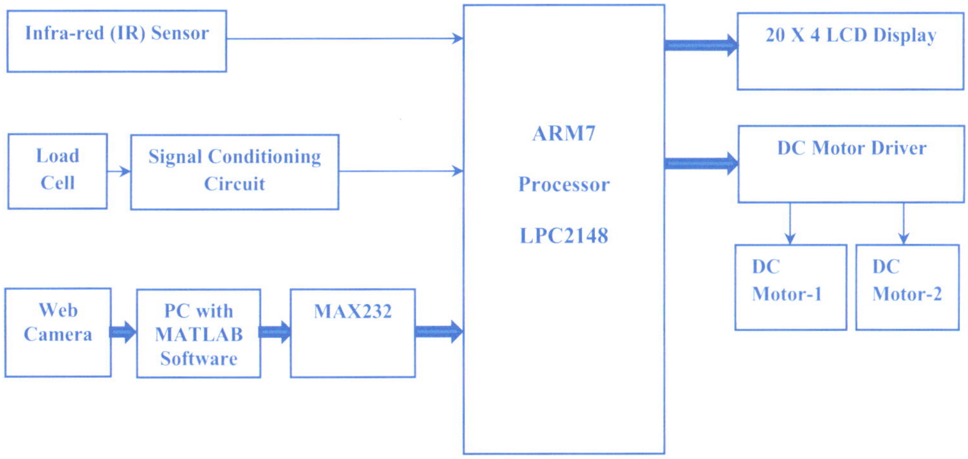

Fig. (2). Block diagram of fruit quality management and grading system.

3.1. ARM7 Processer LPC2148

ARM7 processer is the heart of the system and it performs all the controlling actions related to system projects. ARM7TDMI performs following controlling actions for this system [9].

i. DC Motor Controlling: ON And OFF control.
ii. Serial communication: To receive the MATLAB results.
iii. To display various stages and results of the system on LCD.

3.2. IR Sensor

The Infrared sensor which is mounted on the conveyor assembly board will sense the presence of fruit. As soon as the fruit comes in front of the IR sensor, the ARM processor will stop the conveyor.

3.3. Web Camera

The web camera is used to capture an image of the fruit. It is positioned at the middle of conveyor assembly and mounted at the top of U clamp, on the upper side of a conveyor.

3.4. DC Motor

Two DC motors are used. The first DC motor is used to drive conveyor belt (12v, 30rpm) and the second DC motor is used to rotate the robotic arm used for grading (clockwise and anticlockwise) (12v, 10rpm).

3.5. LCD Display

The 20x4 text LCD is used to display different activities of the project.

3.6. Load Cell

It is utilized to measures the heaviness of the organic product.

3.7. Signal Conditioning

The signal conditioner will amplify the low power signal from load cell and fed to the ARM7 processor.

3.8. Personal Computer

The web camera will capture the image of fruits and fed them to the PC for further processing. The PC equipped with MATLAB software will process the input images. The result of the MATLAB processing is sent to the ARM7 processor through the RS232 cable.

4. SYSTEM HARDWARE AND SOFTWARE SPECIFICATIONS

This segment presents the hardware and software details of the proposed system. The proposed system used ARM7TDMI as a Processor, a 16 MP Web Camera, an IR Sensor (Input 5V, Output 4.7V and range 12 cm), a DC Motor (12V, 10/30 rpm), a Load Cell (Single Point Load Cell-5 to 60kg) and 20 x 4 text LCD Display.

The Keil µVision3 software is used for programming of ARM7 and MATLAB 7.0 is used for image processing.

5. SYSTEM FLOW CHART AND WORKING OF SYSTEM

This section presents the system flowchart and the working of proposed framework.

5.1. System Flow Chart

Fig. (**3**) presents the system flowchart of the proposed framework.

5.2. Working of System

This section explains the working of the proposed system. At the point when the framework is turned on, the transport line begins moving. The organic product which is kept on the transport line will be conveyed alongside it. The Infrared sensor which is mounted on the transport gathering board will detect the presence of a natural product. When the natural product comes before the IR sensor, the ARM processor will stop the transport. Then, at that point, the picture of organic product will be caught by a web camera, which is additionally shipped off a PC for picture handling. The MATLAB programming will handle the picture of organic product for the boundaries like tone, size (edge discovery), and so on. The consequence of picture handling [10] is shipped off the ARM processor with the assistance of a serial port (Universal Asynchronous Receiver Transmitter (UART)). When ARM gets the sign (for example result) from MATLAB; it will begin the transport. At last, the organic product arrives at the heap cell get together for the estimation of weight. Subsequently, contingent on the above boundaries for example variety and weight; the nature of the organic product will be chosen and evaluation is completed.

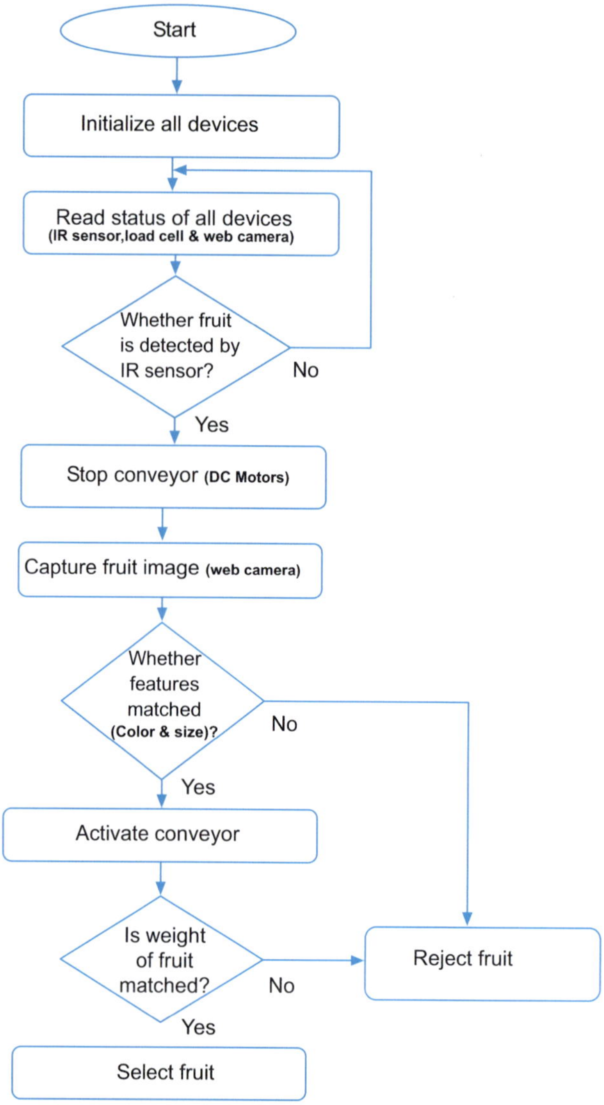

Fig. (3). System flowchart of the proposed framework.

6. RESULTS AND DISCUSSION

This part presents and examines the consequences of the proposed framework. Fig. (**4**) shows captured input image-I of Tomato and Fig. (**5**) shows its corresponding edge detected image-I. Fig. (**6**) shows captured input image-II of Tomato and Fig. (**7**) shows its corresponding edge detected image-II.

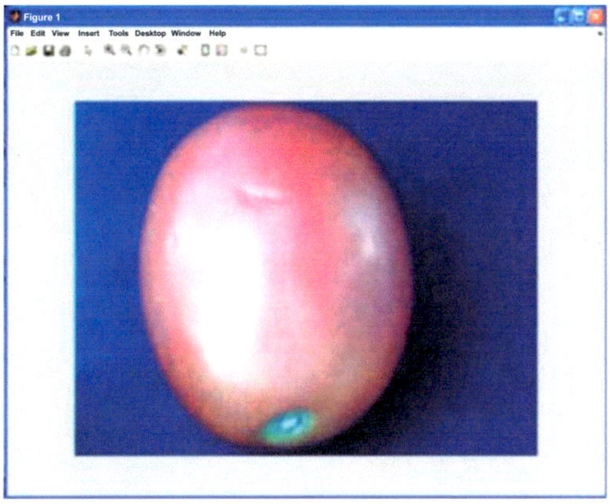

Fig. (4). Captured input tomato image-I.

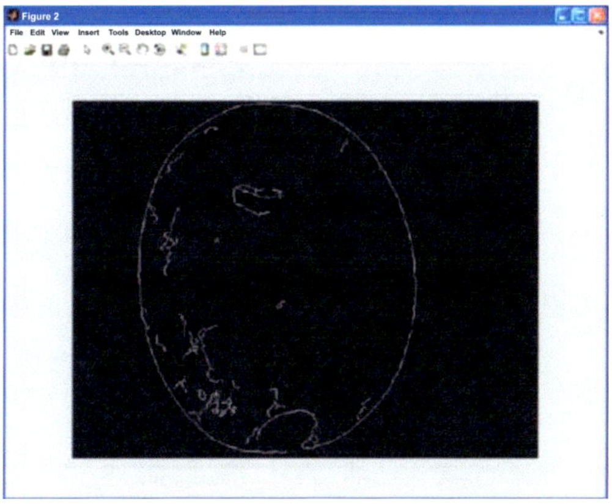

Fig. (5). Edge detected image of the captured input tomato image-I.

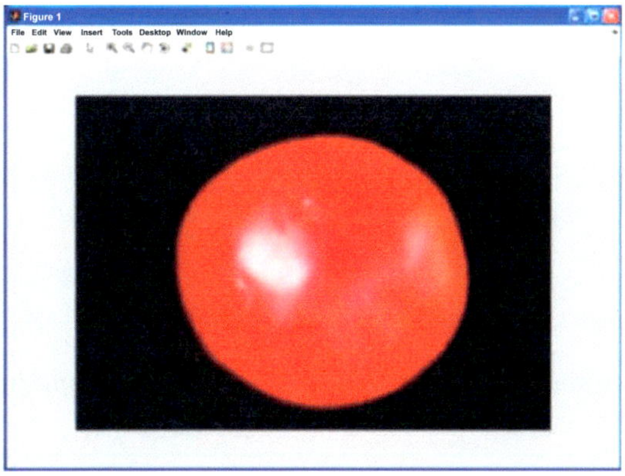

Fig. (6). Captured input tomato image-I.

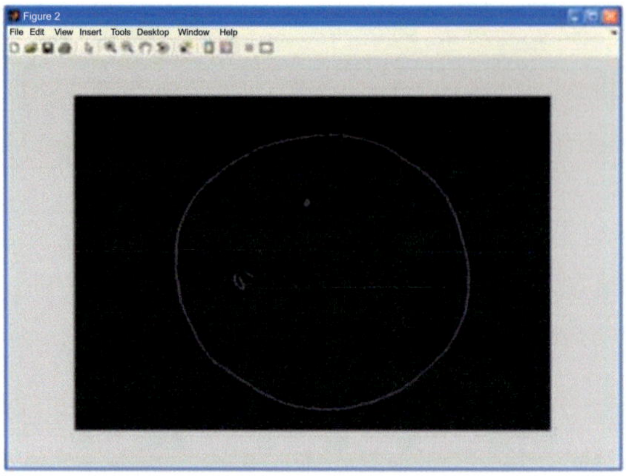

Fig. (7). Edge detected image of the captured input tomato image-I.

Fig. (**8**) shows the color and size coding combination of the captured fruit image. Further, to demonstrate the different combinations of color and size of the fruit, following coding combinations/assumptions are taken into consideration.

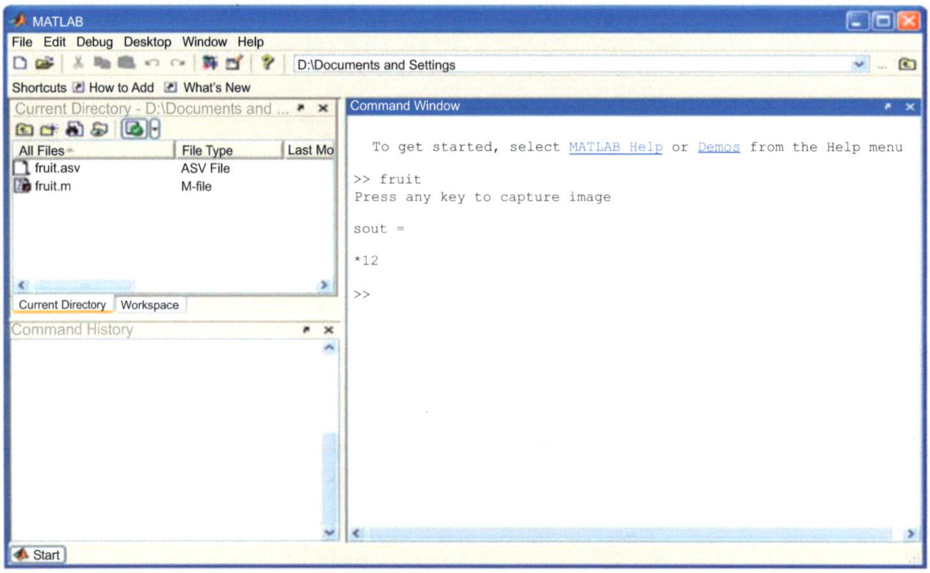

Fig. (8). Shows the color and size coding combination of the captured fruit image.

a. Color coding of Fruit
   - Red Color Fruit = 1
   - Green Color Fruit = 2

b. Size coding of Fruit
   - Size of the fruit bigger than the standard fruit size = 1
   - Size of the fruit smaller than the standard fruit size = 2

The different combinations of color and size coding of the fruit is shown in Table **2**.

Table 2. Different combinations of color and size coding of fruit.

Parameters	Color	Size
1.	1	1
2.	1	2
3.	2	1
4.	2	2

The result in Fig. (**8**) shows that the fruit is red but it is small in size. Similarly, the other results are taken and the data is sent to the ARM processor through the serial port.

Finally, fruit grading is achieved based on the grades such as A, B, C and D. Thus, depending upon the color, size, shape, and weight of the fruit, the quality of the fruit is decided and further, fruits are graded and sorted accordingly.

CONCLUSION AND FUTURE SCOPE

In this paper, we have proposed a fruit quality management and grading system. In the first place, the organic product picture is caught by a web camera and it is handled by a PC outfitted with MATLAB programming. The software finds different features of tomato's image such as the color and size of the tomato. The load cell estimates the heaviness of the tomato. Finally, depending upon the color, size, and weight of the fruit, the quality of the fruit is decided and further, fruits are graded and sorted accordingly. Thus, the system is successfully implemented and tested for fruit quality management and grading. The system is automatic and thus lightweight, simple hardware and inexpensive, with increased speed of operation, and limited manpower and mistakes. This system is very beneficial in various agricultural areas and focused on bringing the revolution in the field. The proposed system can be used in various applications such as selecting specific fruits for making juice in various industries, selecting fruits for making chips, to ensure quality for exporting fruits and grading of fruits for trading.

ABBREVIATIONS

ARM7	Advanced RISC Machine-7
IR	Infrared
LCD	Liquid Crystal Display
MATLAB	Matrix Laboratory
UART	Universal Asynchronous Receiver Transmitter

REFERENCES

[1] S.M. Iqbal, A. Gopal, P.E. Sankaranarayanan, and A.B. Nair, "Classification of selected citrus fruits based on color using machine vision system", *Int. J. Food. Properties.,* vol. 19, no. 2, pp. 272-288, 2016.
[http://dx.doi.org/10.1080/10942912.2015.1020439]

[2] Chandra Sekhar Nandi, Bipan Tudu, and Chiranjib Koley, "A machine vision technique for grading of harvested mangoes based on maturity and quality", *IEEE Sensors. J.,* vol. 16, no. 16, 2016.
[http://dx.doi.org/10.1109/JSEN.2016.2580221]

[3] S.R. Dubey, and A.S. Jalal, "Robust approach for fruit and vegetable classification", *Procedia Engineering,* vol. 38, pp. 3449-3453, 2012.
[http://dx.doi.org/10.1016/j.proeng.2012.06.398]

[4] Md. Tarek Habib, and A.Z.M. Anup Majumder, "Machine vision-based papaya disease recognition", *Journal of King Saud University – Computer and Information Sciences.* vol. 32, pp. 300-309, 2020.
[http://dx.doi.org/10.1016/j.jksuci.2018.06.006]

[5] "Fruits and vegetables quality evaluation using computer vision: A review", *Journal of King Saud University – Computer and Information Sciences,* 2018.

[6] H. Dang, J. Song, and Q. Guo, "A Fruit Size Detecting and Grading System Based on Image Processing", In: *Published in IEEE-Second International Conference on Intelligent Human-Machine Systems and Cybernetics.* Nanjing, Jiangsu: China, 2010.
[http://dx.doi.org/10.1109/IHMSC.2010.120]

[7] J.B. Njoroge, K. Ninomiya, N. Kondo, and H. Toita, Automated fruit grading system using image processing. Published in IEEE Proceedings of the 41st SICE Annual Conference. SICE, Osaka, Japan, 2002.
[http://dx.doi.org/10.1109/SICE.2002.1195388]

[8] N. R. Rane, Automated fruit grading system using image processing. Published in IEEE Proceedings of the 41st SICE Annual Conference. SICE, Osaka, Japan, 2002.

[9] Available from: https://www.nxp.com/docs/en/data-sheet/LPC2141_42_44_46_48.pdf

[10] R.C. Gonzalez and R.E. Woods. Digital Image Processing, 4th Edition.

CHAPTER 9

Internet of Things-based Smart Sensing Mechanism for Mining Applications

Nilesh P. Sable[1,*], **Vijay U. Rathod**[2], **Parikshit N. Mahalle**[3], **Jayashri Bagade**[1] and **Rajesh Phursule**[4]

[1] *Department of Information Technology, Bansilal Ramnath Agarwal Charitable Trust's, Vishwakarma Institute of Information Technology, Pune, India*

[2] *Department of Artificial Intelligence and Data Science, G H Raisoni College of Engineering and Management, Wagholi, Pune, India*

[3] *Vishwakarma Institute of Information Technology, Pune, Maharashtra, India*

[4] *Department of Information Technology, Pimpri Chinchwad College of Engineering, Pune, India*

Abstract: According to the English lexicon, mining is the extraction of coal or other natural minerals from a mine. Extracting these natural minerals is extremely risky, and employees' lives are at stake. Mining workers are exposed to a dangerous underground environment that can cause harm or even death. Some of these injuries or fatalities can be traced back to human error. However, several physical factors or reasons for such a subterranean environment might be blamed for these mishaps. It is not easy to monitor without endangering someone's life. Previously, companies depended on manual processes where an individual would physically inspect the situation, make observations, and submit a report. This technique was too hazardous since the person monitoring a specific threat may be harmed by the same hazard. As a result, this has been the mining industry's most serious challenge for a long time. A smart system can detect problems and communicate information to the relevant authorities before anything hazardous occurs due to this procedure. This smart network system uses wireless sensors and an IoT platform. Gas, temperature, humidity, and vibration sensors are the various types of sensors used to detect the presence of any toxic gas, monitor the temperature, identify the amount of humidity in the air, and monitor subsurface tremors, respectively. All of these sensors are linked together, and the data collected by these sensors is subsequently sent to the cloud for processing. This analysis will assist the system in understanding subsurface behavioural changes, and as a result, it will be able to provide warnings of impending dangerous circumstances. The Raspberry Pi and the Raspberries operating system are used for data analysis. This smart system intends to lower the risk of accidents and infections, benefiting workers and the company's economy.

* **Corresponding author Nilesh P. Sable:** Department of Information Technology, Bansilal Ramnath Agarwal Charitable Trust's, Vishwakarma Institute of Information Technology, Pune, India;
E-mail: drsablenilesh@gmail.com

Parikshit N. Mahalle, Gitanjali R. Shinde and Prachi M. Joshi (Eds.)

Such IoT architecture in the mining industry, which combines operational technology (OT) and information technology (IT), provides a safer mine site for workers, reliable mining operations, a highly integrated environment for both traditional and innovative sensors and equipment, automation that can reduce human intervention and covert surveillance. This research aims to increase IoT adoption in the mining sector by combining a high-level architecture, complying with all industry standards and guidelines, and addressing the mining industry's specific challenges.

Keywords: IoT, IIoT, Mining Industry, Operational Technology, Wireless Sensor Networks.

1. INTRODUCTION

The Oxford vocabulary describes mining as "the process or industry of extracting coal or other minerals from a mine". Risky activities are carried out in order to obtain these mineral resources. Mine workers are exposed to a dangerous work environment that puts them in danger of dying or suffering life-altering injuries. Many of these deaths and injuries are caused by human error.

However, these situations are determined by underlying natural conditions, and these malfunctions can be attributed to them. It is challenging to monitor such circumstances without endangering lives. Fig. (**1**) illustrates how mine monitoring was done by sending someone to the mine and having them report back. However, this approach is risky because the person watching a specific potential threat could also be hurt by it. This level of close observation is inappropriate.

Fig. (1). Mining area [1].

Particular technologies or strategies are created to protect workers from harm in these challenging conditions. "Occupational health and safety" is more formal and describes these procedures. This standard intends to lower the frequency of occupational illnesses and injuries, which will benefit mine workers and the broader economy. These errors may result in underground mining damages due to early retirements and higher insurance costs. The majority of the largest mining businesses in South Africa have been certified, demonstrating the importance of this standard's cooperation. This benchmark can be strengthened using contemporary technological policies to achieve the best results.

As shown in Fig. (**2**), information technology and intelligent framework implementations have enhanced, and the number of devices connected that use the Internet of Things technology (IoT) has increased significantly. Smart grids are one of the smart city's foundations, and IoT technology is used in several applications. IoT is a technical framework that imagines a globally interconnected network of devices and machinery. Smart home devices, smart metropolitan areas, agricultural sectors, automobile sectors, medical services, the manufacturing industry, and public transit are all affected by the IoT. It is estimated that between fifty and one hundred billion smart things and objects will be linked to the internet by 2023. The manufacturing industry is being further developed to reconsider its mechanisms from this perspective, which can inspire primary production developed early.

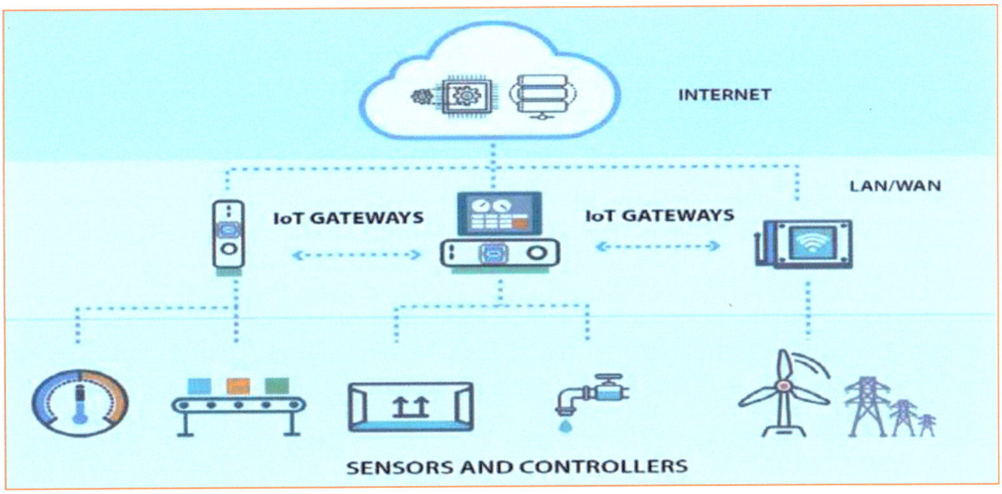

Fig. (2). General architecture of IoT [1].

Industrial Revolution 4.0 includes the Industrial Internet of Things (IIoT), which is an implementation of IoT in the industry sector. The IIoT, which integrates the strong points of the mature industry with the internet, emphasizes the notion of constant digitalization and interconnection of all production units. Fig. (**3**) depicts the IIoT as a hybrid of information and operational technology. The IIoT is a network of physical devices and things that contain electronic parts and sensor systems. The IIoT is a type of industrial network connectivity that enables a network to gain more value and service by data transmission with the manufacturer. IoT tools are now integrated into commercial uses, including home automation, connected vehicles, and wearable technologies. The IIoT is designed to revolutionize several industries, such as industrial production, petroleum and gas, agricultural production, and mineral extraction. The IIoT is designed to revolutionize several industries, such as industrial production, petroleum and gas, agricultural production, and mineral extraction.

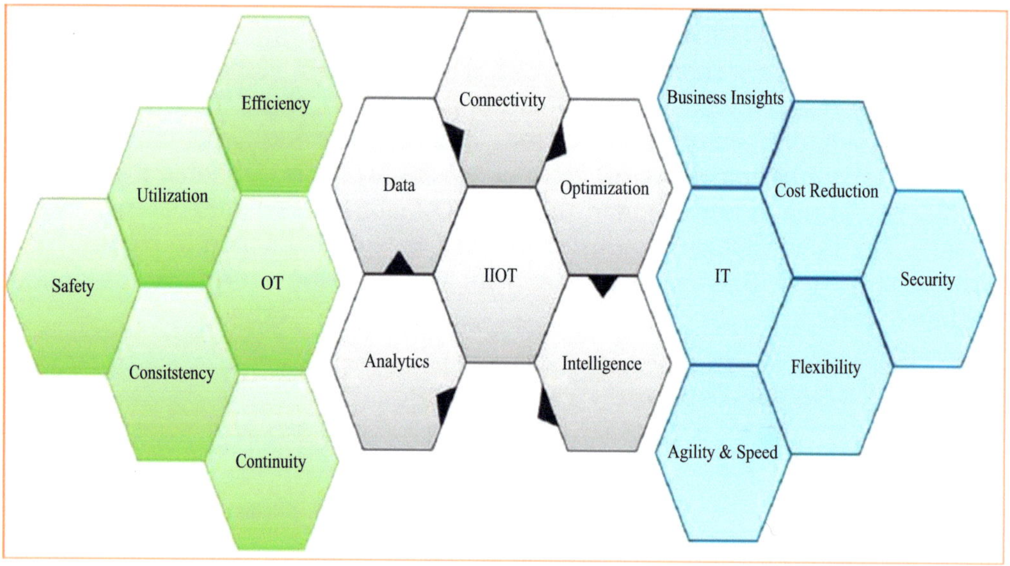

Fig. (3). OT and IT = IIoT [1].

This study focuses on the application of IIoT in the mining industry, particularly in underground mining. The following are some of the industry's complexities and unique challenges:

- Heterogeneity depending on the natural conditions, every miningindustry has a dissimilar design.
- Heavy transport combined with confined spaces is a major reason for disaster.
- It is not possible to communicate wirelessly across shafts and stops.
- A sequence of blasts that would dismantle gadgets if they were moved so every

time.

- Face drilling is a kind of drilling that alters the design on a regular basis.
- Failure, completed and independent actions are necessary to confirm the manufacture and protection in the event of catastrophic failures, among other things.

2. LITERATURE REVIEW

Operations established in contaminated areas, including such mineral extraction, need an active incentive to invest in the industry in sequence to prevent severe significant damage [1]. Identification robots could be employed in underground mining to undertake environmental investigation and survey work, discover hazardous gas leaks, and assist traditional rescue personnel in mine shaft accidents [1]. Implementing current WSN techniques is one of the safety precautions to tackle this dilemma. Cloud computing is used in an IoT-based wireless system for data transmission and storage parameter values acquired from a wireless module with a Zigbee functionality [1]. The WSN spotlighted in comparative analysis a recently developed mine security surveillance framework of a typical cabled surveillance framework [1].

This paper examines the existing condition of information technology in the mining industry and recognizes vertical fragmentation as the main challenging task [2, 3].

The authors suggested an IoT framework for smart building structures and all associated benefits [4]. This ground-breaking research demonstrates the new framework application model, including its processing components [4]. (Sable *et al.*, 2017). For more clarity, performance measures are assessed with cloud and cloud fog arrangements [4].

Applying modern IoT technologies in the power grid is meaningful way to accelerate the industrialization of the electric grid, as well as for efficient electric grid network connectivity [5]. One of the most significant essential IoT implementation sectors is emergency protection and power distribution system [5]. The developed IoT detection and communication technology can successfully prevent or decrease power transmission destruction due to natural disasters. Also, it can increase power transmission reliability while lowering costs [5]. The focus was on the characteristics of smart power system development and construction. This study discusses the use of IoT in a power transmission line online surveillance system [5].

The forthcoming IoT communication infrastructure is anticipated to prepare innovative road applications in smart metropolitan areas, smart metering, and so on [6]. To support such a wide range of applications, a set of rules for communication must be adaptable and intelligent [6].

Several developments necessitate localized calculation to improve the overall performance, protection, and cost reductions [7]. IoT devices have ushered in a new era of computing and communication in recent years [7].

Several research publications on WSN and cloud computing have addressed IoT communication issues [8]. On the other hand, the subject matter of high-level end-to-end connectivity IoT technologies is much less frequently the focus of research [8]. Reliability sounds much better than communication, especially at the application layer [9]. In addition, this research indicates that the networks utilized in IoT systems are frequently virtual and software-based [10].

3. SMART MATERIAL

3.1. Methodology

In this research, a WSN is implemented for parametric evaluation correctness and protection to reduce the number of people killed by mine explosions and unintentional deaths. Each mine worker is given a personal caretaking unit to detect hazardous conditions. If an explosion occurs, information is sent to an emergency care center as soon as possible to let them know the position of the mine labors. Before a detonation occurs, maximum assistance is provided. In this mechanism, investigators employ modern WSN technologies for elevated transmission data at the mine site. The writers use a robot to watch on the mine site alteration. If there are any conceivably harmful situations at the mine site, mine laborers are informed. An individual caretaking unit, including a helmet, is given to each mine employee. Sensor systems built into the helmet notify the user of modifications in attribute values.

A Section dedicated to Robots: In the robotic section, temperature, gas, tilt, humidity, and obstacle sensors would be installed, as shown in Fig. (**4**). All of these sensors would be interfaced with an ARM LPC2148 microcontroller. An institutional ARM control system attached to an LCD displays the parameter values. The ARM supervisor is attached to the transmitter Zigbee component in the direction to send data to the receiver Zigbee component in the ground workstation if any parameter differences arise in the mining region.

Fig. (4). The autonomous mine vision of mining robots [4].

Section of the Helmet: Helmets are personal protective equipment worn by mine workers. Mine workers' helmet contains temperature, heart rate sensor and an obstacle sensor to detect changes in parameter values that exceed the threshold level. If any hazardous conditions occur in the mining area, the helmet is equipped with APR, which provides voice notification to mine workers. A Zigbee wireless configuration was connected this section to the ground workstation.

Concentration Node: To gather information from the cloud through IoT, the concentration node consists of a ground workstation wirelessly joined to a Zigbee receiver component.

Provide safety precautions for mine workers when dangerous conditions arise in the mining area. This section would provide information to nearby hospitals to save mine workers.WSN will help to improve coal mine safety. WSN is more capable of adapting and reduces the need for electrical wiring. Furthermore, information transmission efficiency in the coal mining industry has dramatically improved. Because the parameter values are saved in the workstation in this application, the saved values can be used to detect dangers before they happen. Researchers are informing the personnel about the precautions to be taken in the event of a risk. It will be advantageous for them to save their lives before anyone comes to help them exit the mine. Besides manufacturing a high-level construction, the authors hope to improve IIoT adoption in the mining industry.

They are using industry standards as a guide and addressing the mining industry's unique challenges as shown in Fig. (**5**).

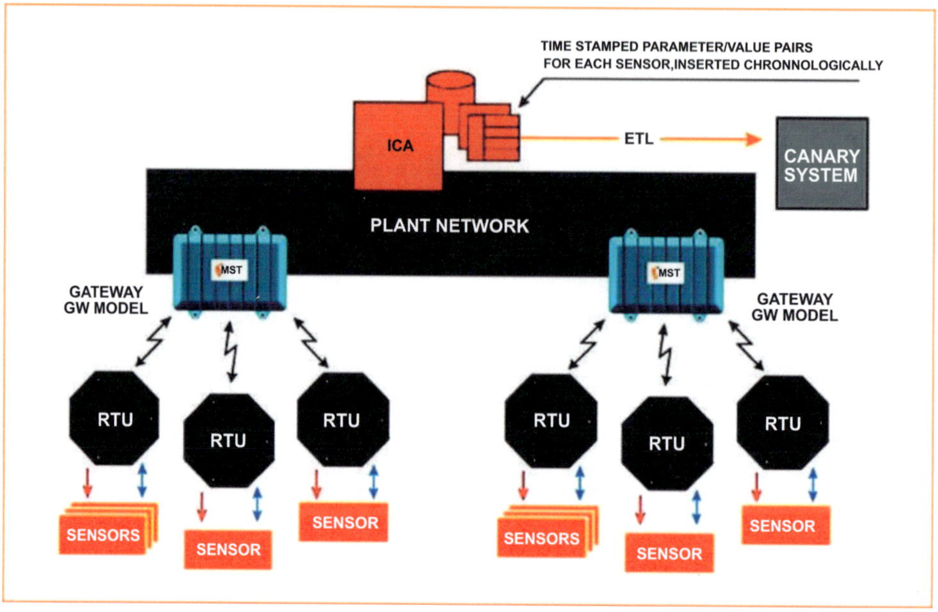

Fig. (5). The WSN is the industry standard for IoT in mining [2].

3.2. Stages of Mining Life Cycle

In this subdivision, the authors explain the phases of the mining life cycle and how the mining industry works. The five stages of a mine industry life cycle, as shown in Fig. (**6**), have commonly been used to compare a series of events in advanced mining. The five stages of a mine industry life cycle are I. Prospecting, II. Exploration, III. Development, IV. Exploitation and V. Reclamation.

Prospecting: Prospecting is searching for coal or other valuable minerals that are not metallic minerals. It is the first step toward making use of a mineral deposit. Mineral deposits can be found on or beneath the surface of the earth. Prospecting techniques are used both directly and indirectly.

Exploration: The second phase of a mine industry life is exploration. The phase's primary function calculates the mineral deposit's size and value. As precisely as possible, techniques similar to but more refined than prospecting are used.

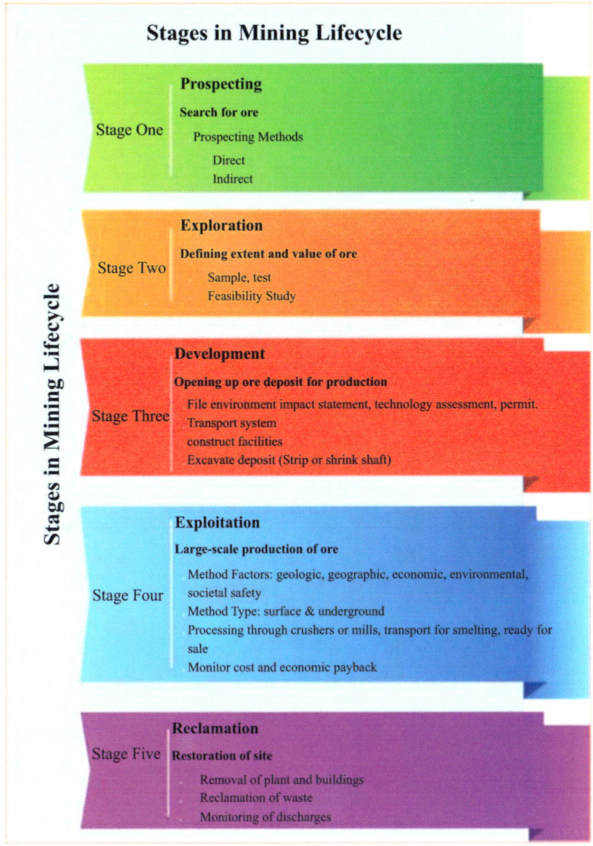

Fig. (6). Stages in the mining lifecycle.

Development: The third stage in this life cycle is the development for preparing a mineral credit for exploration.

Exploitation: With the help of the exploitation stage of mining, large amounts of minerals are extracted from the mine site. Even though development is ongoing, the focus is now on the production stage.

Reclamation: Reclamation is recounting, revegetating, and restoring the water and land values during the final stage of the mine life cycle. It is best to start the mine reclamation process before the first excavations. Mine planners should plan the mine so that the reclamation process is factored in. With the help of the reclamation stage of this life cycle, the total cost of mining has been reduced.

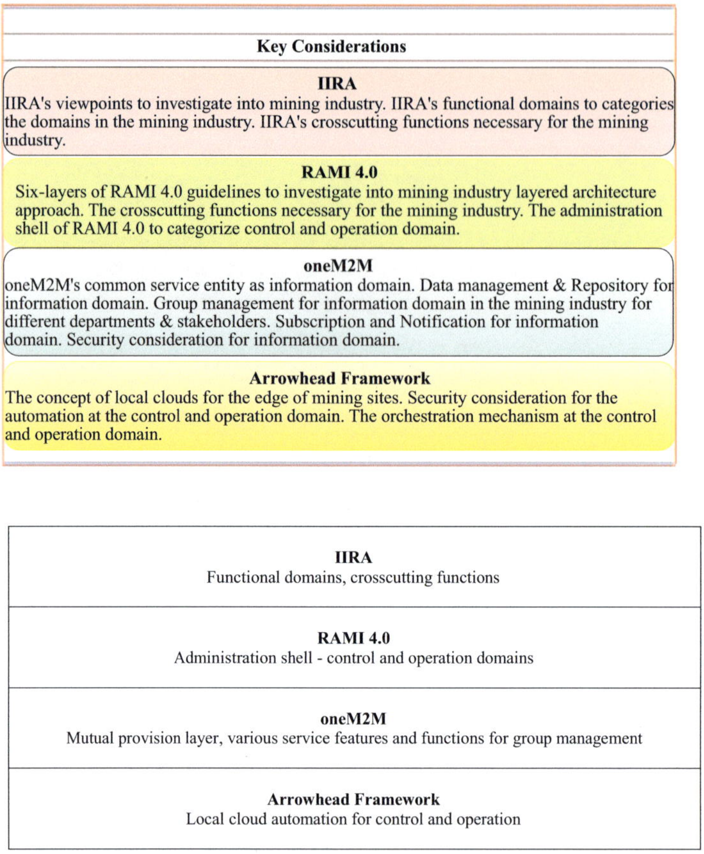

Fig. (7). The importance and usage of IIoT benchmarks for mining [1].

3.3. The Mining Industry's High-Level IIoT Architecture

In this subdivision, the authors try to create a high-level framework based on global practices and standard guidelines. An overview of the important factors derived from industry principles to generate IIoT structure for mining is shown in Fig. (7). The researchers integrated the IIRA's perceptions, functional domains, and crosscutting functions into the design, offering the industry a wealth of guidelines. Various domains of the mining industry's IIoT architecture have been defined as a result of these concerns. The RAMI 4.0 benchmark architectural design for the mining industry has a layered structure and cross-cutting functional areas. RAMI 4.0's administration shell is used for the control and operation domains. The process area manages the tasks in the mine site's control domain. Furthermore, the oneM2M rule includes a mutual provision layer that allows vertical silos to be viewed horizontally.

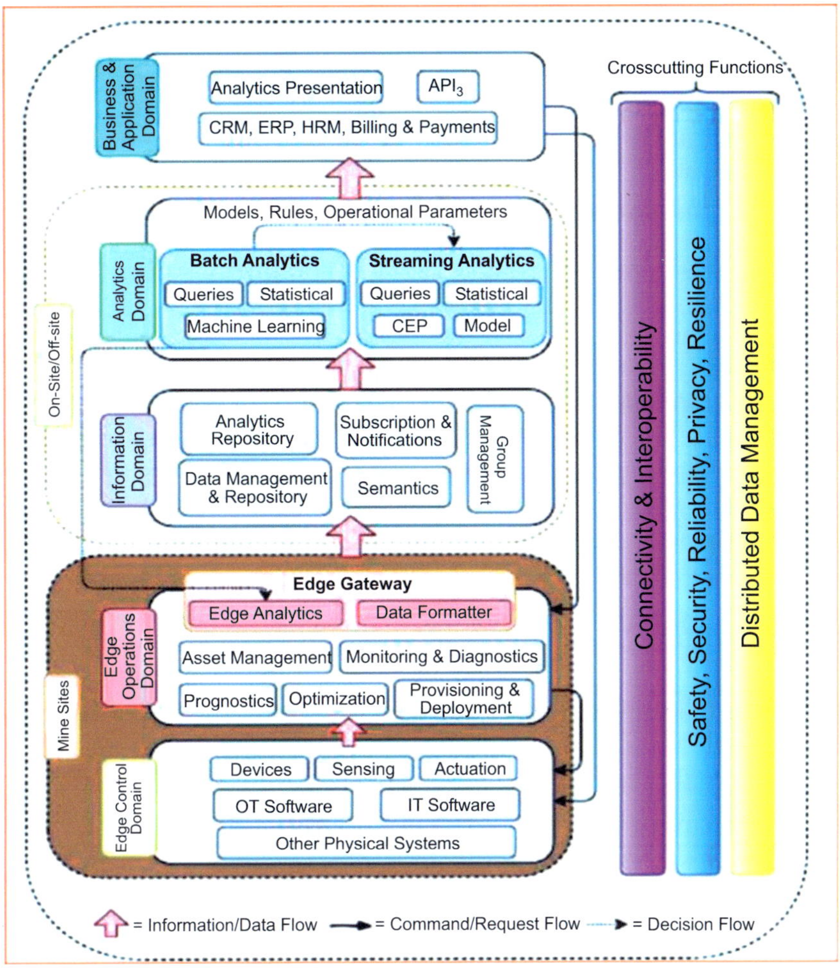

Fig. (8). The manufactured high-level IIoT design for mining industry [1].

The M2M computer science and engineering technique is viewed in this design as an information domain with various service features and functions, such as team management, membership fee and confirmation, information management, database, and safety. Finally, a local cloud automation approach based on the arrowhead framework for mine sites is considered, where many organizations can record and provide service areas. The essential modules of the native cloud can discover and orchestrate these services, allowing them to interact with one another securely.

The layered architecture is divided into five domains, as shown in Fig. (**8**). Every mine site or area is split into two domains: edge control and edge operations.

Domains for information and analytics can be deployed on-site at the mine's edge or off-site in the cloud. The cloud's off-site information domain is linked to all mining areas and domain names. The analytics domain, as well as the business and application domains, are all built above the information domain. Fig. (**8**) shows how unique arrows are used to demonstrate the information flow, commands, requests, and decisions. The following are comprehensive descriptions of each domain.

Edge Control Domain: The control domain comprises various operational and information technology-related software, actuators, sensors, and other physical devices.

This domain is responsible for mine industrial control and robotic organization's various functions. The main responsibility of this domain is to read data from WSN, apply logic and rules, and give commands to actuators to control physical systems. A mining site's control domain usually necessitates high timing precision. Components and devices in the control domain that perform such duties are generally located close to the physical schemes they control, but they can also be distributed in geographical areas. After deploying these devices and physical systems in the mine, staff members may need help accessing them.

Edge Operation Domain: Among the many types of mines available are surface and underground. In case of an underground mine, the operation domain can be located either in the mine or on the surface at the mine's start. The control domain's administration and procedure are the operation domain's responsibility. Procurement and implementation, portfolio management, monitoring and prognosis, optimization, and prediction are all functions of this domain. Procurement and Implementation are a set of functions considered necessary for asset configuration, on boarding, registration, monitoring, asset placement, and superannuation.

Asset administration is a set of activities that enable asset management centers or organizations to send instructions to controller organizations, which are then passed on to the assets. Such commands are bidirectional, meaning the assets can respond to them and send data back to the asset management centers. The detection and prediction of occurrence of issues is carried out by monitoring and diagnostics. This is in charge of analyzing asset core performance metrics in real-time. Asset safety data are gathered and processed using intelligence. To identify the actual cause of a dilemma and alerts about suspicious situations and discrepancies are given. A prognostic is a collection of tasks that IIoT processes provide as a predictive analytics driver in the mining industry, and it is an important consideration. It's based on asset activity, data from the past, and physics asset properties. The term "optimization" refers to functions that improve asset efficiency and performance while lowering energy consumption, by determining how the assets are used to maximize quality and production. It assists in keeping assets operating at their peak performance by identifying output gaps and inefficiencies.

The edge gateway at the mine site is responsible for real-time edge analytics and data-related activity. The edge gateway is also responsible for ensuring that different vertical solutions are connected and interoperable. The primary function of the data format is to convert all data from the operation and control domains into a format that the information domain can understand.

Information Domain: Data management and processing is the responsibility of the information domain. This domain provides an information center point, collecting data from a wide assortment of domains, most noticeably the control and operation domains, and can be located on-site in the mine or off-site on a cloud.

This domain provides the centralized information database for the mining industry, storing information from various departmental systems, including investigation, geoscientists, shredders and grinders, waste disposal, revenues, and industry. To obtain the capacity to accumulate, and transform vast amounts of data into a specific format, data storage for other reasons, including analytics and semantic processing, is part of data management and repository. Group management, responsible for handling group-related queries, is also part of the information domain. Different groups of users from respective units and decision-makers can be formed to obtain suitable direct connections to the information domain.

Analytics Domain: Receiving data from the information domain, maintaining an analytics repository, and performing analytics are the primary functions of the analytics domain. Like the information domain, this domain stored data locally on-site at the mine and remotely in the cloud. The mining industry faces challenges with analytics because the outcomes in the physical domain can affect the procedure and protection of equipment. Such consequences can be unplanned or risky, impacting population livelihoods or causing environmental damage. Batch and stream analytics processing models are available in the mining analytics domain. Batch data analysis is a very efficient way of storing large amounts of data that have been accumulated over the years. Stream analytics relates to the capability to analyze data as it flows from one device to another in seconds.

Business and Application Domain: The business and application domain provides a technical environment where practical enterprise and application logic can be implemented. This reflects business functions that encourage business procedures and administrative responsibilities that an IIoT structure will enforce to clarify end-to-end operational processes. Enterprise resource planning, customer relationship management, and human resource management are just a few examples of business functions. Analytics presentations consume data from the information domain. The analytics domain includes features such as commercial questions, reports, dashboards, report generation, and analysis.

Cross-Cutting Functions: The domains listed above focus on the most common system functions required to support IIoT execution in the mining industry. Additional functionality is required to enable the main system functions. Such supporting features, known as crosscutting functions, must be accessible across several practical components of the architecture, including:

Interoperability and Connectivity: For IIoT schemes, connectivity and interoperability are critical. Because of vertical silos and legacy systems, such problems are especially challenging in the mining industry.

As shown in Fig. (**9**), the synthetically produced design enables a cross-cutting interconnection and interoperability function based on two methodologies. This is done to ensure that systems from different vendors can communicate with each other.

Common Meta-Model: Fig. (**9a**) depicts a common meta-model approach. The conversing stakeholders must be formed using the regular Meta model and Interfaces agreement, which require architectural style integration preparation. There are several approaches to achieving shared met models and interfaces.

Broker Based: Fig. (**9b**) depicts the broker method. It is similar to using a translator between two people who speak different languages. With a small percentage of communicating entities, the broker approach works well. It is the more efficient way of allowing interaction among parties who have been previously designed with independence requirements but now feel the necessity to interact. Furthermore, a broker-based strategy could be used to share information when one system only necessitates specific data from another. In this scenario, a subject-based broker can act as middleware between these systems. When an incident takes place or information arrives in one system, the broker informs the other systems that have already subscribed to that information.

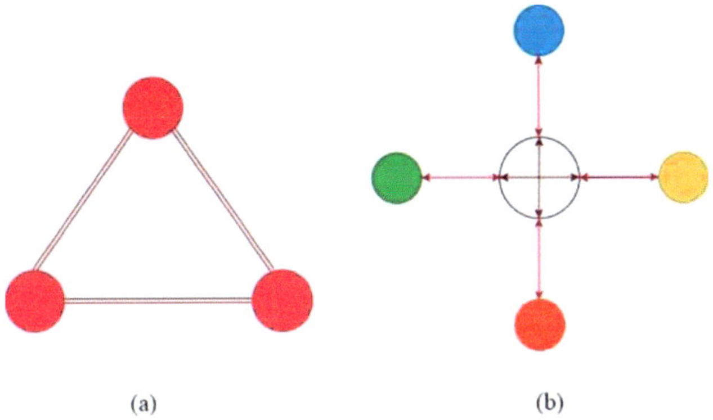

Fig. (9). Models of interoperability: (**a**) Common-Meta model, (**b**) Broker based [1].

Distributed Data Management: The data is spread over a number of mining areas and corners. As a result, the contest of data management produced by a range of devices and implementations at numerous mine sites has been addressed. The DMM can be considered a crosscutting function. The three steps in DMM are collection of data, aggregation of data, and storage systems. The connectivity, on the other hand, is a required feature.

Resilience, Privacy, Reliability, Security and Safety: Security, dependability, privacy, and resilience are all words that come to mind when thinking about safety, security, and resiliency.

Safety: Safety refers to the state of a system that is operating without posing an unreasonable risk of human injury to miners. Traditional OT safety evaluation methods focus on physical substances and events. Risk analysis is used to identify risks in order to avoid incorrect processes and increase system tolerance to unforeseeable events. On the other hand, a software component does exactly what it is programmed to do. Security-related systematic vulnerabilities, on the other hand, can be exploited by adversaries. A remote attacker can take advantage of flaws in mine-connected systems to put a device, such as an autonomous vehicle, in an insecure state. As a result, following safety regulations and practices is critical.

Security: The system's security is a continuous behaviour rather than a conditional statement. In any case, no IIoT system can function safely indefinitely. As a result, it's critical to spell out the specific circumstances that matter and the particular behaviour that stakeholders should expect. The complete form of CIA is confidentiality, integrity, and availability. The qualities that must be maintained in order to provide security are represented by the CIA. In operational technologies, however, availability added the most value. Then there is integrity and confidentiality, which is usually the last thing on your mind. The acronym AIC is formed as a result of this process.

Reliability: The capacity of a device or a system to perform its required tasks for a specified period while meeting specific criteria is referred to as reliability. Analyzing which aspects of system reliability an attacker might affect and putting the system in place can improve the system's reliability. The system's security measures must be implemented to counteract these attacks.

Privacy: Privacy refers to an individual's or a group's ability to control how data about them is retrieved, analyzed, and processed, as well as by whom and to whom it is revealed. Privacy is determined by the stakeholder's desire for the information to be secure or restricted from being used for other legal purposes. Keeping up with new laws and regulations, such as the EU General Data Protection Regulation, is critical.

Resilience: Resilience is a system's changing ability to perform so that it eliminates, accumulates, and manages dynamic confrontational circumstances while performing the assigned duties and then helps restore operative functionalities after causation. When one function fails, it does not imply that others will follow suit. As a result, other options for completing the system's failed task should be instantaneous, quick, and consistent.

4. MINING APPLICATIONS

A. Given the numerous benefits it provides, numerous big mining companies have decided how to begin their digital transformation and digitalization journeys to oversee daily mining operations.

Consider the following scenario: **Cost-cutting and increased productivity**.

Using WSN mining equipment and systems that monitor the equipment's performance has resulted in cost savings and increased productivity. Massive quantities of data are being analyzed in the mining industry to find more cost-effective ways to run operations and reduce overall operational downtime.

B: Ensure that people and equipment are safe

With the help of IoT, the safety of equipment and mines staff is guaranteed by monitoring ventilation and toxicity levels inside underground mines in real-time. It allows for efficient and fast evacuation procedures as well as safety drills.

C: Improved decision-making and decision-making speed (moving from preventative to predictive maintenance)

Nearly every single hour, the mining industry faces an emergency with a high degree of unpredictability. IoT supports balancing situations and making the best decisions where multiple factors are active simultaneously, allowing daily operations to be delegated to algorithms.

CONCLUSION AND FUTURE WORK

The IIoT is a foundation and enabling environment of manufacturing robotics and a source of valuable insights that can be applied to various industries. The mining life cycle is investigated, and current IT practices in the industry are evaluated. Also, the different obstacles in the mining industry are described that can be encountered if a suitable IIoT architecture is implemented. The authors use the guidelines provided by global IIoT standards to address the current issues. It has its own IIoT architecture synthesis projects for the mining industry. The developed IIoT architecture can be used to address the mining industry's technical gaps in interoperability and data exchange. Dissimilar skills, such as OT/IT application domains, IoT gadgets, cloud services, edge computer technology, middleware, big data, and enterprise applications, can be used to implement such high-level architecture.

REFERENCES

[1] V. Henriques, R. Malekian, and Dijana Capeska Bogatinoska, Opatija, Croatia, "Mine safety system using wireless sensor networks", *2017 40th International Convention on Information and Communication Technology, Electronics and Microelectronics,* (MIPRO), no. 5, pp. 515-520, 2017. [http://dx.doi.org/10.23919/MIPRO.2017.7973480.]

[2] A. Aziz, O. Schelén, and U. Bodin, "A Study on Industrial IoT for the Mining Industry: Synthesized Architecture and Open Research Directions", *IoT,* vol. 1, no. 2, pp. 529-550, 2020. [http://dx.doi.org/10.3390/iot1020029]

[3] S.N. Popat, and Y.P. Singh, "Efficient research on the relationship standard mining calculations in data mining", Adv. Sci. Technol. Sci, vol. 14, no. 2, pp. 42-48, 2017.

[4] H. Fayyaz, Z. U. Rehman, and S. Abbas, "An IoT Enabled Framework for Smart Buildings Empowered with Cloud & Fog Infrastructures,", *2019 International Conference on Innovative Computing* (ICIC), pp. 1-8, 2019. [http://dx.doi.org/10.1109/ICIC48496.2019.8966715] [PMID: 19297427]

[5] Q. Ou, Y. Zhen, X. Li, Y. Zhang, and L. Zeng, "Application of internet of things in smart grid power transmission", *2012 Third FTRA International Conference on Mobile, Ubiquitous, and Intelligent Computing,*. Vancouver, Canada, pp. 96-100, 2012. [http://dx.doi.org/10.1109/MUSIC.2012.24]

[6] Z. Nain, A. Musaddiq, Y. A. Qadri, A. Nauman, M. K. Afzal, and S. W. Kim, "RIATA: A reinforcement learning-based intelligent routing update scheme for future generation IoT Networks", IEEE Access., vol. 9, pp. 81161-81172, 2021.

[7] R. Hasan, M. Hossain, and R. Khan, ""Aura: An IoT based cloud infrastructure for localized mobile computation outsourcing",", *2015 3rd IEEE International Conference on Mobile Cloud Computing, Services, and Engineering,* Services, and Engineering, pp. 183-188, San Francisco, CA, USA. [http://dx.doi.org/10.1109/MobileCloud.2015.37]

[8] P. Schauer, and L. Falas, "Communication management for reliable service based IoT systems,", systems,", In: 2020 IEEE 29th International Conference on Enabling Technologies: Infrastructure for Collaborative Enterprises (WETICE), pp. 113-118, 2020. [http://dx.doi.org/10.1109/WETICE49692.2020.00030]

[9] S.N. Popat, and Y.P. Singh, "Efficient research on the relationship standard mining calculations in data mining", *Adv. Sci. Technol. Sci.*, vol. 14, no. 2, pp. 42-48, 2017.

[10] S. N. Popat, and Y. P. Singh, "Analysis and study on the classifier based data mining methods", *J. Adv. Sci. Tech.*, vol. 14, no. 2, 2017.

CHAPTER 10

Explainable Artificial Intelligence (XAI) for IoT

Prashant C. Dhas[1,*], **Parikshit N. Mahalle**[1] and **Gitanjali R. Shinde**[1]

[1] *Vishwakarma Institute of Information Technology, Pune, Maharashtra, India*

Abstract: Artificial Intelligence and Machine Learning are the latest topics across industries. A lot of concentration has been given to these areas and still the adoption has been challenged by users and experts in this field in the search for some kind of solution to be provided that the output can be trusted by all. The purpose of this paper is to focus on the sensor data coming from various IoT devices and how the data can be interpreted by various available algorithms. The ML algorithm is considered a black box with a focus on providing the required output without finding the causes behind the decision and working mechanism provided by that model. In this chapter, we tried to explain various common techniques/models available for eXplainable Artificial Intelligence (XAI) and how those can be used for IoT data.

Keywords: Artificial intelligence, Explainable artificial intelligence (XAI), Machine learning (ML), The internet of things (IoT).

1. INTRODUCTION

Recently, the influence of advanced and sophisticated techniques such as explainable artificial intelligence (XAI), machine learning (ML), and deep learning (DL) on the Internet of Things (IoT) is increasingly intensified. With the increase in the number of connected devices , the IoT usage needs some kind of trust among the users and hence, Explainable Artificial Intelligence (XAI) is an intriguing modern conversation topic [1]. XAI provides a comprehensive analysis of the predicted outputs due to which it is regarded as one of the most prominent techniques in recent times [1]. Regardless of understanding the issue, studies have stated the necessity of understanding the model's process and its predicted output. It is expected that the investigation of XAI and ML models will experience an exponential increase in coming years [2]. It is also anticipated that XAI will overcome the technical difficulties associated with conventional ML techniques.

* **Corresponding author Prashant C. Dhas:** Vishwakarma Institute of Information Technology, Pune, Maharashtra, India; E-mail: prashant.221p0054@viit.ac.in

According to Samke *et al.* (2017) [3] Explainable AI is a collection of tools and frameworks that facilitate understanding and analysis of the predictions made by traditional machine learning models. AI is often defined as the capacity of a model to perform a task that has historically been performed by people using a number of learning techniques. As opposed to this, explainable AI, often referred to as interpretable AI, is artificial intelligence in which the result of the solution is understandable to humans. In contrast, the "black box" concept in machine learning prevents even the designers from explaining why AI made a certain decision.

The Internet of Things (IoT) has significantly impacted people's lives in recent years on the commercial, economic, and social levels, claim Koppula and Muthukuru (2016) [4]. A distributed, interconnected network of embedded systems that communicate with one another across wired and wireless networks is referred to as the [5] Internet of Things (IoT). The development of smart products has substantially modernized modern society's lifestyle and way of life. Because it makes energy automation possible and enhances people's quality of existence, IoT is significant in the modern world (De Luca & Chen, 2021). Despite the fact that IoT networks are vulnerable to threats due to their resource restrictions and ad hoc nature, continuous monitoring and analysis can be used to secure IoT systems, enabling the application of preventive actions, the reduction of possible hazards, and the protection of private data. IoT is essential for the creation of intelligent applications, including smart cities. IoT technology could be used to collect, process, and store data. Also possible are service visualization, monitoring, and device management. However, the security and complexity of IoT have considerably expanded as a result of the ability to share information between devices scattered throughout the globe (Al Hammadi *et al.*, 2021) [6]. Furthermore, a number of security issues have grown as a result of the exchange of extremely sensitive information *via* an IoT platform. Therefore, it is crucial to combine more sophisticated and cutting-edge methodologies, such as AI and ML, with IoT to achieve better performance.

One of the fast-expanding subfields of artificial intelligence (AI) is eXplainable AI (XAI). It refers to techniques that produce accurate and comprehensible models that are transparent, interpretable, and understandable so that people can comprehend the results that are presented (Adadi, & Berrada, 2018) [7]. The purpose of XAI is to offer a means of identifying the origin of the produced output. A younger generation of AI techniques might develop using XAI. In essence, XAI creates a connection between model attributes and results. Explainable models are introduced by XAI's artificial intelligence algorithms, which also guarantee a strong level of learning feedback. It ensures the confidence, security, and privacy of AI partners. XAI employs two distinct modules: an explanation systematically identifies an informative module, in contrast to conventional machine learning techniques. There is a trade-off between explainability and accuracy. Existing models are more precise and efficient, but they are also more complex to comprehend. The implementation of the XAI has the potential to offer the maximum degree of accuracy, efficacy, and explicability. Some of the pioneers in Explainable Artificial Intelligence platforms are IBM, Google, Darwin AI, Flow cast, Imandra, Kyndi, and Factmata [8]. And over 70% of company directors, according to a PwC survey released in 2017, think AI will be beneficial for their companies. It also asserts that by 2030, artificial intelligence would increase the global GDP by up to $15 trillion. As a result, in order to keep up with demand, AI technology needs to become more responsible and reliable, and XAI might be the greatest solution for the AI industry.

Explainable AI is a developing field in artificial intelligence and machine learning. Building public confidence in AI model decisions is crucial. It won't be possible unless the opaqueness of AI algorithms is made more apparent. Explainable AI frameworks are tools that generate reports on model performance and attempt to explain it. LIME and SHAP are the two techniques that we primarily use. In the next subsections, each method is explained in depth.

LIME-Local Interpretable Model-Agnostic Explanations: LIME [9, 10] is one of the most commonly used methods for the interpretation of ML models' predictions. One of the key advantages of LIME is that it is a model agnostics method and could be used for the explanation/interpretation of any model. For the explanation of an ML model, LIME perturbs the input samples and analyzes the changes in the prediction of the model [11]. This simple working mechanism makes it a preferable choice for model interpretation compared to model-specific methods, which require a deeper understanding of the underlying models.

LIME provides local interpretation, which means the model's behavior is described by analyzing the response of a 4 model to changes in a single data sample. Here the intuition is to analyze the cause behind a particular prediction by answering questions like" why was this prediction made?" or" which features caused the prediction?". It produces results in the form of a list of explanations highlighting the contribution of the individual feature as detailed in upcoming sections. We note that the idea and working mechanism of LIME are different from a related concept of" feature importance", which is generally carried out over the entire datasets.

SHAP-Shapley Additive Explanations: Our second explanation approach is based on another state-of-the-art technique namely, SHAPE. The method was introduced by Lundberg *et al.* [9] to address the limitations of the existing methods. Similar to LIME, SHAP provides explanations of individual predictions and could be used for the explanation of any model. However, in contrast to LIME, SHAP provides both local and global explanations. The main difference between global and local explanations lies in the level/scope of explanation. The global interpretations/explanations include complete insights into the general/overall behavior of the model. The local explanations/interpretations describe the causes behind a decision on an individual data sample. Similar to LIME, SHAP could be used for the explanation of ML models trained on different types of data including textual, visual, and tabular data.

Also, there are other frameworks such as, Deep Learning Important Features (DeepLIFT), Explain like I'm 5 (ELI5), What-If tools (WIF), AI Explainability 360 (AIX360), and Skater.

2. MOTIVATION

The Internet of Things (IoT) has significantly impacted people's commercial, financial, and social lives in recent years [5]. There are various XAI models deployed in IoT applications like healthcare, finance, military, and security. Continuous monitoring and analysis can be used to secure IoT systems, allowing for the adoption of predictive and preventative actions, the mitigation of potential hazards, and the protection of sensitive data. The complexity of IoT systems necessitates the use of more sophisticated and cutting-edge methods, like AI and ML [6, 7] along with XAI. The goals of explainable AI are to address the problems that traditional AI has with comprehension, trust, and effective communication. By fusing the best aspects of symbolic AI and conventional machine learning, XAI overcomes these difficulties. XAI supports the quantitative growth of trust. Traditional model-based methods give a clear grasp of how assumptions about a model and input data result in decisions about the output. To be more precise, conventional AI is unable to provide answers to issues like what characteristics of data influence judgments, where better or more data is required, how to improve algorithm design, and when better or more data is not helping to produce the intended results. These reasons drive this study's investigation of explainable AI and associated IoT system algorithms, with a focus on defense measures.

By concentrating on the invention and development of an intelligent algorithm capable of delivering opinions that a human can understand in a particular context and openly explaining such decisions using multiple interpretation methods, XAI seeks to improve AI approaches and methodology. This enables us to look at the underlying intelligent models and make sure that automatically generated judgments are based on recognized norms and principles, enabling decisions to be trusted and their impact to be supported.

XAI intends to enhance AI techniques and methodologies with a focus on creating and developing an intelligent algorithm that can generate conclusions that a person can understand in a given situation and freely explain such decisions utilizing various modes of interpretation. It is possible to investigate the underlying computational techniques and confirm whether automated choices are based on accepted norms and principles in order to ensure that decisions can be trusted, and their influence is justified.

3. RELATED WORK

In this section, we present some recent reviews on explainable AI in IoT contexts and analyse the opportunities and challenges of explainable AI [13]. The study discusses a comprehensive classification system of the XAI process and categorizes the XAI techniques based on the breadth of their explanations, the methodology of their algorithms, and the level or application of their explanations, which aids in the development of trustworthy, explicable, and unique deep learning algorithms. The following section of the article outlines the main theories underlying XAI research and offers a timeline of notable XAI studies from 2007 to 2020. After a thorough examination of each category of algorithms and approaches, the study analyzes the explanation maps produced by eight XAI algorithms using image files. Following a discussion of this method's drawbacks, several new paths for enhancing XAI evaluation are suggested.

According to the authors Al Hammadi *et al.*, 2021 [6], an insider risk assessment system is used for duty security evaluation using EEG brainwave signals with explainable deep learning and machine learning algorithms to classify abnormal EEG signals indicating a potential insider threat and evaluating the fitness for duty. The system is designed to be cost-effective by using an Emotive Insight EEG device with five electrodes. In this study, data from 17 people in different emotional states were collected. The different levels of emotions were mapped and classified into four risk levels, namely low, normal, medium, and high. The data were collected while the subjects were presented with different images from the scientific international affective picture system. The collected EEG signals were preprocessed to eliminate noise from physical movements and blinking. The data were then used to train self-feature learning of two- and one-dimensional convolutional neural networks, Adaptive Boosting, random forest, and K-nearest neighbors' models; the proposed method yielded classification accuracies of 96, 75, 97, 94 and 81%, respectively.

The authors Shukla, A, *et al* , 2020 [13] talked about the possibility of explainable artificial intelligence in aero-plane predictive maintenance. When using Deep Neural Networks for project management, the study also examines the benefits of XAI for predictive maintenance (Pd.M.). The Aerospace IVHM field will be the context for DNN use (Integrated Vehicle Health Management). Since the results of an AI (Artificial Intelligence) solution must be accurately [14] explained and understood by a human operator, the development of an XAI (Explainable Artificial Intelligence) system is important. As a result, the IVHM system would be able to use XAI-based PM to improve the performance of the prediction model. Even if the basic mathematical principles are grasped, they are unable to provide appropriate based structures because they lack understandable insight (*i.e.*, black box). This calls for the creation of a system or process that enables judgments to be visible, explicable, and intelligible. According to reports, XAI research is hastening the use of AI/ML (Machine Learning) in the aviation sector, notably in areas like compliance, transparency, and trust.

Arrieta *et al.*, 2020 [13] examined the existing body of knowledge and technological developments in the field of XAI as well as a hypothetical future state. The article explores prior attempts to define the explainability of machine learning in order to achieve this. After incorporating these preceding conceptual assertions, it provides a definition of explainable machine learning with a focus exactly on the target market. The study suggests and discusses a taxonomy of recent contributions related to the explainability of different Machine Learning models, including those aimed at explaining Deep Learning methods for which a second dedicated taxonomy is built and examined in detail [16].

This critical literature analysis serves as the motivating background for a series of challenges faced by XAI, such as the interesting crossroads of data fusion and explainability. Our prospects lead to the concept of Responsible Artificial Intelligence, namely, a methodology for the large-scale implementation of AI methods in real organizations with fairness, model explainability and accountability at its core. Our ultimate goal is to provide newcomers to the field of XAI with a thorough taxonomy that can serve as reference material in order to stimulate future research advances, but also to encourage experts and professionals from other disciplines to embrace the benefits of AI in their activity sectors, without any prior bias for its lack of interpretability.

4. RESEARCH GAP

Recent interest in XAI emphasizes the importance of AI ethics, trust, and bias, as well as the role of adversarial examples in classifier decision-making. A clarification AI is a technique for verifying an AI agent's or algorithm's output decision. Despite the advantages, there are certain problems related to the implementation of XAI which restrict their adaptation. This research identifies some of the prominent research problems and aims to address these problems while designing an effective and novel XAI-based approach. The problems are listed in the points below:

- Human attention cannot infer XAI explanation maps for decision-making, and there is no quantifiable way to assess how accurate and complete an explanation map is. This suggests that future mission-critical applications should re-evaluate the use of visualization approaches. It would be wise to investigate more effective explanation representation techniques.
- Most of the existing researchers have not focused on the security and data confidentiality concerns associated with XAI. The notions of algorithm property and trade secrets have only been mentioned very briefly in the majority of XAI surveys. These concepts, nevertheless, haven't gotten much attention.
- Other challenges associated with XAI are the high complexity of the algorithms. In general, XAI algorithms use common sense facts to support illogical decisions. In addition, it is difficult to confirm whether the decisions made by the XAI models are fair or not. Depending on the knowledge input provided to AI algorithms, and reasonability, it is logical and takes a distinct stance.
- In addition to XAI, there are certainly other challenges related to IoT such as its "resource" constrained nature, interoperability, secure communication, data privacy, and security.

Although explanations have been found to improve the understanding of machine learning systems among a variety of audiences, it has been questioned if they can foster trust among non-AI specialists. The ideal way to use the explainability to gain the trust of non-AI professionals is currently the subject of extensive research; immersive explanations, including question-and-answer result shows, which have demonstrated dedication. The cost associated with data preparation and computation caused by the addition of the new features or their feature values and so on [15] will be dependent on whether it is feasible to develop such a model. Argumentation [16] can show step by step how the AI model reached some conclusion.

The state of XAI appraisal research at this time shows that it is still in its "infancy" and that XAI strategies should be properly planned and selected. According to user studies, conventional "explanation" maps might not be helpful in decision-making. Human bias may lead to incorrect interpretation of visual explanations for mission-critical projects using XAI to develop a workable XAI-based strategy for IoT contexts, these problems must be solved.

5. ISSUES AND CHALLENGES

Following this, the issues and challenges in XAI for IoT environments are summarized, which need to be addressed.

- The implementation of XAI for IoT-based systems involves a lot of complexities. Most of the time, it is difficult to identify the 'data" "sources" and to access the information, process it and curate the information. This process requires an effective skill set and the ability to handle updated technologies. In addition, XAI-based systems must be trained in a specific domain to get accurate results.
- Training of machine learning algorithms requires large-scale data sets, with minimum biases.
- Data from source systems *via* IoT are more prone to data leakage. It is difficult to protect the sensitive information of IoT devices from unauthorized access.
- Automated preventive mechanisms using XAI are susceptible to frequent failures and require skilled engineers to maintain such complex systems.

6. PROPOSED WORK

The proposed work is on eXplainable AI in an IoT environment.

It can be inferred from existing literary works that conventional ML models fail to provide explainability. Implementing XAI can help the models to achieve high-performance efficiency and can achieve a balanced tradeoff between accuracy, and explainability. Hence the proposed research emphasizes on the XAI for IoT environments. This research intends to address the challenges associated with the implementation of XAI in an IoT environment and contribute to the existing research gap. In this research, instead of using a conventional ML approach, an Explainable ML model is proposed.

6.1. Overview of the Proposed Approach

The workflow of conventional ML models focuses on predicting the outcome without providing the reason. This might confuse and mislead the users and make them believe that the output provided by the machine is accurate. On the other hand, XAI incorporates an advanced process that generates the output with an appropriate explanation of the process involved in the operation. In this case, the user will be provided with additional information about the output which explains the reason for prediction. XAI models contain an extra layer that can explain the output of the model, as illustrated in Fig. (**1**). The extra layer helps in ensuring the accuracy of decision-making because of the explainability module. Any variations in the output can be modified in the extra layer.

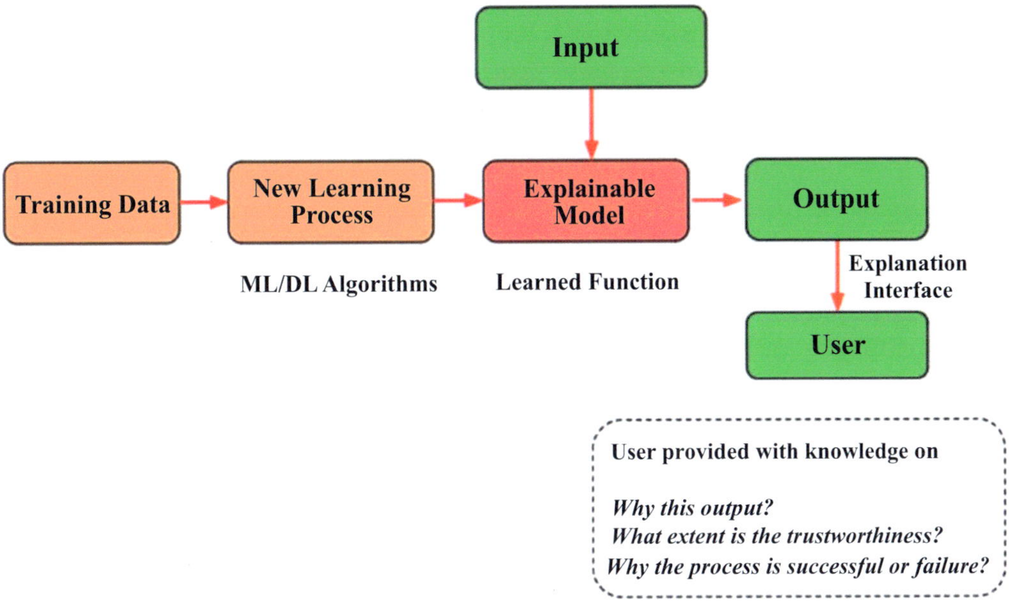

Fig. (1). Workflow of the explainable ML model.

Fig. (**1**) explains the workflow of the proposed XAI for preventive mechanisms using the IoT environment. The proposed framework consists of two modules: (a) feature selection and prediction using ML models and (b) explanation of the prediction.

This research proposes an ensemble learning model. Ensemble learning is a combination of one or more ML models or the integration of ML models with neural networks. For designing the Hybrid learning model, a deep neural network (DNN) is combined with a random forest (RF) algorithm. The proposed model is collectively called as (DNN-RF) model. In the first part, an RF model is used for selecting features and classification and DNN for predicting the failure of machine components. In the second part, two different XAI tools for obtaining an explanation of the model's predictions. Accuracy and traceability are two important attributes of XAI models in this context. This work mainly focuses on the explanation part and aims to address the challenges associated with the implementation of XAI in IoT environments and contribute to the existing research gap.

CONCLUSIONS AND FUTURE OUTLOOK

In this chapter, we explored a few XAI models with their benefits and challenges for XAI in the IoT context. We explored a variety of ML techniques [16], including NNs and conventional ML for predictions. We explored two different agnostic explainable AI strategies to provide an explanation for the models. The explanation provided by these methods is very insightful that could help the stakeholders in making correct decisions in such critical applications. The model explanations may aid future developers, and organizations in addressing the shortcomings of their offered solutions. We anticipate broadening the scope of research by applying start-of-the-art techniques to future operations on various models that are more important. Researchers and industry experts see XAI as a promising technology for overcoming these obstacles. XAI frameworks can add new capabilities and solutions to IoT devices and networks to improve their trustworthiness. We presented a comprehensive survey of XAI solutions for IoT systems in this chapter. We began with an overview of XAI characteristics and key features, followed by a discussion of its role in contemporary use cases. A description of the demand for developing trustworthy systems was provided, with an emphasis to IoT applications and recent standards. Furthermore, we extended IoT frameworks' explainable capability to newer domains, such as IIoT and other smart applications.

LIST OF ABBREVIATIONS

DL Deep Learning

IoT The Internet of Things

IVHM Integrated Vehicle Health Management

LIME Local Interpretable Model-Agnostic Explanations

ML Machine Learning

Pd.M. Predictive Maintenance

PM Preventive Maintenance

XAI Explainable Artificial Intelligence

REFERENCES

[1] D. Gunning, and D. Aha, "DARPA's explainable artificial intelligence (XAI) program", *AI Magazine,* vol. 40, no. 2, pp. 44-58, 2019. [http://dx.doi.org/10.1609/aimag.v40i2.2850]

[2] K. Ahmad, M. Maabreh, M. Ghaly, K. Khan, J. Qadir, and A. Al-Fuqaha, "Developing future human-centered smart cities: Critical analysis of smart city security, Data management, and Ethical challenges", *Computer Science Review,* vol. 43, p. 100452, 2022. [http://dx.doi.org/10.1016/j.cosrev.2021.100452]

[3] W. Samek, T. Wiegand, and K.R. Müller, "Explainable artificial intelligence: Understanding, visualizing and interpreting deep learning models", *arxiv preprint arXiv,* pp. 1708-08296, 2017. [http://dx.doi.org/10.48550/arXiv.1708.08296]

[4] S. Koppula, and J. Muthukuru, "Secure digital signature scheme based on elliptic curves for internet of things", *Int J Elect. Comp. Eng.,* vol. 6, no. 3, p. 1002, 2016. [http://dx.doi.org/10.11591/ijece.v6i3.9420]

[5] G. De Luca, and Y. Chen, "Explainable artificial intelligence for workflow verification in visual IoT/robotics programming language environment", *Journal of Artificial Intelligence and Technology,* vol. 1, no. 1, pp. 21-27, 2021. [http://dx.doi.org/10.37965/jait.2020.0023]

[6] A.Y. Al Hammadi, C.Y. Yeun, E. Damiani, P.D. Yoo, J. Hu, H.K. Yeun, and M.S. Yim, "Explainable artificial intelligence to evaluate industrial internal security using EEG signals in IoT framework", *Ad Hoc Networks,* vol. 123, p. 102641, 2021. [http://dx.doi.org/10.1016/j.adhoc.2021.102641]

[7] A. Adadi, and M. Berrada, "Peeking inside the black-box: a survey on explainable artificial intelligence (XAI)", *IEEE Access.* pp. 52138-52160, 2018. [http://dx.doi.org/10.1109/ACCESS.2018.2870052]

[8] Available from: https://www.pwc.com/gx/en/issues/analytics/assets/pwcai-analysis-sizing-the-p-ize-report.pdf

[9] S.M. Lundberg, and S-I. Lee, "A unified approach to interpreting model predictions", *Advances in Neural Information Processing Systems,,* vol. 30, p. 3, 2017.

[10] T. Khan, K. Ahmad, J. Khan, I. Khan. and N. Ahmad, "'An explainable regression framework for predicting remaining useful life of machines", arXiv: 2204.13574.

[11] A.A. Barredo, N. Díaz-Rodríguez, S.J Del, A. Bennetot, T. Siham, B. Alberto, G. Salvador, G.L. Sergio, M. Daniel, B. Richard, C. Raja, and H. Francisco,"Explainable Artificial Intelligence (XAI): Concepts,taxonomies, opportunities and challenges toward responsible AI", Information Fusion. , vol. 58, p. 2, 2020.

[12] A. Das, and P. Rad, "Opportunities and challenges in explainable artificial intelligence (xai): A survey", *arXiv preprint arXiv,* pp. 2006-11371, 2020.

[13] B. Shukla, I.S. Fan, and I. Jennions, "Opportunities for Explainable Artificial Intelligence in Aerospace Predictive Maintenance", *In PHM Society European Conference* vol. 1, pp. 11-11, 2020.

[14] B. Anibal, and M. Kamal, Proceedings of the European Conference of the phm society,2020.

[15] M. Hopf, H. Bernd, and P. Günther, "Artificial Intelligence for Online Review Platforms", *Data Understanding, Enhanced Approaches and Explanations in Recommender Systems and Aspect-based Sentiment Analysis,* p. 70, 2022.

[16] V. Alexandros, B. Nick, and P. Theodore, "Argumentation and explainable artificial intelligence: A survey", Knowledge Engineering Review, vol. 36, 2021.

[17] V.M. Hopf, H. Bernd, and P. Günther, "Artificial intelligence for online review platforms", Data Understanding, Enhanced Approaches and Explanations in Recommender Systems and Aspect-based Sentiment Analysis, p. 32, 2022.

[18] S.K. Jagatheesaperumal, Q.V. Pham, R. Ruby, Z. Yang, C. Xu, and Z. Zhang, "Explainable AI over the Internet of Things (IoT): Overview, state-of-the-art and future directions", *IEEE Open J. Communications. Society.*, vol. 3, pp. 2106-2136, 2022. [http://dx.doi.org/10.1109/OJCOMS.2022.3215676]

CHAPTER 11

Explainable AI (XAI) for Agriculture

Eudes Smith M. Linheiro[1,*], Gitanjali R. Shinde[2], Parikshit N. Mahalle[2] and Riddhi Mirajkar[3]

[1] *Department of Computer Engineering, Vishwakarma Institute of Information Technology, Pune, Maharashtra, India*

[2] *Vishwakarma Institute of Information Technology, Pune, Maharashtra, India*

[3] *Department of Information Technology, Vishwakarma Institute of Information Technology, Pune, Maharashtra, India*

Abstract: In most nations, agriculture is the main industry providing employment. Agricultural activities used to be restricted to the cultivation of food and crops, but they have expanded over time to include the processing, production, marketing, and distribution of crops and livestock products. Agriculture related approaches or practices must be continuously reviewed with the goal of presenting innovative approaches to sustaining and improving agricultural activities. Currently, agricultural activities serve as the primary source of livelihood, increasing GDP, being one of the sources of national trade, reducing unemployment, and providing raw materials for production in other industries.

Inadequate soil treatment, disease and pest infestation, among other issues, are only a few of the difficulties this industry must overcome in order to maximize productivity. There have been some difficulties with the increased use of technology in this industry, including the need for large amounts of data, low output, and the most obvious difficulty, the knowledge gap between farmers and technology.

When compared to earlier more conventional methods, agricultural practices, and activities have significantly improved since technology entered the field. Technologies like the Internet of Things (IoT) and Artificial Intelligence (AI) have been a few of the technologies that are widely used in these sectors with projects for improving crop production, disease prediction, continuous monitoring, efficient supply chain management, water waste and operational efficiency just to name a few but, this of this project will focus more on AI, more specifically on Explainable Artificial Intelligence (ExAI or XAI).

[*] **Corresponding author Eudes Smith M. Linheiro:** Department of Computer Engineering, Vishwakarma Institute of Information Technology, Pune, Maharashtra, India; E-mail: muassonga.eudessmith@viit.ac.in

Parikshit N. Mahalle, Gitanjali R. Shinde and Prachi M. Joshi (Eds.)

Keywords: Artificial Intelligence , Explainable Artificial Intelligence (XAI) , SHapley Additive exPlanations (SHAP), Local Interpretable Model-agnostic Explanations (LIME).

1. INTRODUCTION

Since it feeds the entire population, agriculture is a crucial component of any nation's economy. If a nation's agricultural base is relatively substantial, that nation is deemed to be socially and economically affluent. The majority of countries rely heavily on agriculture as their main industry. Agriculture used to be solely concerned with growing food and crops, but over time, it has expanded to include the processing, production, marketing, and distribution of crops and livestock products. Currently, agricultural activities serve as a primary means of subsistence, increasing GDP, contributing to national trade, lowering unemployment, and developing the economy as a whole [1]. However, as the world's population continues to grow geometrically, agricultural approaches and practices must be continually reviewed in order to introduce new ideas for sustaining and enhancing agricultural activities.

To maximize productivity, this industry must overcome various obstacles, including poor soil management, pest and disease infestation, and others. There have been significant issues with the increased use of technology in this industry, including enormous data requirements, low yield, and—most notably—the knowledge gap between farmers and these technologies.

Farming entails a great deal of choices and uncertainties, and from season to season the price of farming materials fluctuates, the soil degrades, crops are not viable, weeds suffocate crops, pests damage crops and climate changes occur. Although agricultural practices are broad, farmers must learn to cope up with these uncertainties.

With the introduction of technology in the agriculture domain, there has been great improvements in how agriculture practices and activities are exercised compared to old traditional ways. With projects to improve crop production, disease prediction, continuous monitoring, efficient supply chain management, water waste, and operational efficiency, to name a few, technologies like the IoT and AI have been some of the technologies that have been widely used in these sectors [2 - 6]. However, for the purpose of this project, the focus will be more on ExAI or XAI.

AI, also known as a synthetic version of the human brain that is capable of learning natural language and planning, perceiving, and processing it, has been applied to agriculture with the main objective of creating standards, dependable product quality, control procedures, and the exploration of new avenues for better-serving society at low costs. By enhancing the user experience of a product or service and fostering end users' confidence in the AI's judgment, the purpose of XAI is to clarify what has been done, what is being done now, what will be done next, and to expose the data on which the actions are based.

2. NEED FOR AI IN AGRICULTURE

Plant and animal cultivation is the practice of agriculture. And agriculture was the main factor in the rise of human civilization. Agriculture has a very long history. Agriculture or farming began with the collection of wild crops and the domestication of pigs, sheep, and cattle. Foods, fibers, fuels, and raw materials can be used to categorize the principal agricultural products. Agriculture employs more than one-third of all people on the planet. A tremendous rise in food yield has been achieved by industrial agriculture, mechanization, contemporary agronomy, plant, and animal breeding, agrochemicals like pesticides and fertilizers, and some technological advancements, however, these practices have been inflicting ecological and environmental harm. Aquifer depletion, deforestation, antibiotic resistance, and the use of growth hormones in industrial meat production are a few examples of environmental problems. A drop in crop productivity can result from the agriculture's role in environmental degradation, which includes biodiversity loss, desertification, soil degradation, and global warming.

With the continuous rise in global population and the increased demand for food, traditional ways and the previous advancement in this sector will not be enough to meet the demands of the entire population and also the negative impact that they have on the environment. New ways have been found which promise to deliver good quality while having a lower or no impact on the environment and also maintaining low costs. Amongst these new ways, AI has become so popular in this sector and the positive impact it has, revolutionizing the ways agricultural activities are practiced, to name a few, boosting agricultural productivity, predicting diseases, ongoing surveillance, effective supply chain management, reducing water waste, and operational efficiency.

3. ROLE OF AI IN AGRICULTURE

Over the years, technology has redefined agriculture, and it has revolutionized the agriculture industry in many different ways. Due to the fact that agriculture is a major source of employment in many nations around the world and that only 4% more land will be cultivated by 2050 due to population growth (which the UN projects will increase from 7.5 to 9.7 billion people) [7]. Farmers will have to work harder with fewer resources, and the same poll estimates that in order to feed the additional two billion people, food production should rise by 60%. To meet this enormous demand, conventional techniques are insufficient. Farmers and agro-businesses are looking for novel approaches to boost output, cut waste, and lessen the damaging effects of agriculture on the environment. AI is subsequently progressively becoming one of the key technological advancements in the agriculture sector. In addition to helping farmers and agro-businesses perform better, AI-powered systems and solutions will also enhance quantity and quality in order to satisfy the enormous demand from the additional two billion people. AI in agriculture will bring many benefits such as crop yield prediction and price forecasts, intelligent spraying, predictive insights, disease diagnosis, crop and soil monitoring, and agriculture robots. Fig. (**1**) illustrates the role of AI in agriculture.

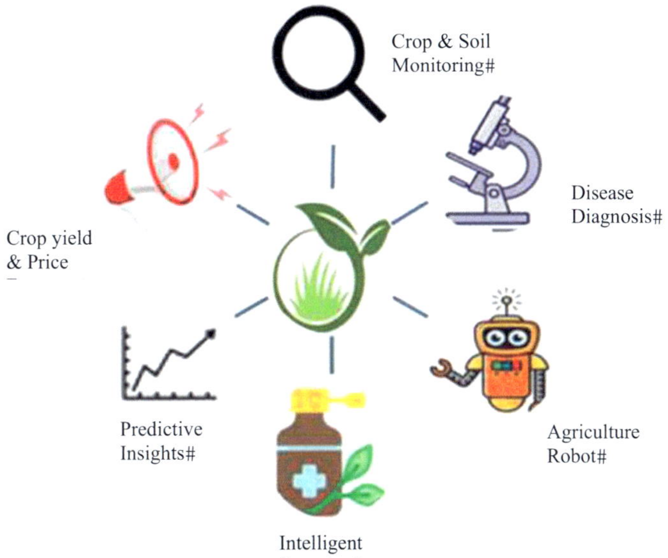

Fig. (1). AI in agriculture.

3.1. Crop Yield Prediction

A crop yield prediction system is a computer-based instrument that estimates the number of crops that will be produced in a given season or year using numerous data sources and predictive algorithms. To give accurate crop yield projections, this method often uses machine learning algorithms that assess data on weather patterns, soil health, prior crop yields, and other pertinent parameters. By estimating crop prices for the upcoming harvest and determining the output yield of crops, farmers can maximize their profits [8]. To create a crop yield prediction system, you'd need to collect and evaluate a large amount of data from many sources. Satellite imagery of farms, weather data from local weather stations, soil samples, nutrient data from agricultural testing laboratories, and historical data on crop yields and agricultural practices in the region may all be included.

After gathering and analyzing this data, you may use machine learning algorithms to create predictive models that can reliably anticipate crop yields depending on a variety of environmental and agronomic aspects. These models can be refined by training them with historical data and testing them against real crop yields in the prior years. Once you've created a solid crop yield prediction system, you can use it to deliver vital information to farmers and other agricultural stakeholders about the predicted yield of various crops in a given location. This information can assist farmers in making educated planting and harvesting decisions, optimizing their use of resources such as water and fertilizer, and planning for future yield fluctuations owing to changes in weather patterns or other variables.

3.2. Intelligent Spraying

Intelligent spraying refers to the use of precision spraying technology to apply pesticides or fertilizers only where they are needed, thereby reducing waste and minimizing environmental impact. Crop yield prediction, on the other hand, is the process of estimating how much yield a crop will produce based on various factors such as weather, soil conditions, and farming practices. Intelligent spraying can be used as a tool to improve crop yield prediction by providing more accurate and timely information about crop health and growth. By using sensors and other advanced technologies, farmers can monitor crop conditions in real time and make more informed decisions about when and where to apply pesticides or fertilizers. By combining data from intelligent spraying with other sources of information such as weather data, soil moisture levels, and historical yield data, farmers can create more accurate models of crop growth and predict yields more accurately. This can help farmers optimize their use of resources and improve their bottom line. Overall, intelligent spraying can be a powerful tool for improving crop yield prediction and helping farmers to maximize their yields while minimizing their impact on the environment. It can employ AI to track the health of crops and spot pests, poor soil quality, nutritional deficiencies, and other problems [9].

3.3. Crop and Soil Monitoring

Crop and soil monitoring are important components of crop yield management. By monitoring crops and soil conditions, farmers can identify potential issues and make informed decisions about how to optimize yield. Here are some ways crop and soil monitoring can impact crop yield:

- Soil testing: Testing the soil for nutrient levels, pH, and other factors can help farmers determine the best course of action for crop management. If the soil is lacking in certain nutrients, for example, the farmer can apply fertilizers or other soil amendments to improve conditions for plant growth.
- Irrigation monitoring: Monitoring soil moisture levels can help farmers determine when to irrigate their crops, and how much water to apply. Over- or under-watering can both have negative impacts on crop yield, so monitoring irrigation is key to maximizing production.
- Pest and disease monitoring: Monitoring for pests and diseases is important for catching outbreaks early and minimizing damage to crops. Early detection and treatment can help prevent widespread damage and minimize yield loss.
- Crop growth monitoring: Monitoring crop growth throughout the growing season can help farmers adjust their management practices as needed. For example, if a crop is growing more slowly than expected, the farmer might adjust the amount of fertilizers or irrigation they're applying to help the plant grow more quickly.

Overall, crop and soil monitoring are essential tools for farmers looking to maximize crop yield. By paying close attention to soil conditions, pest and disease outbreaks, and crop growth, farmers can make informed decisions about how to manage their crops and optimize production. AI can be used to monitor crop health and spot pests, poor soil quality, nutritional deficiencies, and other problems [10].

3.4. Disease Diagnosis

Disease diagnosis is an important component of crop yield prediction. Crop diseases can have a significant impact on yield, and early diagnosis and treatment can help minimize the impact of these diseases.

Here are some ways disease diagnosis can impact crop yield prediction:

- Early detection: Early detection of crop diseases can help farmers take action to prevent or minimize crop damage. By identifying diseases early, farmers can apply appropriate treatments or management practices to prevent disease spread and minimize yield loss.

- Accurate diagnosis: Accurate diagnosis of crop diseases is important for selecting the appropriate management practices. Different diseases require different management practices, so accurate diagnosis is essential for effective treatment.
- Predictive modeling: Predictive modeling can be used to forecast disease outbreaks and potential impacts on crop yield. By using historical data and current weather conditions, predictive models can help farmers prepare for potential disease outbreaks and adjust their management practices accordingly.
- Precision agriculture: Precision agriculture techniques, such as remote sensing and precision mapping, can help identify disease outbreaks and predict potential yield impacts. By analyzing data on plant health and other factors, farmers can make informed decisions about how to manage their crops and optimize yield.

Overall, disease diagnosis is a critical component of crop yield prediction. By detecting and diagnosing crop diseases early, farmers can take appropriate action to prevent disease spread and minimize yield loss. Predictive modelling and precision agriculture techniques can also help farmers prepare for potential disease outbreaks and optimize crop management practices. Farmers will receive advance notice of any plant or crop diseases through crop health monitoring, allowing them to control the diseases through appropriate strategies [11].

3.5. Agriculture Robots

Agriculture robots have the potential to revolutionize crop yield prediction by providing real-time data on crop health, growth, and yield. Here are some ways agriculture robots can impact crop yield prediction:

- Real-time monitoring: Agriculture robots can provide real-time monitoring of crop conditions, including soil moisture, nutrient levels, and plant growth. By collecting data on crop health and growth throughout the growing season, farmers can make informed decisions about when to apply fertilizer, irrigation, or other inputs.
- Precision agriculture: Precision agriculture techniques, such as precision mapping and variable rate application, can be enhanced with the use of agriculture robots. By analyzing data collected by the robots, farmers can optimize the use of inputs, reducing waste and increasing yield.
- Crop scouting: Agriculture robots can be equipped with cameras and sensors to scout crops for signs of disease, pests, or other issues. By identifying these problems early, farmers can take action to prevent or minimize yield loss.

- Harvesting: Robotics technology can also be used for harvesting crops. Harvesting robots can collect data on crop yield and quality, which can be used to make informed decisions about future planting and management practices.

Overall, agriculture robots have the potential to improve crop yield prediction by providing real-time data on crop conditions and growth. This data can be used to optimize the use of inputs, identify and address crop problems early, and make informed decisions about future management practices. It can use AI to monitor crop health to identify pests as well as soil flaws, nutritional deficits, and other issues [9].

3.6. Predictive Insights

Predictive insights are essential in crop yield prediction, as they enable farmers to anticipate potential problems and take proactive steps to mitigate risks and optimize yield. Here are some ways predictive insights can impact crop yield prediction:

- Weather forecasting: Weather conditions play a critical role in crop growth and yield. Predictive insights on weather conditions can help farmers anticipate potential weather-related risks, such as drought or heavy rainfall, and adjust their management practices accordingly.
- Crop modeling: Crop modeling uses historical data and current weather conditions to predict potential yield outcomes. By analyzing data on plant growth and development, farmers can make informed decisions about when to apply inputs, such as fertilizer and irrigation, and adjust their management practices as needed.
- Disease forecasting: Predictive models can be used to forecast potential disease outbreaks and their impact on crop yield. By anticipating potential disease risks, farmers can take proactive steps to prevent or minimize crop damage, such as applying fungicides or implementing crop rotation practices.
- Machine learning: Machine learning algorithms can analyze large amounts of data on crop growth and yield to identify patterns and predict future outcomes. By leveraging this data, farmers can make informed decisions about when to plant, when to harvest, and how to optimize their management practices for maximum yield.

Overall, predictive insights are critical in crop yield prediction, as they enable farmers to make informed decisions about crop management practices and optimize yield outcomes. By leveraging data on weather, crop growth, and potential risks, farmers can take proactive steps to mitigate risks and optimize yield potential. Farmers may save a lot of money and resources if they are knowledgeable about the best time to plant seeds as well as the effects of the weather [13].

4. EXPLAINABLE AI IN AGRICULTURE

The positive impact that AI has on this sector is noticeable, and with all these benefits that it has brought, there is one problem that still remains and that problem is the knowledge gap between farmers and this technology. Because AI and Machine Learning (ML) models are so complicated, often not even their creators can fully explain how an AI came to a particular conclusion. AI being one of the few technologies thriving in this sector, there is a need for these AI/ML models to be trusted as the future technology for agriculture. It requires a lot of expertise in order to understand these non-explainable models. To mitigate this problem, a new AI concept has been introduced. An AI concept that can explain all the reasoning behind a prediction and that concept is called "Explainable Artificial Intelligence (ExAI)". Explainable AI promises to help users in this case farmers perform more effectively, difference between AI and ExAI is depicted in Fig. (**2**). This provides an increased level of understanding between humans and machines, which helps build trust in these AI systems [14].

These four principles—Explanation, Meaningfulness, Explanation Accuracy, and Knowledge Limits—were proposed by the National Institute of Standards and Technology (NIST) as requirements for Explainable AI systems. These four principles will be covered briefly.

- **Explanation:** A system delivers or includes supporting data or justifications for processes and/or results.
- **Meaningfulness:** It should be able to give the required consumer-friendly explanations.
- **Explanation accuracy:** The explanation should appropriately depict the system's process and/or the motivation behind the output generation.
- **Knowledge limits:** A system only operates under the conditions for which it was designed and when it reaches sufficient confidence in its output.

Here are some key benefits of using Explainable AI for its accountability, transparency or fairness and enhanced trust. Being relatively a new area of research, Explainable AI still faces many active challenges. Explainable AI models are more difficult to train and tune and they tend to have lower performance compared to those which are non-explainable AI models, how to generate explanations that are both accurate and understandable, explainability can be at the expense of model performance accuracy and they can be more difficult to deploy since explainability features often need some level of human intervention in the loop.

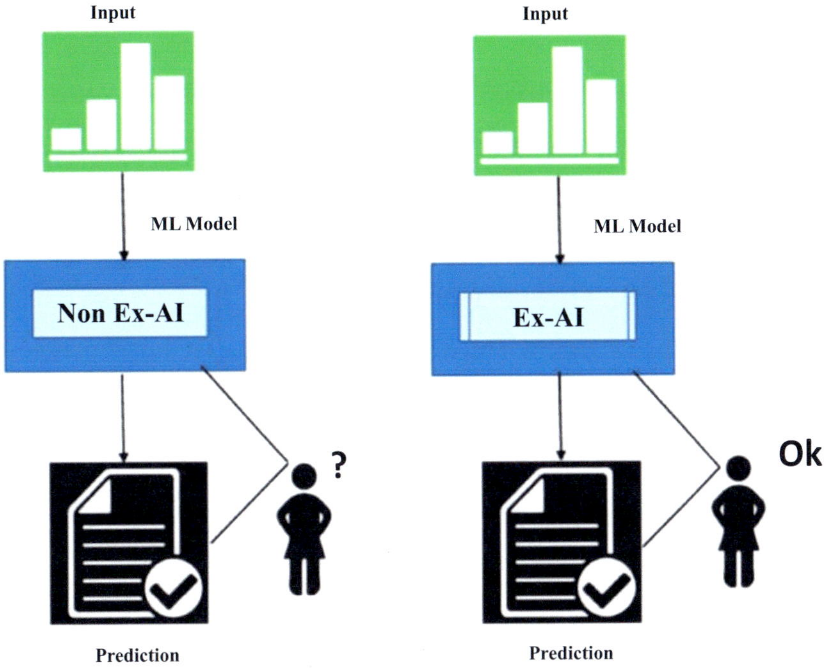

Fig. (2). Difference between ExAI and Non-ExAI.

The most common Explainable AI techniques are SHapley Additive exPlanations (SHAP) [15], Local interpretable Model-Agnostic Explanations (LIME) [16] and Anchor. SHAP and LIME are very similar in terms of their output. These algorithms will produce a feature importance or attribute. It means that they will tell which features are contributing more to the output or predictions. Anchor is slightly different from SHAP and LIME in that instead of creating a feature importance or feature attribute like the other two, Anchor creates a region in the feature space. By coming up with an easily interpretable rule which will guarantee prediction, Anchor will give us a set of information about the given input, rather than feature importance.

5. OVERVIEW OF EXPLAINABLE AI IN AGRICULTURE

An issue with Healthcare 4.0 employing ML and sensors is the analysis of agriculture productivity and climate change consequences in the South Asian region. With major concerns about Global warming and how all the science domains are trying to address it in many different ways, Agriculture is an important element for the survival of the human species and how ML models can predict agriculture yield in order to minimize errors and maximize accuracy and automatically reduce its impact on the environment [17].

The impact of ML in Agriculture, Management, and Healthcare.

Agriculture faces so many challenges and in this research, authors have discussed how technologies like AI will help the agriculture industry perform more effectively in managing the limited resources and increase productivity to meet the demands for food in this growing population while at the same time helping to minimize the effect it has on the environment [18].

The Agriculture Industry Being Transformed by Artificial Intelligence: Towards Future Farming

The Food and Agriculture Organization (FAO) estimates that plant diseases would cost the globe $220 billion in 2019 and that if effective measures are not implemented, this amount will likely increase [19]. To automatically categorize the plant leaf diseases, they suggested a thin Deep Convolutional Neural Network (DCNN) [20]. With the use of artificial intelligence and the Internet of Things, agriculture is becoming automated and digitalized. The Internet of Things (IoT) and Artificial Intelligence (AI) and their impact on the agriculture sector, as well as how eagerly these technologies are able to address the majority of its problems have been discussed [21]. A hydro-economic model with bio-inspiration and AI has been developed for diverse farm management. They used data from the Dharwad district in Karnataka, India for the year 2019–20 to construct a hydro-economic model for varied agriculture management. They integrated a bio-inspired technology with artificial intelligence to achieve this [22]. Classification of plant leaf diseases has been carried out using reliable deep learning and light-chroma separated branches. Drought is one of the disastrous natural hazards and has an impact on agriculture production. Therefore, a drought forecast system has been developed using Long Short-Term Memory (LSTM) and The SHapley Addictive exPlanation (SHAP) to make this system easy to understand or explainable [23].

Explainable AI: A Review of ML interpretability methods.

They deal with the problem that exists in Machine Learning models. Though they have been demonstrating superhuman power and the widespread industrial adoption, but this advancement came by increasing the complexity of the models which made them hard to understand or turned them into "black box models", that may lead to being questioned on the way they make these decisions and how Explainable AI models can be the way solve this problem [24].

A great work has already been done towards solving this problem. What has been noticed, though, is that despite all the marketing hoopla and advantages of Explainable AI in agriculture, there is still a knowledge gap between farmers and the technology. Despite the fact that the approach itself may be explained so frequently, the specialists are the ones who are translating it for the farmers. The farmers greatly rely on the model's expert interpretation than on the model itself. When developing these systems, it should keep the users in mind, with no dependency on specialists, and make the model explanations self-sufficient for the users—in this example, the farmers—to comprehend.

6. PROPOSED WORK

There are many ways or algorithms which you can use in order to make any Machine Learning model Explainable. The two most popular algorithms out of these are SHAP and LIME.

For this project, the goal is to develop and construct a model that will accept a dataset on crop health and crop recommendation as input, which can be in any format (such as csv, pictures, *etc.*), process it, and provide the intended output. A precise forecast of crop health and the ideal time to plant a given crop are the outputs that are required. The model was tested and simplified in this instance, although the outcomes weren't exactly as precise as expected. The SHAP technique was used to generate the basic version of the model on a summer crop recommendation dataset that was downloaded from the Kaggle website. Let's look at SHAP's definition and workings first.

The technique used by SHAP is significantly different; it makes use of game theory findings to pretend that each characteristic is a member of a team and that the prediction represents the award the team receives. After estimating each team member's contribution to the team's success using Shapley values, SHAP then identifies which team members or features made the biggest contributions. This is accomplished by "removing" one team member (one model feature) and evaluating the results.

However, SHAP is more interested in how useful each team member might be in a hypothetical team than just the one they are on currently. As a result, it creates a copy of each team that may possibly exist given the characteristics of the team members, then it subtracts each team member from each team to determine the average contribution of each member to victory. Then, all the libraries required for the implementation were loaded, and the LightGBM classifier was utilized in addition to the SHAP method. Tree-based learning strategies are applied in a gradient-boosting system known as LightGBM. It is dispersed, efficient, and offers the following advantages by design:

- Increased training effectiveness and speed.
- Better accuracy; less memory utilization.
- Support for parallel and GPU learning
- Able to manage massive amounts of data

Kaggle competitions are currently dominated by machine learning algorithms built on decision trees. These contests' winning entries have utilized an algorithm known as XGBoost.

Microsoft unveiled its gradient boosting technology LightGBM a few years ago. These days, it takes centre stage in gradient-boosting devices. Kagglers begin to rely more on LightGBM than XGBoost. XGBoost is 6 times slower than LightGBM.

The LightGBM manual lists a lengthy set of parameters for the relatively new algorithm Light GBM.

The dataset is getting bigger and bigger. Traditional data science methods now have a very tough time producing reliable results. Due to its rapid speed, Light GBM is precededed by Light. Large amounts of data can be handled using Light GBM, which requires less memory to operate.

The popularity of Light GBM is also attributed to its emphasis on precise outcomes. Data scientists frequently use LGBM to build data science applications since it also enables GPU learning.

LGBM should not be applied to tiny datasets. Light GBM is easily able to overfit little data and is susceptible to overfitting. The flowchart of the model is represented in Fig. (**3**).

7. FUTURE SCOPE AND LIMITATIONS

There are still many areas that need to be covered in this project, but it feels like it will be worthwhile if the model can not only predict the health of the crop but also suggest crops that are suitable for a given season, allowing farmers to choose which crops to plant in order to maximize the yield and profit. The future scope of this project is to improve the model's predictions so that they are more accurate in terms of what it was designed for.

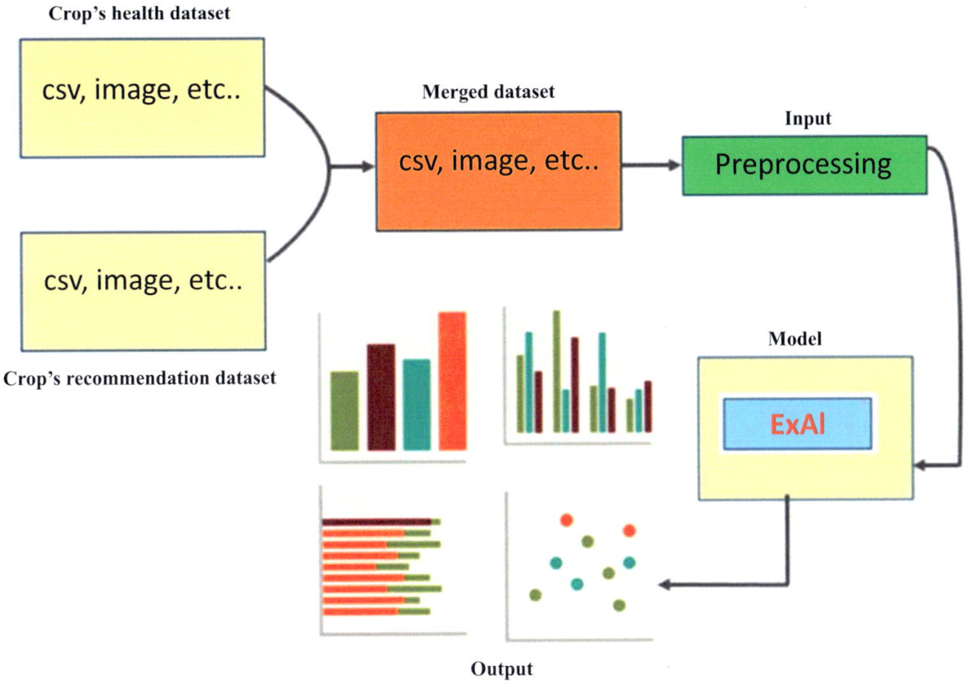

Fig. (3). Flowchart of the model.

CONCLUSION

Although this technology still has a lot of room for improvement, the proposed model for crop health will assist farmers in maximizing their profits and understanding how this model makes predictions. Despite the ongoing challenges this technology is facing, it is anticipated that in the near future, ExAI in agriculture will be as strong and reliable as it is in the automotive industries with self-driving cars.

ACKNOWLEDGMENTS

We would like to thank our colleagues at Vishwakarma Institute of Information Technology for helping us through the paper and providing us with their insights and valued opinions.

We would also like to take a moment to thank our reviewers for giving their valuable time to go through the paper. The generosity and expertise provided by them have helped in improving the quality of the paper.

REFERENCES

[1] S.Y. Liu, "Artificial intelligence (AI) in agriculture", *IT Professional,* vol. 22, no. 3, pp. 14-15, 2020. [http://dx.doi.org/10.1109/MITP.2020.2986121]

[2] D.R. Vincent, N. Deepa, D. Elavarasan, K. Srinivasan, S.H. Chauhdary, and C. Iwendi, "Sensors driven AI-based agriculture recommendation model for assessing land suitability", *Sensors* , vol. 19, no. 17, p. 3667, 2019. [http://dx.doi.org/10.3390/s19173667] [PMID: 31450772]

[3] N.C. Eli-Chukwu, "Applications of artificial intelligence in agriculture: A review", *Engineering, Technology & Applied Science Research,* vol. 9, no. 4, pp. 4377-4383, 2019. [http://dx.doi.org/10.48084/etasr.2756]

[4] I.H. Syeda, M.M. Alam, U. Illahi, and M.M. Su'ud, "Advance control strategies using image processing, UAV and AI in agriculture: a review", *World J. Eng.,* vol. 18, no. 4, pp. 579-589, 2021. [http://dx.doi.org/10.1108/WJE-09-2020-0459]

[5] M.J. Smith, "Getting value from artificial intelligence in agriculture", *Animal Production Science,* vol. 60, no. 1, pp. 46-54, 2020. [http://dx.doi.org/10.1071/AN18522]

[6] E. Alreshidi, "Smart sustainable agriculture (SSA) solution underpinned by internet of things (IoT) and artificial intelligence (AI)", *Int. J. Adv. Comp. Sci. App. (IJACSA)*, vol. 10, no. 5, 2019.

[7] Available from: https://ourworldindata.org/land-use

[8] S. Khaki, and L. Wang, "Crop yield prediction using deep neural networks", *Frontiers in plant science,* vol. 10, p. 621, 2019. [http://dx.doi.org/10.3389/fpls.2019.00621] [PMID: 31191564]

[9] I. Abbas, J. Liu, M. Faheem, R.S. Noor, S.A. Shaikh, K.A. Solangi, and S.M. Raza, "Different sensor based intelligent spraying systems in Agriculture", *Sens. Actuators A Phys.,* vol. 316, p. 112265, 2020. [http://dx.doi.org/10.1016/j.sna.2020.112265]

[10] M.K. Dharani, R. Thamilselvan, P. Natesan, P.C.D. Kalaivaani, and S. Santhoshkumar, "Review on crop prediction using deep learning techniques", In: *In: Journal of Physics: Conference Series* vol. 1767. IOP Publishing., 2021, no. 1, p. 012026. [http://dx.doi.org/10.1088/1742-6596/1767/1/012026]

[11] H. Orchi, M. Sadik, and M. Khaldoun, "On using artificial intelligence and the internet of things for crop disease detection: A contemporary survey", *Agriculture,* vol. 12, no. 1, p. 9, 2021. [http://dx.doi.org/10.3390/agriculture12010009]

[12] S.S.H. Hajjaj, and K.S.M. Sahari, "Review of agriculture robotics: Practicality and feasibility", *2016 IEEE International Symposium on Robotics and Intelligent Sensors (IRIS),* pp. 194-198, 2016. [http://dx.doi.org/10.1109/IRIS.2016.8066090]

[13] V. Lakshmi, and J. Corbett, "How artificial intelligence improves agricultural productivity and sustainability", *Asia Pacific Journal of Energy and Environment*, vol. 6, no. 2, pp. 91-100, 2019. [http://dx.doi.org/10.24251/HICSS.2020.639]

[14] N.L. Tsakiridis, T. Diamantopoulos, A.L. Symeonidis, J.B. Theocharis, A. Iossifides, P. Chatzimisios, and D. Kouvas, Versatile internet of things for agriculture: an eXplainable AI approach.*IFIP international conference on artificial intelligence applications and innovations.* Springer: Cham, 2020, pp. 180-191. [http://dx.doi.org/10.1007/978-3-030-49186-4_16]

[15] aA. Holzinger, R. Goebel, R. Fong, T. Moon, K.R. Müller, and W. Samek, "xxAI-Beyond Explainable Artificial Intelligence", *International Workshop on Extending Explainable AI Beyond Deep Models and Classifiers,* Springer: Cham, pp. 3-10, 2022.bD. Fryer, I. Strümke, and H. Nguyen, "Shapley values for feature selection: the good, the bad, and the axioms", *IEEE Access,* vol. 9, pp. 144352-144360, 2021.

[http://dx.doi.org/10.1109/ACCESS.2021.3119110]

[16] J. Dieber, and S. Kirrane, "Why model why? Assessing the strengths and limitations of LIME", *arXiv preprint arXiv,* vol. 2012, p. 00093, 2020.

[17] M. Shahzaman, W. Zhu, M. Bilal, B.A. Habtemicheal, F. Mustafa, M. Arshad, I. Ullah, S. Ishfaq, and R. Iqbal, "Remote sensing indices for spatial monitoring of agricultural drought in South Asian countries", *Remote Sens.,* vol. 13, no. 11, p. 2059, 2021. [http://dx.doi.org/10.3390/rs13112059]

[18] H. Kalita, K. Kumar, and J. P. Davim, "An overview of machine learning implementation in various industrial scenarios: Agriculture, healthcare and enterprise", *Artif. Intell. Mechan. Ind. Eng.,* pp. 2-20, 2021.

[19] Available from: https://www.fao.org/home/en

[20] E.C. Tetila, B.B. Machado, G.K. Menezes, A. Da Silva Oliveira, M. Alvarez, W.P. Amorim, N.A. De Souza Belete, G.G. Da Silva, and H. Pistori, "Automatic recognition of soybean leaf diseases using UAV images and deep convolutional neural networks", *IEEE geoscience and remote sensing letters.,* vol. 17, no. 5, pp. 903-907, 2020. [http://dx.doi.org/10.1109/LGRS.2019.2932385]

[21] A. Subeesh, and C.R. Mehta, "Automation and digitization of agriculture using artificial intelligence and internet of things", *Artificial Intelligence in Agriculture,* vol. 5, pp. 278-291, 2021. [http://dx.doi.org/10.1016/j.aiia.2021.11.004]

[22] G. Sajith, R. Srinivas, A. Golberg, and J. Magner, "Bio-inspired and artificial intelligence enabled hydro-economic model for diversified agricultural management", *Agric. Water Manage.,* vol. 269, p. 107638, 2022. [http://dx.doi.org/10.1016/j.agwat.2022.107638]

[23] M. Villaret, "Reliable deep learning plant leaf disease classification based on light-chroma separated branches", *Proceedings of the 23rd International Conference of the Catalan Association for Artificial Intelligence* vol. 339, p. 375, 2021.

[24] P. Linardatos, V. Papastefanopoulos, and S. Kotsiantis, "Explainable AI: A review of machine learning interpretability methods", *Entropy,* vol. 23, no. 1, p. 18, 2020. [http://dx.doi.org/10.3390/e23010018] [PMID: 33375658]

SUBJECT INDEX

D

E

F

G

H

N

O

P

R

S

T

V

W

Z

Made in the USA
Las Vegas, NV
03 November 2026

57422506R00117